Southern Christian Univ
1200 Taylor Rd.
Montgomery, AL. 3611

AMRIDGE UNIVERSITY
LIBRARY

POLITICS AND SOCIETY
IN THE THIRD WORLD

ORBIS BOOKS

MARYKNOLL, NEW YORK 10545

00045837

JF
60
.C3513

Calvez, Jean-Yves, 1927-
Politics and society in the Third
World.

POLITICS
AND SOCIETY
IN THE
THIRD WORLD

JEAN-YVES CALVEZ

Translated by M.J. O'Connell

320.917

C 167

74632

Library of Congress Catalogue number: 72-85792

ISBN: 0-88344-389-9

Originally published as Aspects Politiques et Sociaux des
Pays en Voie de Developpment by Dalloz, Paris, 1971.

Copyright © 1973, ORBIS BOOKS, Maryknoll, New York 10545

Manufactured in the United States of America.

CONTENTS

INTRODUCTION

To discuss the political and social aspects of the Third World while avoiding the economic is to limit oneself indeed. But then the reader must recognize that a writer limits himself when he tries to discuss any aspect whatsoever of the developing countries as a group.

In any case, there are many books, even an overwhelming number of them, devoted to economic analysis of underdevelopment and of the first steps in development. There are notably fewer presentations of politics and society in the developing nations. Perhaps then we can render a service by concentrating on these aspects. And precisely because such presentations are relatively rare, the reader may forgive us for speaking of the developing countries as a group and for borrowing elements of our picture from very different geographical areas and assimilating them to each other, even at the risk of barely raising questions which would require whole volumes for themselves.

There is a further limitation we have put on ourselves. To

deal with the political and social aspects of these countries, and thus with underdevelopment and development generally, is already to choose among explanations. It will be clear that we do not regard purely economic factors as negligible. We are convinced, however, that insofar as economy and society are distinguishable at all, economics in the developing countries depends largely on a particular condition and even on a particular form of society (the "traditional" society). This is not really a very radical view. For we are still left with the question of which aspects of society may be the determining ones. Will it be the traditional forms of family and politics, or mentalities, or religions? Or particular historical aspects of the societies in question, for example, the experience of colonialism? We shall try to unravel this twisted skein. We shall not fully succeed, but we shall at least attempt to relate the various factors to one another.

The more specifically political themes will be approached in two ways. First, we shall look at the international scene, the surface of things if you will, for today it is as states on the world stage that the developing countries catch our eye. We must see how they make their presence and organization felt. Here we shall begin our book. Next, in trying to understand the forward movement of these countries despite handicaps, lags, and weaknesses of many kinds, we shall come across the political factor once again, and indeed as the decisive factor. It is at the political level (a social structure, but also a group of men who are the vanguard of the body social as a whole) that the societies and economies of the developing countries are in process of change. This conviction, drawn from our study of the underdeveloped countries, is perhaps the only real thesis of the book.

It is not meant, however, as a permanently valid truth, for we are well aware that in these matters what is true today, may not be true tomorrow. For the political class that today is getting the developmental process started, or at least upsetting the balance of underdevelopment, will soon be replaced. We shall often allude to this fact and shall return to it in the conclusion of the book.

The earlier chapters, which discuss the developing countries on the international scene and in their internal political organization, are the most topical and likely to be the victims of their topicality. In these areas events are quickly dated, and by the time this book is published more than one new event will have unexpectedly occurred. Even in teaching these subjects for several years at the Institute of Social Studies (Catholic Institute of Paris) and the Institute of Political Studies (University of Paris) and in sketching out the material of this book in our courses there, we have been forced several times to change a number of details. But we feel that independently of such details our general observations and discussions will remain valid for a fairly long time. We have therefore been encouraged to retain the early chapters, despite the risk of being dated on several points.

THE
INTERNATIONAL
SCENE

To Paris, New York, or Moscow the developing nations show first of all their international personality: they are states among the other states. Often they are also new states, having only recently won their international independence. But these nations as a group form a majority in the United Nations. Their heads of state are much abroad and often pay official visits to the great capitals. In a word, we cannot but be aware of the international presence of these nations, even when we may know little of their internal social reality.

It is not only to the European or the American that the international activity of the developing countries is primary; they themselves attach exceptional importance to it. Consequently we shall begin our presentation of the developing nations and their problems with their activity on the world stage.

We shall in fact begin by showing the place these nations occupy as a group in international life. This is not because the Third World always has the homogeneity which some ideologies attribute to it. Nor, for that matter, do our newspapers concentrate on the developing countries as a group; we read rather of "Asian Affairs," "African Affairs," or "Latin American Affairs." Sometimes, however, we do hear of the developing nations as a group, or at least of groups of nations which are almost coextensive with the Third World, as, for example, "the 77" of the United Nations Conference on Trade and Development (UNCTAD). And the newspapers often report the activities of the developing nations at the UN. Let us dwell on these two examples, for they help us grasp the importance which the developing nations attribute to their international activity.

The 77 and UNCTAD

"The 77" has been the symbolic name for the developing countries in UNCTAD. The group has a larger membership today, and in fact it already numbered 88 when it met at Algiers, October 10-24, 1967, to write a "platform for common action" for the upcoming New Delhi Conference of February 1968. The platform adopted was called the Algiers Charter. It was at Geneva in March 1964, when the first United Nations Conference on Trade and Development met, that the developing countries were 77 in number. This conference was convoked by the General Assembly and brought together all member states of the UN and of the various international institutions which make up the "UN family" (about 120 members in all). At the conference, since its agenda concerned them in a special way, the developing nations formed a group for promoting their common interests in matters of trade and development.

There was not complete unity and harmony among "the 77" at Geneva. To begin with, the temperate lands producing their agricultural commodities did not have the same interests as the tropical lands. The former were more concerned with abolishing customs and tariffs against their products in the developed countries, while the nations from tropical areas were more concerned with organizing markets and stabilizing prices. The former favored proposals that were Anglo-Saxon in spirit, while the latter favored interventionist policies that were primarily French in origin.

Nor did all have the same interest in "preferences" for the industrial products of the developing countries. The countries whose industrialization was well under way and who were ready to begin exporting to the developed countries of course attached great importance to those preferences; this was true of various Latin American countries such as Mexico, Brazil and Argentina, and of some Asian countries, such as India. But countries with only distant prospects of industrial export to the developed nations did not have the same immediate interest in establishing the principle of preferences.

On another subject opposition, not simply different degrees of interest, existed: the Latin American and Asian countries sought the abolition of other preferences which brought benefits in Europe to many African countries because they were associated with the Common Market through the Yaoundé Convention. But, apart from this particular matter, "the 77" were united in preparing and voting on most of the conference resolutions. The existence of such a bloc was one of the most striking demonstrations of the 1964 Geneva meeting.

At Algiers in October 1967, then at New Delhi in February 1968, the same basic difficulties were evident, but also the same unity. The African states even accepted, in principle, the abandonment of their special preferences, but on condition that they receive equivalent advantages within a generalized system of preferences.

It is worth noting that "the 77" of 1964 were not all from the underdeveloped world. Among them was New Zealand, a producer of foodstuffs and thus as much concerned with liberalization of trade as were the other primary producers. New Zealand was, however, an exception, and her presence does not change the overall significance of the group. A much more noteworthy fact is that for the first time the Latin American governments joined those of Asia and Africa to form a single bloc.

The Algiers meeting of October 1967, and with it "the 77,"

might have run into serious political difficulties. South Vietnam and South Korea were members of the group, while North Vietnam and North Korea (like Communist China) were not. The presence of South Vietnamese delegates at Algiers therefore threatened problems; before the conference began, there had been question of restricting them to participation in the conference sessions. Even greater difficulties might have arisen from the very location of the conference, for Algiers was a symbolic city.

Even before Geneva the Third World had sought to unify itself in a style and framework quite different from those which "the 77" later adopted. The earlier attempt was notable chiefly for the absence of the South American nations. This first effort had led to the Bandung Conference of 1955. It was an Afro-Asian conference, even primarily Asian, and strongly anticolonial in tendency. It paid little attention to economic or trade matters, concentrating instead on demands for political independence. A second conference was planned for the tenth anniversary of the first, in 1965, with Algiers as the meeting place. Major events finally prevented the meeting, especially the arrest of Ben Bella and the takeover by Colonel Boumedienne. Although Algiers had completed most of the preparations, including the building of a large hotel, this second Bandung Conference was adjourned indefinitely. Colonel Boumedienne, however, seemed to have adopted, in essentials, the dynamic international policy of Ben Bella; furthermore, various revolutionary leaders of the Third World had sought asylum at Algiers, and Stokely Carmichael, a Black Panther leader, claimed to have found there his true fatherland. In such circumstances, Algiers might have been tempted to turn this conference, intended as preparation for the New Delhi meeting, into the Bandung Conference that had been adjourned in 1965. So at least some people feared. Magalhaes Pinto, foreign affairs minister of Brazil, had announced that he could not take part in a meeting at Algiers, and similar unfavorable reactions were expected from others.

After the event it had to be acknowledged that if inevitable difficulties arose from the presence, even though restrained, of the South Korean and South Vietnamese delegations, the Algerian government for its part had shown great moderation. The result was to make possible the unanimous adoption of the Algiers Charter. The charter itself, furthermore, contained the well-known clause on the surrender of special preferences by the African states on condition of receiving equivalent compensation. Thus unity won out despite serious threats.

In the face of such manifestations of unity, we must observe that at least at the governmental level there is not complete unity among the developing nations. "The 77" have certain objectives in common, but they do not share all the goals pursued earlier by the Bandung Conference. The Bandung spirit and variants of it have continued, however, to inspire other Third World groups such as the Organization for Afro-Asian Solidarity, or the Organization for Latin American Solidarity. But with such groups we are no longer dealing with governments alone. Instead, we have governments and various other political formations in opposition to them. We will come across these organizations again in dealing with regional institutions in the developing countries. If we take the developing nations as a group, we find unity only with regard to limited goals, chiefly economic, and, above all, with regard to presenting to the developed sectors of the world the claims and protests of the underdeveloped sectors.

At the United Nations

The action of "the 77" within UNCTAD is only a particular case of the presence and action of the developing nations at the UN and in its related agencies (Food and Agriculture Organization, United Nations Educational, Scientific, and Cultural Organization, World Health Organization, etc.). The entry a few years back of numerous developing countries into these organizations had important effects on the organizations' political functioning.

We must realize that the countries which reached independence during the 1958-1960 period attached great importance to UN membership. They regarded membership as a global seal of approval on an indepencence that had been won in bilateral negotiations with the colonial powers; it was to be a sort of international baptism of the new state. The UN had a further special attraction for the developing nations as they were achieving independence: under the joint influence of the US and the USSR, and as the former great colonial powers were taking second place, the UN had been playing a very effective role in the liberation of dependent peoples.

At an earlier time there had indeed been difficulties in the way of admitting new members to the UN, for the rivalry of the USSR and the US had been jamming the mechanism for admission. These difficulties weighed especially on the Asiatic states (Nepal, Lybia, Jordan, South Vietnam, Cambodia, and Laos) between 1950 and 1955. But they lessened after 1955, as the great powers accepted a principle of almost automatic admission. Thus there were hardly any obstacles when the large number of newly independent African nations came seeking admission later on. Mauritania was indeed held up by Soviet veto in 1960, but then admitted in 1961; later on, Kuwait, Togo, and Cameroon were held up, but not for long.

The en masse admission of the developing nations to the UN upset the organization's structure and transformed its meaning. Of the fifty-one states signing the UN foundational charter at San Francisco in 1945, only twelve were Asiatic or African (not counting the Union of South Africa); only four were newly independent. But in 1960 there were already forty-five Afro-Asian states out of ninety-nine members. Today, if we include the Latin American countries, which were founding members but have become ever more closely linked to the Third World, then the statutory two-thirds majority automatically belongs to the developing nations. Such a change is qualitative as well as quantitative.

Admittedly, the Security Council, the Economic and Social Council, and the Trusteeship Council have not been deeply changed in the process. The Third World nations have access to these councils only as members of the geographical groups to which they belong, and so the proportion of Third World nations on the Security Council has not increased despite the entry of newly independent countries into the UN. On November 4, 1960, the Third World nations, at that time forty Afro-Asian and Latin American countries, won a General Assembly vote recommending an increase in the number of council members (thirteen instead of eleven on the Security Council, twenty-four instead of eighteen on the Economic and Social Council), but disagreement within the Security Council left the problem unsolved.

The secretariat itself, however, has undergone modifications, and the developing countries have exercised an important influence in bringing these about. Most memorable is their intervention at a critical moment to save the secretariat as an organ indispensable to themselves and of potential benefit to the smaller powers generally, especially the developing countries. On October 23, 1960, they were confronted with Khrushchev's "troika" proposal. After Dag Hammarskjold's death he urged that a three-member directorate, composed of a "socialist," a "capitalist," and a "neutralist" member, replace the secretary-general. The proposal was calculated to flatter the Third World, since it was fundamentally neutral or neutralist. But the developing nations realized that the proposal also threatened to paralyze the only reasonably effective mechanism in the UN, and they preferred a single secretary-general. To counter the Soviet proposal, they urged instead the creation of three under-secretaries-general chosen "with a view to the main political tendencies of the contemporary world." India, Ghana, and the United Arab Republic backed this proposal. The UN ended up, in fact, with eight assistant secretaries-general, four of them Afro-Asian, one Indian, one Egyptian, one Nigerian, and one Latin American. The secretary-general was also chosen from the Third World: the Burmese U Thant. The solution was a reasonable one and a real success for the developing countries.

However, it is the General Assembly that has been most radically modified by the influx of Third World nations. Due to their numbers there, they have been able to exercise very great influence, greater at times than that of other UN organs. This has been made possible in part by the 1950 peacekeeping resolution which allows the General Assembly to substitute for the Security Council if the latter fails, and in part by the nature of some of the UN commissions. The Trusteeship Committee, for example, with its more traditional composition, is open to all UN member states and is able to replace the Trusteeship Council,

Southern Christian University Library
1200 Taylor Rd.
Montgomery, AL. 36117

at least in defining policy; an especially favorable arena for Third World activity is the Committee on Decolonization, to the activity of which we shall return in a moment.

Within the framework of these institutions, which their very presence modified, the developing countries have tried to conduct a political campaign along three lines: an international détente between the blocs; the liberation of dependent peoples; and later, but with growing emphasis, their own development.

The first developing countries to win independence reached the UN and the international scene right in the middle of the cold war between the West and the Soviet Union. They were not themselves much caught up in this tension and they attempted to moderate it. India especially tried to play this role at a critical moment; later some smaller countries tried to do the same—Senegal, for example, represented by Mamadou Dia at the time. The results were disappointing. It cannot be claimed that a "third force" from the Third World effected any lessening of tension; if East-West relations changed, the change was due to other factors. Besides, if all the newly independent countries were in agreement on principles, they were generally divided along East-West lines when the Soviets and the West disagreed. On the concrete details of disarmament, for example, Israel, Laos, Pakistan, and the Philippines generally supported the West; the Arabs, the Colombo group, Ghana, and Guinea adopted a "neutralist" position which, in fact, often favored the Soviets.

Almost all of the newly independent countries condemned France's early nuclear efforts, except for Laos which abstained and Israel which approved. On the Hungarian crisis in 1956 the rift was greater. A number of countries approved the Western position, while the Arab countries, India, Ceylon, and Indonesia abstained from condemning the USSR. "On the whole," concluded P. Gerbet in 1961, "the newly independent countries want disarmament and the end of the cold war. But they have hardly any means of achieving their purpose. So they seek to escape the cold war chiefly by withdrawing their geographic zone from the intervention of the great powers (cf. the Libyan affair of 1958, the Congo in 1960), but they have difficulty in assuring such a withdrawal, since they are divided among themselves and lack cogent means of action. They count above all on the UN which seems more and more to be serving the small nations."[1]

This conclusion sums up accurately the Third World's changing role in the UN. After a few nations had vainly thought themselves able to make the great powers and the UN listen to reason, the majority began to look rather to making the UN serve their own purposes: decolonization and development. The Third World's most notable activity in the UN has thus been directed at dismantling colonialism and at the progressive deepening of the independence already won by nations in the General Assembly.

Colonialism is an area in which the Third World countries have admittedly experienced many disappointments, to the extent at times of making them despair of the UN. Sekou Touré, for example, in his speech at the opening of the eighth congress of the Democratic party of Guinea (September 1967), complained that "the massacre of the courageous Vietnamese people, the refusal to denounce Israel's aggression against the Arab states, and the persistence of the inhuman policy of apartheid in South Africa are all eloquent proof of the UN's failure." This state of affairs, he added, is due to the right of veto by the five great powers and the lack of effective instruments in the hands of the UN secretariat.

Doubtless not all the developing countries equally regretted the failure to denounce Israel's aggression. At the extraordinary General Assembly dealing with the problem in July 1967, a number of them refused to endorse strong measures, and such measures failed in the end to win a two-thirds majority. Many Third World nations, however, share Sekou Touré's disappointment at the UN's powerlessness in dealing with colonialism. To understand their state of mind we need only look at some proceedings in the UN agencies.

Consider first the Security Council. In early summer of 1967 Congo-Kinshasa complained of the revolt of Katangian mercenaries and police at Kisangani. The council accepted the complaint and Theodore Idzumbuir, the Congolese representative, revealed the "Kirillis plan," drawn up at Madrid with the cooperation of a high-ranking Belgian officer, formerly counselor to Tshombe, for sabotaging the Congolese economy, stirring up mutinies, and murdering General Mobutu (in power since 1965). Several Belgians and Frenchmen were implicated in the conspiracy, he claimed, and the Portuguese and Spanish governments could not be unaware of the plotters' activities. Congo demanded the condemnation of Belgium, Spain, and Portugal, although not of France, despite the implication of some Frenchmen in the affair as the minister presented it. "Realize now," he concluded, "the colonial and racist threat to my country, and do not wait for an army to invade her from sanctuaries in Angola and Rhodesia."

Whether these complaints were valid or not, the Security Council's reply (July 2) took a significant form: the unanimous but very circumspect (no names mentioned) condemnation of states "which allow the recruiting, training, and passage of mercenaries for the overthrow of the legitimate Congo-Kinshasa government." The council went on to invite all governments to give assurances that their territory would not be so used. Before the vote the US representative made explicit the limitations of the resolution, and announced his intention of supporting it "on the understanding that it is addressed to no government in particular."

Here is another example from the same period, this time from the Committee on Decolonization. The developing nations had set far greater hopes on this agency than on the Security Council, but it too only piled up ineffective resolutions and does so still. On September 13, 1967, with twenty-one votes and two abstentions (Great Britain and Australia), a resolution of the committee condemned "the illegal arrest by South African authorities of thirty-seven Africans from South-West Africa in flagrant violation of that territory's international status," and demanded that "the South African authorities cease all illegal acts in the international territory of South-West Africa and immediately release the thirty-seven persons mentioned." Obviously such a resolution could have no practical value.

South-West Africa, formerly a German colony, later became a territory by League of Nations mandate; but since the establishment of the UN, South Africa has consistently refused to heed UN resolutions changing the League of Nations mandate into a UN trust. To the UN, then, South-West Africa is "an international territory," for which South Africa is accountable to the UN. To the Union of South Africa, on the contrary, South-West Africa is a territory wholly subject to its sovereignty. The UN has never managed to make its viewpoint prevail. It obviously did not succeed in doing so in the resolution of 1967 concerning the thirty-seven individuals charged at Johannesburg with terrorism, murder, and the attempted overthrow of the administration for the benefit of the outlawed nationalist movement, Swapo.

There are countless examples of such ineffective and useless resolutions, and of other actions taken at the UN by the developing nations but crowned with little practical success. Yet, taken as a whole, the decolonization efforts of these countries at the UN have not been in vain. Many actions may seem ineffective and yet have a real value, depending on the plan of action behind them. It is almost impossible to act directly by coercive decision at the UN; the General Assembly cannot even adopt decisions that are binding. But it is possible to act indirectly, by using the institution's resources to bring pressure to bear on some important factors in the decolonization process; this is what the developing countries have done.

What are these factors? They are, first, the behavior of colonial populations (ranging from civil disobedience to armed rebellion); second, public opinion in the mother countries; and, third, the action of the superpowers who have various means of exerting pressure, including intimidation. In practice, steps had to be taken, according to Michel Virally, "to weaken the diplomatic position of the colonial power in question (and thereby to lower its capacity for resistance)"; "to encourage native movements for independence (and, should the occasion arise, to strengthen the diplomatic position of their representatives abroad)"; "to strengthen the anticolonial sectors of public opinion back in the parent countries."[2] It was possible to move in these three directions by multiplying public debates and thus bringing the problems of decolonization to public awareness.

In the San Francisco Charter there are only hints of a "right to decolonization"; they occur in the sections on the international trust system (chapters 11 and 12 of the charter) and in Article 73 on the non-self-governing territories. The developing countries were skillful in using these two documents.

The international trust system included the right of peoples to achieve independence or some freely chosen autonomous regime. It also had in view the right to a minimum of cultural, economic, and political development, without which the first right could not effectively be exercised. This system soon came under sharp attack. For it was, in a measure, still linked to the idea of colonization and of the "sacred mission" of civilization. On the other hand, it did truly aim at decolonization, and the charter insisted on the interests of the administered population as distinct from those of the administering power (Article 76). Furthermore, the functioning of the trust system was under international control. It was thus possible to make advantageous use of the charter's dispositions on trusts.

With the charter, then, as its instrument, the General Assembly tried first of all to take some steps towards determining the date for the end of trusts. Among the trust agreements signed after the establishment of the UN, only the agreement on Somalia (1948) had a cut-off date: the trust was to last for ten years. For other trusts the General Assembly began to urge the administering powers to fix a terminal date quickly.

Questions next arose about the lifting of trusts: it was important that this take place according to the desires of the subject people, and especially that these peoples have the effective opportunity of voting for independence. The General Assembly therefore formulated some requirements, including the organization of plebiscites under its control (Togo and Cameroon) and the sending of international missions to prepare for the transition to independence (Ruanda-Urundi). The addressees of these resolutions were, in practice, obliged to accept them.

Though juxtaposed in the charter to the trust system, the status of non-self-governing territories (Article 73) was a much less favorable one. It proclaimed indeed the "primacy of the interests of the territory's people" and required the "progressive development of their free political institutions" as well as of the population's capacity for administering itself. But the word independence was missing. There was but a limited element of international control, in the form of an obligation to furnish information. Moreover, there was no definition of "non-self-governing territory," and the UN had to be satisfied initially with lists drawn up by the colonial powers themselves in 1946. In some instances the administering power stopped furnishing information. This action supposed that the territory had ceased to be non-self-governing. The General Assembly asked for explanation, and tried to formulate a definition of non-self-governing territories, no longer leaving this to the individual judgment of member states. A first list of criteria for non-self-government was approved on January 19, 1952; it was later revised and followed by a new list on October 27, 1953. Furthermore, a nation was to lose its non-self-governing status by winning independence or some "other form of separate autonomy" or by free association on equal footing with the former parent state or with some other country. As a matter of fact, any choice but independence was soon regarded as suspect, though this was the only possibility of which Article 73 did not speak.

A major problem arose in 1965. At that time Spain and Portugal, which had belatedly entered the UN and had not subscribed to the initial declarations of the San Francisco Charter, claimed that their possessions should be regarded as "overseas provinces." A resolution of December 15, 1960, therefore formulated new principles for determining the circumstances under which the states should furnish information. There were twelve principles and they constituted an interpretation of chapter 11 of the charter. Most relevant is the presumption of an obligation to furnish information if the territory in question is "geographically separated or ethnically or culturally distinct from the administering country" (fourth principle). Furthermore, the General Assembly decided that it was itself competent to apply the criteria and to decide whether a member state should furnish information. Another resolution of 1960 defined as "non-self-governing" nine territories administered by Portugal: the Portuguese government was therefore declared obliged to furnish information on these territories.

A little later there was a conflict with the United Kingdom over Southern Rhodesia. The General Assembly on June 28,

1942, declared that the "territory of Southern Rhodesia is a non-self-governing territory in the sense of chapter 11."

Thus there was a series of clarifications of the "right of decolonization." However the developing nations' most resolute intervention in behalf of decolonization was the "Declaration on the Granting of Independence to Colonial Countries and Peoples" of December 14, 1960. This well-known document adverted to "the necessity of a rapid and unconditional end to colonialism in all its forms and manifestations." The application of the declaration is spelled out under six main headings. (1) "The subjection of peoples to a foreign yoke, domination, and exploitation is a denial of fundamental human rights; it is contrary to the United Nations Charter; and it compromises the cause of world peace and collaboration." (2) "All peoples have the right to free self-determination; in virtue of it they freely determine their political status and freely pursue their economic, social, and cultural development." (3) "The lack of preparation is never to be a pretext for delaying independence."

The fourth, fifth, and sixth sections look to more practical and immediately applicable consequences. "There shall be an end to all repressive measures . . . against dependent peoples." "Immediate steps are to be taken . . . to hand over all power to the peoples [of dependent territories] without reserve or condition . . . so as to allow them to enjoy complete independence and liberty." "Every attempt to destroy . . . national unity and territorial integrity of a nation is incompatible with the goals and principles of the United Nations Charter."

The project was presented by forty-three nations and adopted by eighty-nine votes, with no exception but with nine abstentions.

The statement that the dependence of peoples is contrary to the charter is contradicted (as has been pointed out) by chapters 11 through 13 of the charter which provide for such a situation of dependence and furnish a juridical framework for it. "The charter systems," says Mr. Virally, "whether of international trust or of non-self-governing territories, are based on the idea that independence should be delayed until a minimum level of political, economic, social, and educational development is reached."[3] But the offsetting argument offered was that the colonial link perdures contrary to the will of the dependent peoples, whereas Article 7 requires respect for "the principle of the priority of the inhabitants' interests."

Whether or not the declaration was illegal from the viewpoint of the charter, its passage by the assembly helped speed up what seemed to be a lagging decolonization. Even though as a simple declaration it had no binding force, it did have a notable effect.

While effecting the passage of these various resolutions, the developing countries were also working, as we noted earlier, to multiply their means of intervention and discussion at the UN. There was, first of all, the effort to assimilate control over non-self-governing territories to trust control as provided by the charter. In this direction the General Assembly adopted as early as November 3, 1947, a "plan to be used as a guide by member states in preparing the information to be supplied in accordance with Article 73." Next, the assembly found a way to intervene against the exploitation of information collected on the non-self-governing states. It began by bidding the secretary-general to take cognizance of this information in his annual report. Then it established a special committee to examine this information before the opening of the next session. The committee was to be composed equally of administering and non-administering powers. On January 18, 1964, this examining committee became permanent, as the Committee on Information Related to the Non-self-governing Territories.

In fact, since 1948 the committee's report has acquired great importance and provided a basis for many of the General Assembly's resolutions. The assembly sought, moreover, to obtain information, through the committee, on political and constitutional development, "in accordance with the spirit of Article 73," though not according to its letter. The first recommendation along these lines was in 1947, and it was often renewed, especially after 1960. The Committee on Information was thus, much like the Trusteeship Council, an important instrument of control in colonial affairs, and it became, in practice, a major organ of the UN.

A further step was taken in 1961. The majority which had secured the Declaration on Independence of 1960 was no longer satisfied with the Committee on Information, set up as it was on a parity basis. At the 1961 assembly the same majority secured the creation of a special seventeen-member committee to "study the application of the Declaration" and to make any recommendation helpful in implementing it (November 21, 1961). The new committee, unlike the old, soon became the tool of a majority bent on harassing the colonial powers; all but three members of the committee were from the anticolonial powers. Moreover, the committee was given a free hand in deciding its own procedure. It considered itself empowered, for example, to sit between UN sessions; thus it became a kind of permanent organ. It resolved to determine on its own the list of territories it would be concerned with; it drew up a questionnaire for the administering powers; it took to itself the right to receive petitions and to hear petitioners (through a special subcommittee) as well as to send investigative missions to some territories (while recognizing, of course, "the need to obtain the cooperation of the administrative powers involved"). It soon took the name "Committee on Decolonization," in which guise we have already met it.

The first report of the new committee (1962) was 597 pages long and dealt with twelve territories (the two Rhodesias, Nyassaland, Basutoland, Bechuanaland, Swaziland, Zanzibar, British Guiana, Mozambique, South-West Africa, Kenya, and Angola). The report led to a General Assembly resolution on seven of these countries; the report had previously been discussed in plenary session, with no prior examination by an assembly commission. Later on, the Committee on Decolonization continued to be concerned with all the touchy affairs in this area, especially the Rhodesian affair and the affair of the Portuguese colonies.

The resolutions were, of course, in every instance nonobligatory, and this fact often angered the developing nations. Nonetheless, from the view of such nations at least, we can find great value in the efforts they put forth in the UN in the cause of decolonization; they made a voice heard on the public stage which would hardly otherwise have been heard. Even today, such efforts are so important in the eyes of the developing countries that they often give them priority over the third of their objectives, namely, to win all possible concessions for their own development.

Even within the more technical and specialized agencies of the UN, and at the risk of hindering the functioning of these agencies, they take every occasion to harass the remaining colonial powers. In the International Labor Organization and in UNESCO, for example, political problems often take priority, contrary to the primary purposes of the organizations. If all this energy is likely to be less fruitful in the years ahead (we have already heard Sekou Touré's bitter criticism on the point), it is because the effectiveness of international organizations is declining. But at least the UN has been for years a privileged instrument of the developing countries in their struggle for decolonization. They had indeed good reason to attach great importance to their presence in the UN and to their international baptism.

REGIONAL
ORGANIZATIONS OF
DEVELOPING
COUNTRIES

While trying to make their presence felt on the world stage, the developing nations were also trying to organize themselves into coherent groups. The effort was directed, first of all, to forming an all-embracing organization which would enable the developing nations to act effectively at the international level. We spoke earlier of "the 77," who are quite significant in this context. At the same level, there were efforts to unify the developing nations within the UN proper. The efforts met with varying success.

There was a well-known Afro-Asian group in the UN not long ago. It was initially dominated by a strong majority of Arab nations but was reorganized on a broader basis after the Bandung Conference (1955). For a long period it elicited identical and unanimous votes from its members (in two-thirds of the cases involved, according to a statistical study by Thomas Bovet). Unanimity was especially certain in votes for decolonization; we have already seen how the developing nations concentrated on this matter in the UN. In time the group lost its drive for several reasons. First, as the number of developing nations in the UN grew, the need to rally votes became less urgent. Second, the African nations had been entering the UN in large numbers, and after the Accra Conference of 1958, Ghana's initiative led to the formation of an African group to see to it that their continent should project its own personality on the international scene. The Africans, however, were themselves divided from 1961 on, with the Casablanca group on one side ("positive neutralism"), along with Ghana, Guinea, Mali, and Morocco, and, on the other, the Brazzaville group of twelve more "moderate" states, bent on a "united diplomacy" and on common activity within ther UN. States of this second group were, for example, to support Kasavubu in the Congo and to back the admission of Mauritania to the UN, against the opposition of Morocco and the Casablanca group.

Because of these and other developments, such as the failure of the second Bandung Conference which was to have been held at Algiers in 1965, we must record that despite many efforts, the political unity of the developing nations as a whole (the unity of a "third world") has been slow in coming. Even if we look only at the African and Asian states and leave aside the Latin American countries, we must draw the same conclusion. There has been genuine success in organizing a total group only where the members limit themselves to objectives of a more economic kind; such is the significance, once again, of "the 77," from Geneva (1964) to Algiers (1967) and New Delhi (1968).

At the regional or continental level, however, more has been achieved, and we must attend closely to what is taking shape here. The most interesting institution at this level is beyond doubt the Organization for African Unity (OAU). But we must also mention the Organization of American States (OAS) with its special characteristics, and not forget other organizations which are political without being intergovernmental, such as the Organization for Latin American Solidarity (OLAS) which is dedicated to revolution on a continental scale. In Asia, apart from the Arab Mid-East, we do not find any really regional organizations, for the name can hardly be applied to the Southeast Asia Treaty Organization (SEATO) or even to the successive forms of the Maphilindo project (Malaysia, Philippines, Indonesia).

Africa: The Organization for African Unity (OAU)

The OAU was born in 1963 of an effort to overcome the division between two rival organizations of African states, the Casablanca and Brazzaville groups, or "revolutionary Africa" and "moderate Africa," which had both been formed shortly after independence.

The Brazzaville group was formed in 1963 and resulted from a conference of heads of state held at Brazzaville. Houphouet-Boigny expressed its spirit in a statement sharply critical of neutralism: "There are those who want a 'positive' neutralism which both blocs would respect. But we are realists and are therefore determined to concentrate on real solidarity in defense matters in order to confront neo-colonialism, such a solidarity as will force the sorcerer's apprentices of neo-colonialism to respect us." This seems to mean, in fact, the internal consolidation of an African neutral zone rather than an active political effort (as was implied in "positive neutralism"). But Houphouet-Boigny came out much more clearly on March 24, 1961, in the weekly journal *Fraternité*: "We want Africa to become a large Switzerland, with its neutrality guaranteed by all. But we are not children. We know that the world is divided into two camps and that Africa is a central concern of both . . . . The Brazzaville Twelve have chosen the Western camp." Not all the twelve went so far perhaps, but Houphouet-Boigny's remarks nonetheless do express a clear-cut opposition to another political thrust which aimed at a rapprochement between Africa and the Eastern bloc.

The latter political goal was represented by the Casablanca group which included Morocco, Ghana, Guinea, and Mali. Morocco, it is true, belonged to the group only because of the support it received from the other members and from the USSR in its territorial claims to Mauritania. Guinea and Mali, on the contrary, pursued a quite explicit policy of neutralism which was in fact rather favorable to the Eastern bloc and hostile to the Western world and the former colonial powers.

Thus in their search for pan-African unity the African nations were divided. But each was apprehensive of the consequences for itself of such a division, namely the danger of subversion and plots engineered from neighboring countries. This explosive situation, vividly felt by the majority, led to the search for an organization which would embrace all the African peoples. The search ended with the establishment of the OAU at Addis Ababa in 1963. The Brazzaville and Casablanca groups agreed to dissolve; their dissolution caused no great difficulty since neither was a structured organization. The Afro-Malagasy Union, however, was a more delicate matter. The Union, close in spirit to the Brazzaville group, included the former French colonies (except for Togo, Mali, and Guinea) and had a much more articulated structure. It had various agencies for cooperation: the AMU proper, in the political area; the Afro-Malagasy Organization for Economic Cooperation (AMOEC) in the economic sector; and there was even an embryonic military organization. But after some hesitation the AMU agreed to dissolve, provided that certain agencies for cooperation should be established within the new scheme. Addis Ababa was thus a great conference of mutual rediscovery by revolutionary Africa and moderate Africa, and by black Africa and white Africa as well. Today there are thirty-eight member states in the OAU.

The circumstances which led to the reunion also gave the new organization a somewhat conservative style. Its prime concern was protection from divisions and their consequences, and the OAU can be described as a Holy Alliance, similar to the one that emerged from the Council of Vienna in 1815. The OAU's first and most important act was to give solemn guarantees to existing frontiers and thus to reject territorial claims which could lead to a series of conflicts among the African states. Two years later, at Accra, the OAU adopted resolutions on political refugees and on subversion. The member states pledged themselves to tolerate no form of subversion by political refugees and no subversive activity against a member state. They obliged themselves not to engage in a press and radio campaign on any situation within a member state of the OAU and not to cause dissension within states or among them by encouraging or aggravating social, religious, ethnic, or other disagreements. The member states also agreed to observe the principles of international law in dealing with political refugees and to encourage refugees to return home with their own and their country's consent. At the same time, of course, they promised to guarantee the security of political refugees from nonindependent African territories and to support them in their struggle for the freedom of their native land. All these resolutions were adopted in order to save the OAU from the severe tensions which threatened its existence. Eighteen French-speaking African states had refused to attend the Accra conference on the grounds that Guinea was promoting subversive activities against them. But in taking these resolutions the organization also confirmed its character as a Holy Alliance; the OAU thus preserved its existence, but it also limited its effectiveness, since it has tended not to intervene in the important issues of the day.

In practice, the OAU still survives, ten years after its creation, but it has a uniformly difficult existence. At one point, some members feared it would become the private instrument of Nkrumah, president of Ghana, in his campaign for pan-Africanism. A case in point is the way the organization kept Tshombe out of the way at the Cairo conference of 1964 by confining him to his hotel. But the uneasy members received reassurance from the resolutions of the Accra conference in 1965, and the chief source of danger was removed by the fall of the Ghanian leader whose ambitions no one else inherited. Nonetheless the organization is far from having fulfilled its promise. Since its establishment in May 1963 (Abbis Abada) it has held regular summit conferences: Cairo (July 1964), Accra (November 1965), Addis Ababa (November 1966), Kinshasa (September 1967), Algiers (September 1968). But most of the meetings have taken place in an atmosphere of tension. Thus, for various reasons, the number of participating heads of state has steadily dwindled: twenty-six out of thirty-eight at Accra in 1965, twenty at Addis

Ababa in 1966, sixteen at Kinshasa in 1967. "Disenchantment" was the explanation.

The Kinshasa conference of 1967 offers a rather significant example. When the conference opened, no one expected anything important to come from it. If we may believe the foreign observers, the conference intended to pass over in silence all divisions among the states: the Nigerian war of Biafran secession; the civil war in the Sudan. Major General Gowon, head of the Nigerian federal government, had several times declared that the conflict between the Lagos authorities and the separatist government of Biafra was a strictly Nigerian affair. In the Sudan, Mr. Maghghoub had stated his opposition to a conference with a majority of black heads of state taking cognizance of a conflict between his government and three Southern provinces where the population was almost entirely black. Nor could there be any question, it seemed to the conference, of officially discussing the frontier quarrels of Algeria and Morocco, and Algeria and Tunisia, which had lately been brought before the organization and were still not settled; or the territorial dispute between the Republic of Somalia and Kenya on the one side and Ethiopia on the other (concerning Ogaden); or finally the quarrel over hostages, in which Guinea and Ivory Coast were at loggerheads. The issue in this last case centered on some Ivory Coast fishermen who were stopped and examined by Guinean authorities in Guinean waters during February 1967 and on two Guinean ministers who were arrested in reprisal at Abidjan airport at the end of June.

The foreign observers were perhaps prone to pessimism and spite. But even the president of the conference, Dior Hamani (Nigerian head of state), showed himself quite reserved: "This summit meeting must be a realistic conference. The member states have their own internal problems. I am among those who regard such problems as primarily problems of development . . . . By reaching unanimity on what unites us, we can eliminate what divides us."

In addition, the Kinshasa conference expected to be subject to more absenteeism than previous meetings. There would be the absence, to begin with, of most French-speaking heads of state (among them Houphouet-Boigny, Senghor, and Tsiranana);

Dior Hamani, presiding at the conference, would have to represent the "French-speaking club" all by himself. Expected, too, was the absence of Modibo Keita and Sekou Touré, both doubtless kept at home by the domestic situation in their respective countries (Mali and Guinea); of most heads of state from the Maghreb (especially Boumedienne who had no desire to discuss the recent disappearance of Tshombe); of Doctor Kamazu Banda, president of Malawi, a pan-African but also not desirous of being forced too soon into sanctions against Rhodesia and South Africa. Since the conference would be taking place in the Congo, it was expected to find in attendance, along with General Mobutu, the heads of state of neighboring countries: Rwanda, Central Africa, and Congo-Brazzaville, along with Emperor Haile Selassie and President William Tubman of Liberia, the two "historical figures" of African unity.

In the end, the conference exceeded expectations. The Republic of Somalia and Kenya decided to renew diplomatic relations, and their border conflict could thus be settled. Furthermore, the conference did take up the question of Biafra and appointed a commission to "mediate" in the Nigerian struggle, even if this move came only at the last minute, a few hours before adjournment. The resolution stated: "The conference condemns every act of secession within a member state and, while recognizing that here this is an internal matter the resolution of which belongs primarily to the Nigerians themselves, it renews its faith and confidence in the federal government of Nigeria" and "determines to send a consultative mission, made up of six heads of state, to the president of the Nigerian federal government in order to assure him of the conference's wish to safeguard the peace and territorial integrity of Nigeria." The mission included Emperor Haile Selassie, Presidents Dior Hamani (Niger), Ankrah (Ghana), Ahidjo (Cameroon), Tubman (Liberia), and Mobutu (Congo-Kinshasa). The mediation effort was ineffective, but at least henceforth the OAU would be concerned with the Biafran situation.

A further decision at Kinshasa dealt with the subject of mercenaries in the Congo. A committee was formed which brought together all the states bordering on the Congo (Congo-Brazzaville,

Central African Republic, Sudan, Uganda, Zambia, Tanzania, Rwanda, Burundi) in order to examine ways and means of helping Congo-Kinshasa. In practice, the committee spent its time trying to work out a way of evacuating the mercenaries and providing sanctuary for the Katangian police.

U Thant, the UN secretary-general, was present at the Kinshasa meeting, and at its end, despite the positive results achieved, felt obliged to warn the members against "fragmentation" and "provincialism." He added: "The members of the OAU, the charter of which is based on common principles and ideals, must avoid the danger of narrowing their vision and must keep a right balance between collective efforts for Africa as a whole and the duties incumbent on them as members of the world community of nations. A narrow nationalism has no place in our age, twenty years after the birth of the United Nations; the world today has entered the era of interdependence." And still more sternly: "Everyone agrees that in the last few years your organization has not made all hoped-for progress towards its goals." The concession that followed did not weaken the criticism: "In a continent containing such cultural and ethnic diversity, slow progress is neither surprising nor discouraging. The Organization for African Unity is a young organization. We can only hope that it will achieve its objectives in a few years' time."

The Algerian summit conference of 1968 was not to belie these critical judgments on the OAU. Nigeria and Biafra were again on the agenda. The supporters of Biafra were obviously left unconvinced as primary stress was put on Nigerian unity. The conference president, Mr. Boumedienne, in particular, exerted all his authority in behalf of Nigerian integrity, but to little purpose. Guns were to settle the matter in the end.

The insistence of many members of the OAU on Nigerian unity is easy to explain: the organization has its roots chiefly in the instinct for self-preservation of the heads of state and of the states themselves. Each one is aware that his own situation becomes precarious as soon as frontiers are anywhere threatened or a government is overthrown. The OAU, of course, finally accepts as legitimate any new regimes that achieve stability (in

Togo, Ghana, etc.), but it does so only after a period of waiting and application for recognition, so as not to encourage rebellions against the established government. We must conclude that to the majority of states mutual security is of greater value than a dynamic political orientation and that the assured unity of the continent as a whole is worth the sacrifice of many important political goals. The OAU has not thus far proven this diagnosis false, but at least it continues to be an agent of unity for the continent.

Such unity as the OAU stands for is admittedly loose enough to allow regional organizations, especially economic ones. Thus, in the French-speaking countries, the Afro-Malagasy Union has ceased to exist, but the Afro-Malagasy Organization for Economic Cooperation has been replaced by the Organization for Afro-Malagasy Cooperation. In another organizational framework the finance ministers of the thirteen French-speaking Afro-Malagasy countries regularly work together on monetary matters; these are the countries whose currency is guaranteed by the French franc. For example, at Dakar in 1967 the ministers met with Messrs. Debré and Yvon Bourges to prepare for the general conference at Rio of the International Monetary Fund and the International Bank for Reconstruction and Development. Present at Dakar were the seven members of the West African Monetary Union (Ivory Coast, Dahomey, Upper Volta, Mauritania, Niger, Senegal, and Togo) and the five members of the Monetary Union of Equatorial Africa and Cameroon (Cameroon, Central African Republic, Congo-Brazzaville, Gabon, Chad), along with Madagascar. Mali was at this time reentering the West African Monetary Union and was represented at the 1967 meeting by an observer.

There are other, analogous efforts at cooperation but all of them have economic goals and limited scope. Only the OAU is a political organization with a broader horizon. Its effectiveness is indeed limited by its politics of self-preservation, and it has little interest for those whose political goals are more daring or more revolutionary. But perhaps in this present stage of consolidation after winning independence, the primary objectives of the African nations are bound to be political stability and respect for frontiers. How long must such a state of affairs last? The question arises in the mind of every observer of the OAU and doubtless in the minds of responsible Africans as well.

South America

When we first turn to Latin America, we may think there is a parallel between the OAU which unites the African states and the Organization of American States (OAS) which unites the American states. However, we soon notice the fundamental difference between the two organizations and begin to understand the special situation of the Latin American continent: only the African states belong to the OAU, whereas the OAS includes, along with the Latin American republics, the United States, and the latter bulks large indeed in the organization. We might think that there is a similar situation in the union of Common Market Europe and the "associated" African states; the great difference, however, is that only economic agreements are involved here and that Europe is not a member of the OAU, the political organization.

For some years now, or, more exactly, since the death of President Kennedy, the OAS has seen United States efforts to use it as a bulwark against revolutions. Consider, for example, the twelfth conference of OAS foreign ministers at Washington in September 1967. The meeting was requested by Venezuela after an infiltration attempt by guerillas, some of them Cuban. The Bolivian foreign affairs minister Walter Guevara Arce tried to prove with photographic evidence that Ernesto Che Guevara, who had disappeared from Cuba in April 1965, was the chief organizer of the Bolivian revolutionary underground and that he was in Bolivia a short time before the infiltration. Che in fact died near Camari, Bolivia, a few weeks after the Washington meeting. According to the Bolivian minister, other "close collaborators" of Fidel Castro had been active with Che in Bolivia since 1966.

The meeting was thus primarily devoted to an investigation of the Castroite threat, and Dean Rusk, who backed the Venezuelan resolutions, asked that the Cuban policy be "condemned and denounced as a flagrant violation of international treaties, of the principles of international law, and of the basis of the relations between states." The American secretary of state went on to say: "The countries of the Northern hemisphere will not allow a handful of agitators to draw them away from their main purpose: to effect a peaceful revolution with the help of the Alliance for Progress." The conference thus represented another step along the political line followed by the United States: a solemn denunciation of "Castroite subversion"; an appeal to friendly countries to stop regarding the Cuban regime as legitimate; a recommendation to countries touched by the Cuban "menace" to join hands and increase their exchange of "services" in the anti-guerilla struggle; finally, an invitation to boycott ships engaged in trade with Havana.

But four South American countries refused to let the inter-American system be changed into an anti-Communist or an anti-Castroite organization: Mexico, Chile, Colombia, Uruguay. A still larger number feared that in following the US lead they might simply be paving the way for interventions like that of the US in the Dominican Republic, not long before. Had not General Harold Johnson, American army chief of staff, declared in 1967: "The United States has in reserve highly trained forces, superior to those used in Santo Domingo, which it can quickly send to Latin America in answer to a call for help from an allied government"? Such forces, the general added, made the establishment of an "inter-American force" unnecessary! The "inter-American force" had been for several years a major objective of the US within the OAS, but the reluctance of several countries (especially those mentioned above) effectively prevented its establishment.

Th OAS situation, which has lasted for quite a few years, suggests some reflections. Clearly evident is the powerful and obviously "asymmetrical" pressure exerted by the North American partner in the organization. But we may ask whether in the absence of the US there would be fewer tensions than the organization has experienced in recent years, for these occurred every time the US pushed the struggle against Castroite subversion or the establishment of an inter-American interventionary force.

We may be inclined to answer this question with a "yes," if we look back to the organization's tranquil days in the Roosevelt and post-Roosevelt periods, when in the name of good neighborliness the US was politically much less active on the Latin American continent. However, we must take into account that among the South American states themselves the OAS experienced tranquillity only as long as it, too, was a kind of Holy Alliance, somewhat after the manner of the OAU, with each country looking primarily for the security which nonintervention guaranteed.

Nowadays, within Latin America, Cuba no longer adheres to the principle of nonintervention, or at least it has exposed itself to the charge of intervention. It has been excluded from the OAS and would probably have been excluded even from an interstate organization made up only of Latin American nations. In further contrast to earlier days, the South American states are generally becoming more and more divided along political lines. On the one side are countries like Chile, Mexico, and Uruguay, whose political stance is more favorable to social change and to independence of the United States. On the other are those, especially the military regimes (with Brazil at their head today), which are more conservative and less uneasy about dependence on the United States. Venezuela, after suffering so much subversive activity in the last few years, seemed ready to join the second group, at least until the election of Raphael Caldera as president of the republic (December 1968); Caldera immediately showed that he wanted peace with Cuba.

Both groups are now politically active. The activity is not enough to break up the OAS, for the security afforded by nonintervention is valuable to all of them, but it is enough to create strong tensions within the organization, even independently of the presence of the United States whose very active policy under Johnson increased the disharmony within the OAS. In short, even if we leave aside the United States' position within the OAS, it can be said that despite interesting efforts at economic organization (such as the Latin American free exchange area), continental unity is presently much weaker there than in Africa.

A confirmation of this judgment may be found in the existence for the last few years of associations of parties and underground

groups which claim to represent another kind of continental policy. These exist alongside the inter-governmental organizations.
Such associations have no real parallel in Africa today.

We must indeed be realistic about the strength of such organizations. Consider the Organization for Latin American Solidarity
(OLAS), denounced by Dean Rusk at the tenth conference of
OAS foreign ministers in 1967, as a "tool of the Cuban regime"
(the OLAS had just had a meeting in Havana).   Rusk added,
however: "The Organization for Latin American Solidarity shows
a deepening rift between extremist elements and the orthodox
members who follow the Moscow line and prefer a peaceful
approach."

Just at the time Rusk spoke, the outlawed Brazilian Communist
party expressed opposition to the OLAS and removed Carlos
Magelha from his office. He had claimed to represent the Brazilian
Communists at the Havana conference of the OLAS in July.
But the party, it was announced, "had sent no represenative to
the OLAS conference in Havana." The Chilean Communist
party, too, had just sharply criticized the policy of Cuba and
of the OLAS. The party's secretary-general, Luis Korvalan, published an important article in *Pravda* at the end of July. In it
he tried to show that revolutionary movements in each Latin
American country have their own special conditions of development and action and that the leaders of such movements "know
better than anyone else what they can and ought to do." He
added that if brotherly advice is useful, models imported from
abroad are not necessarily useful as well. He insisted, further
—against the OLAS view—on the necessity of securing unity
of action within each country between the Communist party and
other revolutionary forces, especially those springing from the
lower middle class. "It is impossible to create a revolutionary
avant-garde in an arbitrary or artificial way around a leader or
around men who individually adopt the most radical positions
(at least as they themselves see it) and are prepared to engage
in this or that revolutionary action." Again: "The Cuban revolution shows that it is impossible to generalize from the specific
details of one or other experience. It would indeed be wrong
to deny that the general characteristics of the Cuban revolution

may be repeated elsewhere, but the concrete forms will be different." Therefore he warns against "risky undertakings which cause
the death of valuable revolutionaries and end in setbacks." The
article ends with what might be called a declaration of independence from Castroism: "The Latin American Communist parties
came into being at different periods and act in different social
and political circumstances. Some parties attempt to bypass the
phase of the assimilation of socialist ideas. But Communists do
not think that such an approach is the only possible one."

The OLAS Conference of July, 1967, had to open without
Communist delegates from Venezuela, Argentina, and Brazil,
although the organizers of the conference had promised that all
the Latin American Communist parties would participate. The
Chilean and Colombian party delegates did come, but showed
dissident views from the outset. As a matter of fact, the OLAS
no longer consisted only of radical groups which agreed with
the more intransigent Cuban views. All anti-imperialist movements had a right to membership if they accepted the resolutions
of the "Tricontinental Conference" (Havana, 1966). In fact, those
groups did not join which refused to see in guerilla warfare and
in the immediate creation of a new Vietnam the only revolutionary
solution.

After the Mid-East crisis of early summer, 1967, and after
the Kosygin-Johnson meeting at Glassboro, Raoul Castro, Fidel's
brother, had announced defiantly: "Cuba is no one's satellite."
The coolness of the USSR had in fact already been shown at
the time of the Tricontinental Conference, and since then the
rift had continued to widen between the orthodox Communist
parties and the groups that adopted pro-Cuban principles. Where
will revolutionary recklessness end, asked the orthodox, as they
pointed to the defeat of the guerillas who had launched an attack
in Peru a year before and whose leaders were now on trial. Where
will the procrastination policy of the orthodox Communist parties
end, asked their opponents. The latter could point to the hypocrisy
of the Argentinian party whose leader, Victorio Codovilla, had
advocated armed struggle at least as a "last resort," but had done
nothing when President Ilia was deposed by the Argentinian
army. They could point to the Brazilian Communist party's sub-

missiveness to the middle classes. The Cuban periodical *Theory and Practice* said on this last subject: "The coup d'etat which overthrew Joao Goulart and brought Castelo Branco to power was possible only because the Communist party was unable to show the necessary independence."

The continental revolutionary movement thus suffers from deep schisms, reflecting schisms within the Communist world as a whole. At times, moreover, the "pro-Chinese" themselves show a real disaffection toward Cuba, thus creating a three-way split. Nonetheless, the OLAS has at least existed and has been able to promote guerilla uprisings at various places on the continent. For this reason it deserves consideration, along with the inter-governmental OAS, among organizational efforts in the continents of the underdeveloped world. Its presence, alongside an inter-governmental organization which itself is in a state of tension, underlines the great difficulty of uniting the Latin American continent behind any single policy; the schism within the revolutionary forces themselves only highlights the difficulty even further.

Asiatic Organizations

Asia, it need hardly be said, does not enjoy such a unified policy either. In fact, it enjoys it even less than the other continents: either as a whole, or in its Western or Eastern sectors.

In the West the Arab League, established after the Second World War, has passed through serious crises since Nasser came to power. It has seen the rivalry between Nasser's Egypt and Saudi Arabia, which was intensified during the war in Yemen. It has been further rocked by Bourguiba's denunciation of Arab intransigence towards Israel, for this intransigence was the only bond uniting the League once the rivalry between Egypt and Saudi Arabia had begun.

On the eve of the last Arab-Israeli War (1967) there was a spectacular reconciliation of Saudi Arabia and Egypt, but it did not last long. At the ensuing Khartoum Conference new divisions were already evident, especially on some new issues resulting from the war. Confronting Nasser, who had been won over to moderation, was Syria, supported by Algeria; they were raising the flag of intransigence. Again in 1969, at the Rabat Conference of the Islamic countries, deep rifts in Arab unity were evident. All this means that while the Arab nations have no choice but to cling together on the international scene and to support each other against Israel, they are far from forming the single-minded bloc which Nasser was promoting.

As for South-East Asia, we mentioned in passing, early in this chapter, a project for uniting a number of countries in the area. In its most ambitious form, the project involved Malaysia, the Philippines, Thailand, Indonesia, South Vietnam, Burma, Cambodia, and Laos. All these countries, after all, had a stake in the South-East Asia Friendship and Economy Treaty (SEAFET), which the Malaysian prime minister, Tunku Abdul Rahman, proposed in January, 1959. In fact, however, the neutralist nations kept aloof from the beginning. The nations most involved in the new project seemed compromised by membership in the South-East Asia Treaty Organization (SEATO), founded by John Foster Dulles as a pendant to NATO: the Philippines and Thailand were members of SEATO, and Malaysia had military agreements with Great Britain. Hanoi and Peking immediately branded SEAFET and SEATO as "two imperialist schemes." By 1960 it was clear that only the Philippines, Thailand, and Malaysia could sign the SEAFET agreement. The treaty was renamed the Association of South-East Asian States (ASAS), and then ASA after an intergovernmental conference at Bangkok in 1961. According to the declaration issued by the conference, the association was concerned with cooperation in cultural affairs, in the use of natural resources, and in international exchanges.

But the Communist countries still voiced opposition. Indonesia was reserved, and this was a serious matter in view of her importance for organizing the tin and rubber markets. Neutralist Burma also wanted to stand aside, and this hindered the organization of the rice market. In the end, the undertaking had but limited success, because the great nations of Asia did not cooperate and British business groups, especially the airlines, were cold to the association. Then, to complicate the situation even further, there arose the dispute between the Philippines and Malaysia about North Borneo (1962). The meetings of foreign affairs ministers, called for by ASA, were rescheduled several times and finally put off indefinitely in 1963. Relations between the two countries improved later on, but the future of ASA or any similar organization remains uncertain. The later development of Indonesia might seem to favor a revitalized organization. But the simultaneous division of South-East Asia by the Vietnam War has shelved all such projects. Thus, under the heading of "regional organizations" there is very little to say for Asia up to now.

Generally, then (although with nuances according to continent), and despite great energies expended on the morrow of independence, political divisions between the developing nations have run too deep for cooperative political projects to be possible. The only organizations that endure are those concerned with mutual security and non-intervention; at least they endure where no one is very tempted to intervene, as in Africa, and where security is prized above all other political goals.

The result of such a situation is a serious one for the underdeveloped nations: they can pursue no large-scale political aims. Not too long ago, the Third World united within the UN in efforts to speed independence; today it can unite only in its pursuit of economic development, as in "the 77," but then the unity lacks effectiveness because there is no genuine common political will behind it.

This is one of the key weaknesses of the Third World, and it is more serious for the immediate future than all the economic indicators of which so much is made: lagging growth of agricultural production and of international trade, decreasing value of money, etc. Since independence, the Third World has not spoken with one voice as it did at Bandung, nor has any single continent so spoken. This is one of the greatest distresses of the distressed continents.

THE THIRD WORLD
AND THE GREAT POWERS

The developing countries, despite the high hopes they set on their international activity, have not succeeded in forming a truly political Third World nor even in establishing genuinely active political forces on a continental scale. Thus they have often found themselves thrown back on their relations with the great powers: the United States or the Communist powers, Russia and China. How do these relations stand today?

In like fashion, many developing countries, once they have become independent, have had to enter into new relations with the great powers which were formerly their parent states. Often, after a period of crisis, they have reestablished cordial relations. It is important for us to evaluate these relations too. It must immediately be noted also that relations with former parent states are somewhat disquieting for the developing countries. At times, then, to counterbalance these close links or to be able to stand up to the parent states at critical moments, the developing countries have turned to other powers which had not played the same colonial role toward them. These two sets of relations then cut across each other.

41

Our aim is to gauge the strengths and weaknesses of the developing countries, and in this chapter we shall be forced to recognize that the hopes of the developing countries in their relations with the great powers have not been fully realized.

Relations with Former Parent States

In regard to former parent states, the first effort of the new states was generally to establish their independence on a solid basis. In several instances, the new nations even sought to break all ties. Doubtless they did not want to provoke all the crises that arose, but they did want room to move freely. Once the crises were past, many countries had to enter into renewed relations with the parent states. Resignation was often their frame of mind in this, even when the renewal was outwardly cordial enough.

In short, even where independence was peacefully achieved, the links with former parent states were at first steadily reduced, and there was a general lessening of the close relations that marked the time of independence itself. Then, in a second stage, relations became progressively normalized.

Let us recall, then, first of all, the close ties which united many newly independent countries to their former parent states. Many circumstances favored such close relations, despite independence: habits, institutions, customs, sometimes a common language, along with various practical considerations (belonging to the same military defense area or to the same monetary zone, with the mutual advantages these brought with them). Habit and immediate interest led to the establishment of privileged relations between the independent countries and their former parent states. This happened, for example, between the United States and the Philippines and between France and the majority of those African states which had been part of the French empire.

Some agreements of this kind were reached even before independence, as between France and a number of countries that emerged from her sphere of sovereignty. Nothing like this happened in the trust territories, however; for them and for countries that became separated from the United States, Great Britain, and

Belgium, agreements were negotiated and signed only after independence.

Among the new relations, there were few formal treaties. At times, however, there was the reality of a treaty, translated into the form of privileged diplomatic relations that were to be guaranteed by high-ranking representatives instead of ordinary ambassadors. The same reality found expression in cooperation between diplomatic services and in agreements on information and mutual consultation. All this took place within the framework of the French Union (later the French Community) or the Commonwealth. At times, military cooperation was maintained, at least for defense purposes. Agreements of this kind existed between France and several nations of black Africa, and were applied, for example, in the Libreville troubles in Gabon (1964) and in Chad (September 1968, and July 1969).

Most importantly, there was financial and technical cooperation through common monetary zones and agreements for technical and financial assistance. There was the privileged status accorded individuals in the territory of the other country, along with extraordinary procedural guarantees. There were agreements on business establishments, involving equal rights and reciprocal treatment for individuals of the two countries.

Close relations of this kind were kept or established with almost all former colonies, except for Guinea, and with the former mandates and trusts, except for Syria and Libya (France), Jordan and the Sudan (Great Britain). There were military agreements between the Philippines and the United States, between Malaysia, Ceylon, and Great Britain, between the African states which were members of the Community or belonged to the Entente, and France.[4]

The sequence of events is rather uniform: rupture, denunciation, and in every case later renewal and revision of relations. Here is a pessimistic summing-up from 1961. "The Holland-Indonesia union was broken in 1954, and nothing is now left of the agreements the two countries made in 1949. The French-Guinean agreements of 1959 have never been applied. French relations with Morocco and Tunisia are quite different today from what was anticipated in the agreements drawn up at independence. Agreements between Belgium and the Congo will surely never be applied . . . . Initial relations tend to deteriorate as the advantages originally granted to the former parent state are gradually reduced."[5]

The development was less unfavorable for the majority of African states. Yet in 1961 it was possible to say: "The very favorable atmosphere should not blind us to the fact that every revision of relations tends to reduce the advantages initially granted to the former parent state, or to increase its obligations, which amounts to the same thing. The influence of the dominant power grows ever less, and its privileges are gradually watered down. Gradually the former parent states become no different than other countries."[6]

In general, the weakening of relations has chiefly affected the privileged status of persons and property, or military advantage (the French bases have vanished from most North African countries). Financial and technical cooperation—which evidently favors the new nations—has been much less affected. The burdens on the Third World countries were the more easily thrown off as they appeared, or could appear (as in the case of the military bases), to be a prolongation of the former overlord's domination.

Developments did not affect only the content of the relations. The new nations wanted not only to cast off burdens, but also, and above all, to avoid all bilateral relations with particular countries. A universal international society was on the horizon and much was expected of it. But special relationships to a former colonial power were, more than others, a subject of reproach. "Beyond all else the issue is the bilateral nature of cooperation. It is noteworthy that the complete failures (Indonesia, Congo), the partial ones (Indo-China, North Africa), correspond to situations in which a newly independent country confronts the former dominant power. The merits of the Commonwealth or Community formulas are in this respect greater than is generally allowed."[7]

In any event, relations with former parent states have admittedly deteriorated, and a few years ago the process seemed almost irreversible. Yet the tendency was reversed, and reknitting of relations was soon evident, along with a general improvement in the atmosphere.

Here are some examples. The Holland-Indonesia Union was formed in 1949, but was shattered by 1954. Nothing was left of the 1949 agreements. Yet after the events that shook Sukarno's Indonesia, quite normal relations soon existed between Holland and Indonesia again.

Guinea with its refusal of the Community had broken with France. France, on its side, had drawn rather drastic conclusions from the refusal: assistance cut off, personnel brought home. Guinea did not draw back in the face of these seemingly irreparable actions; not only did it leave the French franc zone but made use in neighboring countries of the bank reserves expropriated at Konakry. Even today, attempts to restore full relations have failed. Yet the last three or four years have seen the beginnings of such restoration. In 1967, at the end of the eighth congress of the Democratic party of Guinea, Sekou Touré expressly stated his desire to renew connections with France. Negotiations followed and some steps have already been taken.

Mali, too, had broken with France, at the time when the federation with Senegal had split up. It had withdrawn on the diplomatic, military, and monetary fronts. Yet a few years later, much sooner than Guinea, it was looking for normalization of relations again.

The same thing happened with Congo and Belgium. All sorts of incidents punctuated this difficult relationship. As late as 1967 there was an outstanding example in the affair of the "mercenaries." *Le monde's* editorial for August 22, 1967, said: "Though it firmly denies any share in the mercenaries' activities, Brussels' hands are perhaps not quite so clean of their recruitment." But less than three years later the climate had changed enough for General Mobutu to pay an official visit to Brussels.

On the other hand, the still unresolved Rhodesian affair encumbers Great Britain's relations with a number of African nations which are geographically more or less close to Rhodesia. The key event will still be readily recalled: on November 11, 1965 the government of Ian Smith took independence for Rhodesia before the measures were adopted which Britain wanted for guaranteeing the black population's political role in the new state. Economic sanctions were proposed under UN auspices and were approved by Great Britain, but they were to prove ineffective. In any event, they did not force Ian Smith to yield. As a result Great Britain was put in a continuing uncomfortable position vis-à-vis the African states, especially those of the Commonwealth.

However, this situation and others like it ought not make us forget the widespread normalization of relations between former colonies and former parent states. Things are now quite different than they would have been, had the tendencies which were manifested in the numerous ruptures of relations on the morrow of independence gone unchecked. But perhaps the reason for such a gradual renewal of relations with the former colonial powers is the difficulty the African nations have had in establishing close and profitable relations with the other great powers.

Relations with the Other Great Powers

It looked at the beginning as though the relations of the United States with many developing countries would be quite favorable after independence. The United States even moved openly in some instances to take over where the European powers were leaving off: to replace France in Guinea and Belgium in the Congo. The United States was rightly seen by the developing nations as a noncolonial, even an anticolonial power. This image was still alive around 1960, and Kennedy's short time in office promised to strengthen it even more.

Today that image is completely obscured by the prolonged Vietnam War in which the United States has become mired, and by the virulent racial conflict in the States during the last few years. The image of an anticolonial America is thus wholly forgotten by most people in the Third World, and the United States seems aware of this, for it is making hardly any use of its diplomatic advantages, at least in Asia or Africa. In Latin America it maintains good relations only where governments heed United States warnings of the danger of Castroite subversion.

The other superpower, the USSR, has not won hearts either nor achieved especially privileged diplomatic position in the former colonial states. Many of the USSR's expectations have proved illusory in Africa. This occurred first in the Congo after

Lumumba's disappearance; then in Guinea where euphoria was followed by touchiness and irritability, and in Ghana where Nkrumah's fall brought cooler relations with the USSR. In the Mid-East, cooling off and warming up in relations seems to depend a good deal on the varying intensity of the "Israelite menace."

The situation is better in parts of Asia, especially in India, where the Soviets have left pleasant memories of their mediation in Tashkent after the Indo-Pakistani conflict of 1965.

In Latin America privileged relations with Cuba have had their ups and downs. Today, as we noted earlier, Moscow prefers the orthodox Communist parties which do not share the Cuban viewpoint.

Around 1963 or 1964, many developing countries found relations with China much more promising than relations with the USSR. Yet these relations, too, have failed to develop harmoniously, especially since the Cultural Revolution. There was a real development of such relations with Tanzania and Congo-Brazzaville, for example, and for a while in Burundi as well. But the Chinese were soon expelled from a number of countries, including the Central African Republic, and in many countries distrust was growing even before the events of the Cultural Revolution.

One episode in this history of distrust took place in Kenya. In 1968 the African Union of Kenya adopted a strong resolution proposed by Tom Mboya, minister for economic planning and development, for breaking off diplomatic relations between Kenya and the Chinese People's Republic. The Chinese ambassador to Kenya, it was claimed, had "impertinently intervened" in Kenya's ideology. "The Chinese," according to the resolution, "have insulted Kenya and its government out of jealousy of our country's peace and stability . . . . If we must study anyone's thoughts, they will be those of President Kenyatta, who led us to independence." Mboya further accused the opposition party (the People's Union of Kenya), with former Vice-President Oginda Odinga at its head, of being China's mouthpiece.

Kenya's action led to several incidents: one of these was a violent demonstration outside the Kenya embassy in Peking after an occurrence involving a Kenyan diplomat. China threatened to "crush" the government of Kenya if it did not stop its hostility. Yet diplomatic relations were not in fact broken off.

China's relations with nearby Tanzania remained better. Yet here too, the enthusiasm which was aroused by Chou En-lai, the Chinese foreign affairs minister, when he preached, from Bamako to Dar es Salaam, the extension of the revolution to the African continent has long since passed. There has thus been more than one setback to Chinese-African relations.

Passing over to Asia, we find Chinese relations with many countries to be quite tense and at times paradoxical. There is paradox, for example, in China's support of Pakistan against India, since Pakistan was involved in a military agreement with the United States whereas neighboring India was observing neutrality and was even haughty toward the United States.

China's relations with India have long been deteriorating. The most recent major incident occurred in 1967 when, on September 11, India and Chinese troops skirmished at the Himalayan pass of Nathala, on the Sikkim-Tibet frontier. The fighting stopped there and was replaced, a few days later, by a war of photographic propaganda, centered on the exchange of dead soldiers after the skirmish. The Chinese pictures of the pass seemed to show Indian corpses on the Chinese side of the barbed wire (the Indian stringing of the wire had doubtless led to the fighting). The Indians replied that corpses "had been recovered on both sides" and claimed that the bodies of Indian soldiers recovered from within the Chinese lines "had doubtless been carried behind the Chinese lines to suggest that the Indian army had been the aggressor."

Soon there was nothing left of the incident but this shabby debate. Yet there had been great fear, at least on the Indian side. For since July China's policy toward India had been hardening, with threats leveled chiefly at the government of West Bengal (the capital of which is Calcutta) for being the tool of a "reactionary" central power ruled by "Dange's clique." Dange was the leader of the pro-Soviet Indian Communist party. Further, there had been the June agrarian uprising in West Bengal at Naxalbari, near Nepal and East Pakistan. On this matter the leftist (pro-Chinese) Communists were divided, the extremists backing the uprising, while the "pro-government" members sought to limit the disorders lest they provoke intervention by the central government as at Kerala in 1959. Radio Paking defended the uprising and said that it was inspired by Mao Tse-tung's thought.

We can readily understand India's fears, then, at the September border-incident at Nathala. The Indians feared a Chinese advance southward toward Darjeeling and Naxalbari in order to establish the first "red spot" on Indian soil. India also remembered 1962 when Chinese troops had descended from the Himalayan passes and set up their standards in Assam, only to withdraw soon after. And they recalled an incident in 1965 when during the Indo-Pakistani War the Chinese issued an ultimatum to India over the Sikkim-Tibet frontier, an ultimatum forgotten after the India-Pakistan armistice.

The September 1967 incident strengthened the hand of those in the Indian parliament and government who were urging a break in diplomatic relations with Peking. The assistant prime minister, Morarji Desai, doubtless exceeded his competence in letting it be noised abroad that India might recognize the "theory of the two Chinas." Such recognition was not about to be given, but it is significant that the idea could be even entertained.

Chinese relations with Burma, too, have been tense. During the Cultural Revolution China suddenly issued sharp accusations against the Burmese government of Ne Win: it was stirring up "anti-Chinese" feeling and was engaging in "reactionary" politics in collusion with Moscow and Washington. The *People's Daily* for June 30, 1967, said: "The clique now governing Burma took power in 1962 by a military coup and is imposing a fascist, milita-rist rule on the country and controlling economic channels under pretext of nationalization." Such accusations were the more sur-prising because in previous years the *People's Daily* had only praise for the Burmese regime. Then Chinese authorities often visited Rangoon, and the Burmese paid frequent friendly visits to Peking. Besides, Burmese policy was explicitly neutralist.

With Cambodia, likewise a neutral or neutralist country, China has also had its difficulties. Prince Norodom Sihanouk had to denounce Peking's interference in Cambodian affairs, to dismiss two ministers for "pro-Chinese" tendencies, and to suspend the publication of journals showing similar tendencies. Even though until then he had been esteemed at Peking for his "anti-imperialist" views, the prince unhesitatingly stated, "China disputes Cambodia's right to be its own master, tries to drive a wedge between regime and people, and takes the side of her enemies." The situation was to change, of course, in 1970 when the prince was deposed at Phnom Penh and sought support at Peking.

A final entry may be added to the dossier. It concerns Nepal. Like Ne Win's Burmese regime, King Mahendra's worked on the principle of allowing no quarrels with the Chinese. Yet his regime too has been the object of a propaganda offensive by Peking and of pro-Chinese demonstrations at Katmandu.

Were all these occurrences in 1967 part of a wide-ranging Chinese strategy? "The feeling of many Indian observers," wrote Jean Wetz in *Le monde* (September 14), "is that Peking now sees its progress barred by the increasingly massive American presence in Vietnam and by Hanoi's desire for independence. In these circumstances, Mao and his friends—it is thought here—might seek to break through their 'encirclement' by turning to Burma from the North, which would offer an avenue into the always unstable North-East of India and into East Pakistan which is agitated by the desire for 'autonomy' in relation to Rawalpindi." In this interpretation, Peking did not hesitate to change its attitude in a spectacular fashion, even toward the Burmese government which had always bent over backwards to avoid a confrontation with China. Whatever the validity of this hypothesis, it cannot be denied that relations between China and many Third World nations have seriously deteriorated. Up to the present there has been no real renewal.

The conclusion to be drawn from this panoramic view of China's relations with the developing countries, and from the earlier remarks on US and USSR relations with the same countries, is that the developing countries have found no sure and solid diplomatic footing with the great powers, Western or Communist. They remain rather isolated in the world.

The Smaller Countries: Israel and Yugoslavia

For a complete overview of the foreign relations of the developing nations we must add, at least for Africa, their relations, close at times, with powers which although small play a unique role on the international scene. We have in mind here Israel and Yugo-slavia especially.

Yugoslavia, long cast off by the official Communist world, has readily aligned itself with the developing nations. The policies of the underdeveloped nations and of Yugoslavia are admittedly not always alike. A Yugoslavia-initiated conference at Belgrade not too long ago showed clearly how the two sets of concerns do not coincide. But there has nonetheless been political complic-ity between Yugoslavia and many underdeveloped countries.

Israel has, for its size, pursued an extraordinarily active policy in Africa, entering into numerous cooperative agreements with African states. In financial terms its help represents only .05 percent of all that the African nations receive; but in the help given, Israel has shown inventivenss and ingenuity. Much of its aid takes the form of very practical kinds of instruction, and it refuses to try to rival the great powers at the university level. The training it offers takes place in Africa itself, which represents a great saving of expense and allows Israel to reach the masses rather than the elite. Finally, Israel passes on its know-how in problems which it itself has had to solve and which the African countries often face—for example, the problems of irrigation in Tanzania and Ivory Coast. Furthermore, driven as they are by their own frontier mystique, the Israelis have often been able to awaken in African youth a pioneer spirit which helpers from other countries are rarely able to communicate.

Israel's policy first affected the states of West Africa, which were the first to win independence. Specifically it was initiated in 1957 in Ghana, the first nation to reach independence after the Second World War. In a second phase Israel established lasting contacts with the English-speaking countries of East Africa. Its most privileged relations are doubtless with Ethiopia, due to the fact that this country, like Israel, has had to face a double threat from important Muslim minorities within its own borders and from Nasser's policies. But in practice Israel has had close relations with every sub-Saharan African state, about thirty in all.

In its relations with these states, Israel claimed to prescind from all political considerations. During the Israeli-Arab War of 1967 and during the process that followed upon it at the UN, some African states sent messages of support to President Nasser

(Tanzania, Guinea, Mali, Mauritania), and a large number were noncommittal (seventeen abstained in the General Assembly vote). In response, Israel said it held grudges against none. Similarly, when a decision was taken in Guinea to expel Israeli nationals, Israel avoided all retaliatory moves. On the other hand, eight African nations voted against the resolution condemning Israel: Madagascar, Togo, Botswana, Gambia, Ghana, Lesotho, Liberia, and Malawi. These were doubtless enough to warrant a continued active policy in Africa. And this policy has generally been well received. The Israelis are, after all, less formidable partners than 190 million Americans and 800 million Chinese.

But in the final accounting, Yugoslavia and Israel are small states, and the African states owe their close links with them to the special situation of Yugoslavia and Israel. Furthermore, Israel's position has deteriorated somewhat since 1967. But we must repeat that the friendship of the great powers, Eastern or Western, has appeared a rather dangerous thing to the African states and to the other nations of the underdeveloped world. If such countries have not achieved a definitive diplomatic status, it is basically to their honor that they have been unwilling to sacrifice their independence as the price of such status. But the result has, nonetheless, been their isolation.

In the last analysis, the Third World nations find what security they have within the diplomatic system of the former parent states, and, although formalities are carefully observed, the reality is that at times they are under the protection of these parent states. The surface facts are not in doubt here. At the same time, however, we must not see more than is there, for after some unhappy experiences the former colonial powers have tended to keep hands off the internal affairs of the new states. But this very fact, once again, reinforces the isolation of the Third World countries. This isolation is another expression of their distressful condition.

The real hopes of the developing countries rest on the bonds that exist among themselves, on the continental scene and on the world scene. We come back to "the 77," who are perhaps the most potent symbol for international relations in the Third World. This is the line along which these nations must advance.

Confronted with the United States' preoccupation with the Vietnam War and with the divisions of the Communist world and especially with the development of China since the Cultural Revolution, the Third World nations will do well to play down various political ambitions and to link arms with each other, even at the cost of sacrifices, in a world of powers not wholly favorable to them.

NATIONAL UNITY
AND INTEGRATION

What is the nature of these states that have suddenly appeared on the international scene within the past few years? They are states of the Third World, the underdeveloped world. These newly independent nations enter a category already occupied by the South American nations which have been in existence somewhat longer. We shall now consider this aspect of the matter in some detail.

To begin with, these states are not robust, but suffer from various weaknesses and especially from serious national weaknesses. Perhaps we must even say that the newest at least of these countries have put but little energy into securing an international position and playing a role on the world scene, precisely because of their national weakness. Consequently, before going on to speak of other characteristics in their political regimes, we must look more closely at the national weakness that is typical of many of these nations. A large number of them, in fact, face difficulties of integration. At times they do not admit these problems and try to evade them by the kinds of international self-projection of which we have spoken. Yet the internal problems are often the radical ones and color all other preoccupations.

It has been remarked of these countries that we often see states being born while the nation is still unborn. Or else the national idea is pushed by a small group long before it has any chance of taking root in the population as a whole. Yet it is certain that in the long run a political community's existence can only be founded on an adequate convergence of the interests of the various groups making up the community and on a sense of common destiny and mutual obligations.

In this respect serious obstacles existed in the societies of the Third World when they reached political independence. These societies were generally marked by ethnic, linguistic, and historical pluralism; this was true of large states like India no less than of very small ones like many of the African states.

Pluralist Societies

Let us look first at India. The history of this huge subcontinent is one of successive invasions. In recent centuries alone the Persians, the Muslim Moguls, and the British have entered. In addition, Northern India faces Western Asia, while the South, cut off by the Vindhya Mountains, has always been oriented more to the sea and to South-East Asia (it exported Buddhism to the latter). India thus brought with it to independence an astonishing diversity of cultures and religions. The diversity remains even after the partition of 1947 which gathered up a good part—but only a part—of the Muslim population into Pakistan.

In the Indian Union there are three great religions: Hinduism, Islam, and Buddhism. The current political division of South-East Asia roughly corresponds to this religious distinction, Pakistan being 86 percent Muslim, India 85 percent Hindu, and Ceylon 84 percent Buddhist. But within India the Muslims and Buddhists are well represented, to say nothing of an important Christian minority, especially in the East, and of the Parsi, Jain, and Jewish minorities. The Muslims alone form 10 percent of the population.

Linguistically the complexity is no less remarkable, and linguistic groupings are at times very important. For example, in Pakistan and India together more than seventy million people speak Bengali. In India alone the 1950 postindependence census gave the following figures for spoken languages: 42 percent spoke Hindi, Urdu, Hindustani, and Punjabi (all forms of Hindi but distinct enough to be mutually incomprehensible); 9.3 percent spoke Telegu; 7.6 percent Marathi; 7.4 percent Tamil; 7 percent Bengali; 4.6 percent Gujarati; 4.1 percent Kannada; 3.8 percent Malayalam; 3.7 percent Oriya; and 1.4 percent Assamese.[8] These figures are enough to suggest how important particularisms are in India (people there prefer to speak of "communalism"). Finally, the caste system must not be forgotten.

India's national unity was thus very shaky when independence came. Violent disturbances of religious origin marked the first few months, and disturbances of a primarily linguistic origin have occurred periodically. Linguistic divergence forced the division of Bombay State into Gujarat and Maharashtra. The desire to impose Hindi as a national language (which the constitution declared it to be) was to be the chief cause of frequent disturbances, both in the South, which wanted to keep English as a language for communication, and in Bengal, which prided itself on its own language being no less important a bearer of culture than Hindi.

Moving from India to Africa we find many parallel situations and, very soon after independence, significant conflicts. One example is the conflict that arose in early 1960 at Nouakchott (Mauritania) between the Moors of the interior and the blacks of the Senegal valley when the government tried to impose the teaching of Arabic throughout the country. The same divison between animistic blacks or Christians, on the one hand, and Muslims (Moors or blacks), on the other, can be seen in the Sudan, Chad, Cameroon, and Nigeria.

In the East and South (as well as in Madagascar), the blacks (or Malagasy) find it difficult to get along with the Indians, the Chinese, and at times the whites. No less important is the polyethnicism of the blacks themselves, a characteristic of almost all the countries of the continent. The different tribes with their different customs and distinct languages can be counted by the tens in most countries. Tribal patriotism remains a very strong sentiment. Lively oppositions arise on a tribal basis, and conflicts from some other source find support in ethnic differences: Bahutu and Batutsi in Rwanda and Burundi; Ashanti and Fanti in Ghana (Nkrumah was Fanti, many of his opponents Ashanti); Yorubas, Ibos, and Hausas in Nigeria. Liberia and Sierra Leone show a further cause of heterogeneity: former slaves from the Americas established themselves on the coast in the nineteenth century and dominated the tribes of the interior.

There are also the tragic cases of tribes, sometimes important ones, divided by colonial frontiers which later became the frontiers of modern states; thus the Ewe were divided between Togo and Ghana, just as much earlier, in the South American Andes, the Aymara Indians were divided between Peru and Bolivia.

A number of Latin American countries are familiar with great heterogeneity: white, mixed, Indian and black populations. In Peru there is practically no communication between the people of the coast and the Indians of the altiplano who speak Quechua or Aymara and live in very different geographical and climatic conditions.

Such heterogeneity renders difficult any common political life. Out of such disparate elements nations had to be formed—not commanded into existence by fiat. Political life, after all, is in large measure a matter of communication (administrative communication, exchange of opinions and influences). But this essential function is made very difficult by ethnic diversity and by cultural and linguistic particularism, to say nothing of considerable differences in degree of adaptation to modern culture and in economic level. As soon as a richer group is asked to make sacrifices for a poorer group, there is trouble because the groups feel no genuine affinity to one another.

The Pluralist Societies in Recent Times

The situation just described was often aggravated in recent times, and especially during the colonial period. Some groups were more favored by the colonizer or profited more from his presence, while others were distrustful and remained faithful to their traditional way of life or were ignored by the colonizer. Sometimes it was the former aristocracies that were favored; more often, ethnic groups formerly less successful seized the opportunity to advance. In such circumstances, independence and the period following it were often a time of new changes in the respective positions of various groups.

A frequent case is the opposition of coastal dwellers who profited more by colonialism, and the peoples of the interior, who were less favored or, as descendants of higher and more brilliant cultures, less willing to be corrupted. On the morrow of independence the peoples of the interior try to recapture their old dominant position; at times they have difficulty in winning it because they have difficulty in adapting to a new economy and new ways or are simply unwilling to do so.

In India, for example, there is opposition of this kind between the coastal areas, chiefly in the South, and the interior or North. The coast was the first area to undergo Western influence. A reversal in favor of the North and the interior began indeed in 1920, well before independence, as the North gradually developed a large middle class of lawyers, doctors, educators, and especially administrators. In this way the state of Uttar Pradesh, Nehru's home, achieved decisive importance. Independence continued to favor the progress of the heavily populated interior regions. But this progress brought numerous adverse political consequences for the coastal areas and explains, in part, the hostility of the coastal peoples to the introduction of Hindi as the official language. The official status of Hindi, of course, makes it easier for Hindi-speaking youth to secure administrative and governmental positions. But unemployment is already high among the educated classes of Bengal and Madras, and many of them feel that the introduction of Hindi will close the doors even more to them. In these two states, consequently, hostility to Hindi has been most in evidence. On the other hand, the coastal peoples feel that the taxes they contribute to the central government far outweigh the financial benefits they receive in return. The government distributes public funds on the basis of population, so that Uttar Pradesh and Bihar, for example, receive relatively more than Madras, West Bengal, or Kerala.

In Ceylon, too, there has been some compensation for the Buddhist and traditionalist middle classes up-country which had hitherto been neglected in favor of the coastal peoples. A similar tension has existed in Madagascar since independence, between the coastal dwellers and the Merina people of the high plateaus who traditionally dominated but today must face competition.

Thus, not only is there great cultural or ethnic diversity in many Third World countries, but independence has often brought reversals in the relative political situations of the various populations. Such a displacement of political forces gives rise to resentment and tension. Often too it has social significance, since group struggles are struggles for relative social status. But differences in social level are all the more serious when built on ethnic, cultural, linguistic, religious, or at times even territorial foundations. The unity of the nation within the map-drawn frontiers is thus weaker than the unity European nations possessed in the nineteenth century, even when they were being torn by the social struggle of the industrial revolution. Or, rather, the nation has not yet found a genuine unity to overcome an extreme pluralism, aggravated by inequalities which colonialism and, later, independence set up between segments of the population.

Even in Latin America national unity suffers from the same stresses. Circumstances of economic or political history have excessively favored one sector of the population or territory at the expense of the others; here too there have been some remarkable reversals. One need only think of the traditional hostility between the inhabitants of Buenos Aires (the "Porteños") and of the interior, and of the reversal that took place when Peron fell; or of the numerous secessionist attempts of the Paulists in Brazil, at least until 1930.

The problems thus raised for the Third World nations are not unlike those which arise out of new or traditional tensions in the old nations of Europe or North America: between the South and North of France, between North and South in the United States, between the two Canadas, or between Prussians, Saxons, and Bavarians in Germany. But the situation is often more serious in the Third World countries. They have no long common political history and have therefore not even begun to find a resolution. Thus the first order of problems to be faced and energetically attacked are those of national integration.

Linguistic, Administrative, and Political Problems

In this area there are many practical problems which will be on the agenda for a long time to come. First, there is the linguistic problem. People feel the need of a common language for communication. But how is such a language to be imposed without attacking the personality of the various populations within the state? What status should be given to the local mother tongues? Are they to be taught in school and systematically cultivated or to be relegated to purely familial and domestic use?

Difficulties arise no matter what solution is adopted. It is not easy to keep the language of the former colonial power as a language of communication. Yet this is generally the only way to have a universal means of communication, and one which, in addition, facilitates the acquisition of scientific advances and contacts with the rest of the world. It is more difficult still to impose one of the country's native tongues as a national language, because the members of other linguistic groups see this as a move to achieve a dominant position. Such is the case in India with its attempts to impose Hindi; in Mauritania with Arabic.

The recruitment of administrative personnel is likewise a very delicate matter. New states have urgent need of the most qualified personnel. But they must also preserve a nice balance between the sectors of the population. In a country like Lebanon, despite the different cultural levels of the Christian and Arabic communities, the government has tried to recruit the same number of members from the two groups. In practice this means recruiting a surplus of civil servants from the various communities, independently of their qualifications, in order to maintain a show of balance.

There are also economic and budgetary problems. The relatively richer part of the population pays the greater part of the taxes and is always likely to look with jaundiced eye on measures that would expend a disproportionate share of budgetary resources on poorer regions and populations in an attempt to speed up their development.

Beyond these more limited problems there is a large one which concerns the very structure of the state. Heterogeneity of populations, for example, is one argument used to defend a single-party constitution. We will return to this point in a later chapter. More generally speaking, the apparatus of the state, which is established before anything else, often tries to resolve the problem of national integration by imposing a unitary and centralized governmental structure. To this point, too, we shall return.

The opposite view is that to stretch the spring too much is to break it and that it makes more sense to build up federal or decentralized structures in order to meet the reality of heterogeneous and pluralist societies. This reality has, in fact, dictated a certain measure—at times, a very large measure—of federalism, at least in a first stage in the history of developing states. However, despite its advantages, federalism is not always easy to maintain.

Federalism played an important role in several South American countries. Even today it is a political reality in Brazil, despite the advance of the central power since 1930. India since independence has been a federation, under the name of the Indian Union.

In Africa, Nigeria is a very important example of internal federalism, and it is worth our while to dwell on it briefly. Nigeria was created as an antidote to the balkanization which was threatening here as in many other areas of Africa. But in this huge collection of populations there was no other resolution possible except a decentralized structure that could preserve sufficient unity while respecting the particularities of heterogeneous peoples.

In practice, power in Nigeria was divided between regional and central levels. But even at the federal or central level, power had to be composite, open to influence from the various federated entitites which thus share in its exercise. The need was met by a system of national parties, each of them the privileged (though not the exclusive) expression of a particular region, although at the regional level there was practically a single-party system. Thus at the time of independence (1960), 150 seats out of 312 in the Federal Assembly went to the Northern Peoples' Congress (NPC) and its allies, 89 to the National Council of Nigerian Citizens-Northern Elements' Progressive Union (NCNC-

NEPU), and 73 to the Action Group. The NPC represented chiefly the North, but had eight seats at Abadan (in the West). The Action Group represented chiefly the West (34 seats there), but also had 24 seats in the North-West and in the Middle Belt, 14 in the East, and 1 at Lagos. The NCNC was the Eastern party, but also had 21 seats in the West and 2 at Lagos. A coalition cabinet was formed on this basis: 10 members from the NPC and 7 from the NCNC (3 from the East, 3 from the West, 1 from Lagos). The Action Group, however, remained an opposition party at the federal level, a fact not unrelated to the difficulties the Federation later met in Nigeria.

The first advantage of such a structure of essentially regional parties which also have a certain national significance was to assure the representation of regional interest up to the cabinet level. In addition, despite the Action Group becoming an opposition party, the West was not left completely voiceless because like other regions it had its own autonomous government.

The system also had the advantage, at least in principle, of preventing the silencing of small ethnic groups within each region. The Action Group profited by Yoruba irredentism in the North; in the East it consolidated the non-Ibos of Calabar, originally represented by a special party but later integrated into the Action Group. Finally, as one commentator noted, perhaps too optimistically, the federal structure "allows the functioning of a multiparty system and even of a parliamentary regime, which has proved inadequate in all the unitary black-African states."[9]

The federalist structure of Nigeria might at least be viewed as an apt response to the need for regional autonomy and for the protection of ethnic and religious minorities. In addition, it springs from the typical situation of a pluralist society, common to so many Third World states. But, despite the federalist bond, ethnic and religious pluralism in Nigeria was so strong that it led to the Biafran secession and a terrible war, to which we shall return shortly.

If we look only at solutions adopted at the time of independence, we must note that unitary formulas (highly centralized government) prevailed in the states that emerged from the old French empire. But these were small states. Let us pause for a moment to consider the advantages and disadvantages of small states. It can certainly be said that from an economic viewpoint the multiplication of small states (due, for example, to the failure of the Western African Federation, then of the Mali Federation) has numerous disadvantages. The economic advantages of large groupings are clear. They generally offer a variety of resources and thus allow for a balanced economic development. They involve a larger population, which assures a sufficient working force (especially if density is favorable). A large state offers, above all, the possibility of a large domestic market which stimulates development more readily than a potential foreign market. A large state, finally, is able to support large revenue-producing units, especially in the area of heavy industry. All these advantages, however, remain more possible than real if the corresponding political unity is too weak. We saw this to be true, in the early years at least, in Congo-Kinshasa, where size and variety of resources proved profitless without a minimum of national unity and political order. It is precisely in the political area that, in the absence of viable federalist or decentralist solutions, the small state offers the least troublesome answer and even has some advantages: it is easier to undertake national unification and to establish a satisfactory administrative organization. We might thus think of recommending, for the first stage of development, a large-scale economic organization, especially for the coordination of investments, but also, under this umbrella, a breakdown into small political units.

Worsening of Domestic Tensions

In any case, it is a fact that a decade or two after independence the Third World states, especially the larger ones, are still greatly hindered by problems of national integration. For evidence enough we need only turn again to India and Nigeria.

In India, recent political developments seem to have increased the difficulties of national integration. In the years after independence the fact that one party dominated at the federal level and, apart from rare and temporary exceptions, within the various states as well, was a guarantee against the hardening of particularism. Little by little, this restraining influence has been disappearing. One by one, many states of the Union have adopted coalition governments, made up of dissidents from the Congress party along with members of the nationalist right or the socialists or even the Communists, all of them in opposition to the Congress party which continues to be dominant at the Union level (after the general elections of February 1967). Coalition governments took over, for example, in Uttar Pradesh and Madya Pradesh, two of the largest states. A group of states containing two-thirds of the Indian population, or 300 million people, are now in the hands of opponents of the Congress party.

At times this development in one or other state is attributed to parochial disputes. In Madya Pradesh, for example, the quarrel would be between Maharani Vijaya Raja of Gualia and the Congressist prime minister (Mishra). But the noteworthy thing is precisely that many states do not hesitate to put "communal" or even more particularist concerns before the national interest.

A very significant event occurred at the beginning of September 1967. The minister for foreign affairs, Mohammed Ali Currim Chagla, the first Muslim to direct India's foreign affairs, resigned because (he claimed) of the government's linguistic policy. The minister had certainly been criticized for his own foreign policy during the Mid-East crisis, and his resignation might be thought due to that, in part, since the Indian government was now attempting to backpedal after getting too involved in defense of the Arab cause. However, the linguistic question was also a primary topic of discussion; the cabinet had just decided on the principle of replacing English with the regional languages in all higher education within five or ten years.

Up to this point, the great effort had been to impose Hindi, as provided by the Indian constitution. Convinced no doubt that they would never win out in great sections of the country, especially in Bengal and the South, the partisans of Hindi thought they could achieve their goal indirectly by using all the regional languages.

Obviously, the substitution of regional languages for English, if applied not only to higher education but to the administrative and judicial systems as well, would create a Tower of Babel.

This was the point Chagla made at his resignation. Someday, he said, the people of India would be able to communicate with each other only through interpreters. The cabinet's policy, he concluded, "threatens and even undermines the nation's unity." It was clear, of course, that this policy would not be enforced any more than many earlier decisions on linguistic matters and that the linguistic problem would continue to be an apple of discord.

Twenty years after independence, religious communities, too, still confront each other in India. Among countless incidents, some very serious, this one was reported in a news dispatch in the summer of 1967: "Units of the Indian army have been rushed to Srinagar, capital of Kashmir, where for three days tension has been high between Muslims and militant Hindus of the Jan Sangh party. On Thursday there were some minor altercations in the city. Now it is feared that the situation is rapidly deteriorating and there may be outbreaks of violence. Primary and secondary schools have been closed. Police and troops patrol the streets around the clock. The tension between the two communities began a month ago with a marriage between a young Muslim and a young lady of the Hindu Brahman caste. The Jan Sangh militants claim the young girl was kidnapped and forced to marry. Several party leaders came to the city and delivered violent speeches which caused a sharp reaction in the Muslim community." In many instances there was worse than tension; there was a great deal of bloodshed.

In Africa, too, we read from time to time in recent years of tensions involving the Asiatic minorities in East Africa. In Kenya a campaign was mounted which led to the deportation of the Asiatics. They were accused of having "exploited their opportunities" to take control of the national economy. The Union of Postal and Telegraph Employees declared: "Asiatics have no right to live in Kenya, for our people are not responsible for the difficulties they might have met in their homeland."

Despite official silence it is increasingly impossible to overlook the struggle between the Sudanese Muslims of the North and the black animist or Christian tribes of the South. The same kind of tensions are less violent and still largely latent between

North and South in Chad and Cameroon. Cameroon has, in addition, the problem of the Bamiléké tribe. It continues to be a delicate problem after the conclusion of an atrocious civil war which caused about seventy thousand deaths from 1958 to 1965. The Bamilékés are an aboriginal tribe, too poor in land (they say) to survive; they have therefore spread out through the rest of the country and have become too successful in commerce and administration for the peace of mind of less dynamic but landed peoples.

The Biafran affair in Nigeria, more than any other in recent years, has underlined the difficulties of national integration in Africa. On March 30, 1966, the Eastern region, with Ibos in a strong majority, proclaimed its independence and took the name of Biafra. Its leader was Lieutenant-Colonel Ojukwu. The Mid-West (with its capital at Benin City) joined the secession for a while, since Biafran troops had taken up positions in the area. For a brief moment, it seemed that the West, with its Yoruba population, might follow suit. But the Western leader, Chief Awolowo, one of the most honored architects of independence in 1960, finally refused to follow the secessionist trend; he was opposed to secession but probably feared also that the Ibos of Biafra might become dominant. The result of the secession was the war between Biafrans and federalists, long ignored by world opinion but forced upon the attention of all in its brutal final phase. It ended only in January 1970, after three and a half years of fighting.

But we must go beyond these events and recall the great state of fifty or sixty million people which from 1960 to 1965 had been a pilot state for moderate Africa and a constitutional model for all of Africa. We noticed earlier the salient traits of a federal system which seemed to maintain a fairly good balance betwen the various forces in a country ethnically divided between the Hausa or Fulani of the North who were Muslims, the Yorubas in the West, and the Ibos in the East. But the far more numerous Northerners had held power from the beginning at the federal level. They held it legally through Prime Minister Abubakar Tafawa Balewa. Their hold on it behind the scenes was even stronger, because the prime minister was regarded as the tool of the greatest feudal lord of the North, the *sardauna* of Sokoto (Sir Ahmadu Bello). The Southern peoples, educationally more advanced and more "modernizing" in their views, were restless under the domination of a traditionalist overlordship. Difficulties and disturbances began in 1965, first in the West, in Yoruba country, then more seriously in the East among the Ibos.

The crisis came in January, 1966, with a coup d'état which was a settling of accounts between Northern and Southern authorities, the latter chiefly Ibos. The federal prime minister, Tafawa Balewa, and the feudal prince, Ahmadu Bello, were assassinated, while numerous Ibos in the North provinces were victims of pogroms which caused at least tens of thousands of deaths.

Power then fell to General Ironsi. He thought the solution to the problem lay in centralizing the federation. He looked energetically for this but found in his path, once again, the Ibos who feared that centralization would be to the profit of the more numerous Northern population. Five months after taking power, Ironsi, too, was assassinated.

Then the present head of government, Major General Gowon, came to power. He was certainly more prudent than General Ironsi had been, but nevertheless he failed to master the separatist tendencies of the Ibos, now intensified by the massacres. The separatism had numerous causes. Apart from the ethnic particularism of the Ibos and the Catholicism many of them professed, there was the considerable natural wealth of the East, especially petroleum and gas, which afforded the prospect of an island of prosperity and economic realism amid a huge unstable Nigeria. In this respect, Baifra's secession inevitably reminded people of Katanga's, five years earlier.

Was Gowon right in launching military operations against the Biafran secessionists and starting so great a civil war? He was afraid, in fact, that the secession would spread. Had not Chief Awolowo, leader of Western policy, declared that if the East left the federation, the West would soon follow it? It was only later on, once military operations had started, that Awolowo modified his position and joined the federal government.

Nigeria after the secession is still confronted with a serious problem of national integration; indeed, reconstruction may be more difficult than the original construction, the building of the federal state in 1961.

The Period of the Guerillas in South America

Latin America has not yet experienced situations quite like those of Africa. The Indian peoples, for example, have nowhere begun to play the role of the Ibos or the Bamilékés. There is, however, the case of the half-breeds of Arequipa in Peru and their long struggle with the white middle class of Lima; and there is the rivalry, already mentioned, between the Porteños of Buenos Aires and the people of the hinterlands of Argentina.

Above all, however, there are the fairly analogous situations recently exploited by guerilla movements, though the latter are generally still at the stage of simple peasant uprisings. This description fits Juliao's peasant band in North-East Brazil, 1963-1964; it fits Peru 1965-1966, Bolivia in more recent years, and Venezuela and Colombia over a long period. To round off this chapter on problems of internal unity in the developing countries, we must speak briefly of this guerilla period in Latin America, for it has struck all observers and will alert us to the inherent difficulties of national integration.

Accuracy of statement is necessary here, for we are dealing with quite different kinds of sequences. In Colombia, for example, fighting originally took the form of a classic civil war, quite different from the guerilla warfare that succeeded it. The civil war lasted from 1948 to 1953 and was fought between the liberals and conservatives. The starting signal was the assassination of Liberal leader Jorge Gaitan in the streets of Bogota during an inter-American conference (April 8, 1948). The result of the initial disturbances was five thousand dead. During the next five years three hundred thousand more died in the country areas. Starting in 1953, the dictator Rojas Pinilla (a Colombian-style Peron) managed to pacify the country for a while, but the newspapers were soon again reporting bandit raids and burning villages.

Pinilla fell in 1957 and was succeeded by a National Front government. According to a truce agreement of 1958, each outgoing president of the republic (after a four-year term) would make way for a president from another political party. This was a pleasant political game which covered up the continuing disturbances. The latter, however, gradually developed into guerilla movements in the full sense. "Independent republics" were established for a while at Tolema and Huila in the South, in accordance with orders from the Communist party in 1959. Such republics grew out of the peasant jacqueries. Peasants had organized the redistribution of the land, and the autonomous administration and armed defense of the inaccessible mountain areas. The independent republics were under systematic attack by government forces in 1962, 1964, and 1965. Only after fearful struggles did the army finally become master of the situation.

In the same areas the Colombian Revolutionary Armed Forces (FARC) next appeared on the scene. These were genuine armed forces, not armed peasants, and were supported chiefly by the Communist party. The party was not outlawed, but numerous arrests of Communists were made in 1967, including that of Gilberto Vieira, secretary-general of the party.

An Army of National Liberation (ELN) also came on the scene in 1964 or 1965, and was active north of Bogota, in the Santander district. This was the underground group joined in January 1966, by a priest, Father Camillo Torres Restrepo, formerly chaplain of the Catholic students at the University of Bogota; he was slain by government forces on February 15, 1966. The ELN continued to operate in 1966 and 1967, capturing some small villages, attacking mail trains, etc. Its final activities were located chiefly in the Giron region, a leading tobacco-growing area.

The repression of these various underground groups seems today to have succeeded. But after such a history of violence, who can say it will not flame up anew?

In neighboring Venezuela, several groups have been active since 1961: the Armed Forces of National Liberation (FALN), made up of Communist party militants; the Movement of the Revolutionary Left (MIR), founded by the left wing of the Democratic Action group, which had abandoned Betancourt; and various worker and student groups. The origins of the whole underground movement were much less clearly peasant in character than in Colombia. Further, the scene of action has often been the cities (for tactical combat units), at least as much as the countryside. Venezuela is, of course, 72 percent urban. Another notable characteristic of the movement in Venezuela is that the principal initiative had been with the Communist party. In 1966, however, after numerous failures of the underground and the jailing of most of its own leaders, the Venezuelan Communist party adopted a new policy: the end of armed combat and a return to lawful political action. As a result the government freed a number of interned Communist leaders in 1968. Only a hard-core fraction of the Venezuelan Communist party still supports the underground, thus breaking the instructions on moderation issued by the local party and by Moscow.

Bolivia had experienced large-scale miners' strikes, especially in 1942 and 1964, and had put them down with bloodshed. The revolutionary struggle seemed crushed for a long time to come. It began again in early 1967 only because of the activity of Che Guevara who died there in autumn of the same year.

In Peru, from 1958 to 1962, a guerilla movement, supported by Indian peasants, was led by Hugo Blanco. The latter managed for a while to establish a sort of independent republic in the valley of the Convencion, but the movement was suppressed in 1963 and Hugo Blanco was arrested. A new movement sprang up in the same area in 1965, under the impulse of a Peruvian MIR, a dissident offshoot of the American Popular Revolutionary Alliance (APRA), under Luis de la Puente Uceda. The MIR was a Castroite guerilla movement with the slogan "the land to the peasants." Still another group, independent of the MIR, was active in the South (Ayacucho) during the autumn of 1965, under the leadership of Hector Bejar, who has since been captured. Recent military operations seem greatly to have hampered the effectiveness of the Peruvian guerillas.

To the foregoing countries we must add Guatemala, where underground movements have existed since 1962, but where suppression has been equally active. In most other countries guerilla action has been more sporadic. In Brazil, Argentina, Mexico, Chile, and Uruguay there is opposition to the government from the revolutionary left, but it always chooses other courses of action.

Concluding the panorama, we must repeat that the situation in Latin America is different than in many countries of Africa or Asia, since in the latter it is ethnic, linguistic, and religious differences that threaten national unity. But the parallel needed nonetheless to be drawn in order to have a full picture of the various smoldering situations which imperil national unity in so many developing nations. It must also be remarked that the great period of guerilla warfare, which seemed about to lay waste the South American continent, is now past. Yet everywhere there remain small fires which could blaze up into civil wars as devastating as the Nigerian-Biafran conflict. The Third World nations continue to be threatened by civil divisons and, for the foreseeable future, will have to face difficult problems of integration.

PRESIDENTIALIST

REGIMES

In contrast to their frequent weakness in national unity and integration, the political regimes of many developing nations are apparently of a "strong" type. What we find, in fact, is a rather general tendency to adopt presidentialist forms of political power. For a current knowledge of the developing countries this important characteristic must be spelled out in detail. Whether the apparent strength is genuine or often hides many weaknesses is of course another question. This aspect of the problem will also receive our attention, especially in the next chapter on the single-party systems.

South America

The Latin American political regimes are the oldest among those to be considered. In some instances they have lasted a long time. Thus the examination of their general characteristics is of great interest.

Latin America has, in fact, had a large number of constitutions:

between 180 and 190, for twenty republics, in the course of a century and a half. This figure does not include numerous amendments which at times change the very nature of a regime; thus in Chile in 1891 and Brazil in 1961 amendment meant the substitution of a parliamentary regime for a presidential one. From this large numer we must not, however, conclude to an infinite variety of constitutional models. The numerical inflation occurred chiefly in the first years of independence, up to 1850. Furthermore, in the large countries (Brazil, Argentina, and Mexico which contain two-thirds of the continent's population) the number of constitutions has been very limited—nine in all (whereas since 1850 there have been sixty-six for Bolivia, Dominican Republic, Haiti, Nicaragua, and Venezuela, which together have less than twenty-five million inhabitants). It is thus possible to reduce the apparent variety of constitutions to a few basic forms. There are exceptions, of course, to these few: Uruguay's democratic institutions have long been like those of Switzerland; Cuba has recently turned to the institutions of people's democracy; Haiti has perhaps not yet emerged from its organizational chaos. In the rest of the continent, however, we find relatively stable forms and characteristics.

The first of these characteristics is the tendency to centralization, a departure from the federalism generally promoted in the first period of independence. Only Brazil still has truly federalist institutions; yet even here ever greater powers of intervention are being allowed the government in matters hitherto reserved to the federated states. The tendency to centralization has often been due to efforts at national integration. It is being reinforced today as the state takes over larger responsibilities for economic development.

Much more important is another widespread characteristic, on which we must dwell: the preponderance of the executive power. An observer recently made the general remark: "Despite the fact that in the nineteenth century when Latin American institutions were being formed there was a powerful movement to extend the powers of assemblies, Latin America has had only very brief experience of parliamentary regimes and has had to turn to presidential ones in which it has been necessary to broaden the presidential powers, in fact or by law. Thus the normal regime in Latin America, in periods of regular institutional functioning, is a regime of preponderant executive power, rightly called a regime of presidential preponderance."[10]

An exception, already mentioned, was Uruguay, until its recent constitutional modification (1967). From 1919 on (except for the 1930-1938 period) executive power was in the hands of nine-member national council of government, in which three members had to be from the opposition party; members of the majority party presided in rotation. The recent constitutional revision, however, has been in a more authoritarian direction.

Latin American constitutional theory is generally one of separation and equality of powers (legislative, executive, and judicial). The theory is formulated even more strictly than in the United States. But in reality the balance is not assured. Even apart from frequent cases of suspension of the constitution, the president (head of state and of the executive) has a genuine preponderance. Only in Chile can the congress exercise a real independence and try to use the powers recognized for it by the constitution. For a long time (1890-1925) Chile had a parliamentary regime of the French type; during that period the congress acquired its tradition of aggressiveness which not even the Popular Front presidents, Aguirre Cerda and Jose Antonio Rios (1938-1946), could break.

In Brazil "presidential domination is less fully accepted than in Spanish America."[11] Is this an echo of the parliamentarianism practiced under Don Pedro? Or is it the effect of federalism, which gives opposition parties a solid footing? In any event, there is a tendency to presidentialism and it came to the fore in the referendum of January 1963, in favor of Joao Goulart, after the interim parliamentary regime which followed upon the departure of Jânio Quadros.

In Mexico and Argentina there is hardly any restriction on presidential power (except the protection of the army); congress can take no legislative initiative without the president and can hardly amend laws he proposes. The president always easily manages to secure ample legislative delegation. The rule of constitutional law is officially established but hardly practiced; the judiciary is hesitant to intervene in political matters.

The drawback of the system is not so much that it begets dictators (other systems do that, perhaps just as easily) as that it camouflages them. Jacques Lambert notes that "the difference between a president respectful of the constitution and a dictator must be less in the extent of the powers at their disposal than in the use they make of them: only the dictator acts arbitrarily, but both can be equally authoritarian."[12]

All of this, we have said, represents a tendency. We must add further that there has been a real evolution along these lines, away from regimes which at many periods have been close to a parliamentary system, at least in principle. Thus in the background of many presidential regimes there is the substructure of a multi-party—often a bi-party—system of parliamentary nature; the parties have usually been a liberal and a conservative party, vying with each other for power since the nineteenth century. But the very violence of the struggle between parties which were like clans is what has led to the strengthening of presidential over parliamentary power in order to save national unity. Everywhere the need was felt "of establishing a stronger executive power than in Europe, in order to prevent the breakdown of the still young states" (J. Lambert).

We must also realize that the old political parties and their parliamentary interplay involved only a small part of the population, since only a few had the franchise. Consequently, when new levels of the population won entry into political life (first the middle classes, then the proletariat, especially the workers —with the peasants hardly affected even today), they found it difficult to express themselves in the framework of the old party system. Since the system continued however to exist (facilitated by delay in extending the franchise further), the new sectors of voters obtained some representation through the president, making up thus for their lack of representation in parliament. Presidential power has thereby been consolidated. It is not surprising, then, that this power should often have a populist character, found in extreme from in Vargas of Brazil and Peron of Argentina.

In Brazil, the electoral system now used for parliamentary elections favors states with small populations, those with a high percentage of illiteracy, the most economically backward ones, and those in which political groups represent family or clan struggles rather than ideological or economic divergences, as in the more advanced areas of Brazil. "The rural oligarchies who dominate the backward regions enjoy an assured representation in congress, allowing them to secure themselves against the claims of the urban populace."[13] On the other hand, for the election of the president as practiced until 1964, the electoral district was Brazil in its entirety. "The popular vote," it was noted, "became the decisive factor." This has long been true: popular support for Vargas in 1950 and Quadros in 1960 even came into play independently of the great party machines. We can understand, then, why the decision was taken to have the president elected in the autumn of 1966 by the congress, not by the people. But the decision ran counter to a thirty-year development in the Brazilian form of government.

The central executive power has been further strengthened in Latin America by the fact that the state has more and more taken over the task of economic development. Here again Brazil is a good example, for under Vergas, then under Kubitschek, the state has engaged in the construction of a whole industrial infrastructure.[14]

It is noteworthy, however, that with few exceptions (Peron's Argentina, Castro's Cuba) the trend toward strengthening the executive has not been accompanied by a trend to a single-party system. The parties have indeed been modified; we have seen the birth of rather large national parties alongside the old liberal, radical, and conservative parties. Such newer parties are, for example, the Brazilian Labor Party, the (Brazilian) Social Democratic Party, and the (Brazilian) National Democratic Union (all now defunct); various socialist parties; the American Popular Revolutionary Alliance of Haya de la Torre and the Popular Action of Belaunde Terry in Peru; Betancourt's Democratic Action in Venezuela; Eduardo Frei's Christian Democratic Party in Chile. But the dual system of parliamentary representation (which expresses more the interplay of the traditional parties) and a more popular representation through the presidential executive has nowhere completely disappeared. This makes it very difficult to pass over to a one-party system.

LIBRARY — ST. BERNARD

We must note also how Latin America tries to arm itself against abuses of the presidential system. The problem takes this particular form: how to guard against the temptation for the holder of executive power to become a dictator? "This temptation is especially strong in view of the hero-worship and devotion of backward peoples to the person of their leader."[15] It is a temptation that reappears with populist allegiance to a presidential leader.

The temptation is met by an essential element, often unappreciated abroad, in the South American presidential system: the time limit on the presidential mandate. The powers of the president are hardly limited in scope, but they are limited in time. Many precautions are taken against attempts at reelection (whether direct reelection of the president himself or indirect reelection through a figurehead). The terms of his mandate is generally a little more than in North America (five years in Brazil and Venezuela, six in Argentina, Mexico, and Chile), but, given the prohibition of such reelection as often extends the United States' president's term to eight years, the real duration is somewhat less in South America.

It may happen, of course, that the reelection statute is suspended for this or that president. This happened with Porfirio Diaz in Mexico from 1884 to 1911 and for Peron whose 1949 constitutional revision was aimed at legalizing reelection. Consequently, many constitutions prohibit amendment of this clause. Mexico forbids reelection entirely, even after a period out of office. The reason is that Calles had tried a clever system: he obtained the election as his successor of Portes Gil, who resigned a year later, then of Ortiz Rubio, whom he forced to resign in order to succeed him himself; he failed only with the more independent Cardenas.

"Presidential self-succession," says Jacques Lambert, "has surely been one of the most serious defects in Latin American political life. Today, however, the president no longer tries to prolong his term openly, except in the less developed Latin American countries. In those countries which contain most of Latin America's population—Brazil, Chile, Mexico, Argentina, and Colombia—the rule of no reelection is one of the laws most generally respected. This fact represents a success in effort to guarantee a democratic regime, and its great importance ought not to be underestimated."[16]

Another remark of Lambert's has a broader bearing and touches the heart of our problem: "If it be admitted that a strong executive power is necessary in the social climate of South America, then an essential problem in guaranteeing the democratic character of such authoritarian regimes was to secure the time limit on the presidential mandate."[17] On this point Latin America has adapted the North American system to its own ends. Thus, says Lambert, "the system of presidential preponderance admittedly does not work perfectly, but can anyone prove that more democratic regimes would work better in such difficult circumstances?"

Let us note, finally, that the system of presidential preponderance has been established more by custom than by the constitution. In many instances the constitution contains an embryonic idea of ministerial responsibility to parliament. "In Costa Rica, Panama, and Nicaragua, congress can censure ministers; in Cuba under the 1940 constitution, in Peru under that of 1933, in Bolivia under that of 1938, and in Ecuador under that of 1946, a vote of censure forced the cabinet to resign."[19] In practice, however, such provisions remain pretty much paper law, since presidential preponderance is guaranteed by other means.

Africa

Africa, too, in the first years after independence saw a rash of constitutions,[20] and this trend is not yet past. The speed of constitutional change at some moments are very rapid, but in recent years it has slowed somewhat. The change at first took the form of strengthening presidential power, with an accompanying tendency toward a single-party system. But observers could see a change of heart after the first revolutions had occurred.

The constitutional traditions of the parent countries generally had great weight at the time of emancipation, and Africans tried to transpose European institutions into a new setting. "Within the Commonwealth formal imitation went so far as to set the white wig of British justice upon black heads."[21] The imitation was, however, more complicated than a passing glance might suggest. In the former British territories, for example, men imitated the real working of English institutions rather than their formal appearance. The formal appearance is the balance of legislative and executive; consequently we do find in the first African constitutions of former British territories such provisions as the appointment of the prime minister by the head of state, or the responsibility of the prime minister to the parliament and the right of dissolution. But the real functioning in Great Britain involves the exercise of full and entire executive power by the majority party; this, too, was imitated in Africa in the form of cabinet dictatorship.

French parliamentarianism, itself in process of development, offered a rather complex inspiration. At the moment when the African states were attaining independence, France had just adopted the Gaullist constitution of October 4, 1958. This, rather than the parliamentary regimes of the Third and Fourth Republics, is what the Africans imitated. Thus they were imitating what Duverger called "inegalitarian parliamentarianism." Consequently we find in Africa various provisions regulating, in a draconian fashion, the exercise of political responsibility (delays, qualified majorities, etc.). We find, too, limitations on the scope of law, along with regulatory powers given in principle to the government; a system of extraordinary powers which allow the government to ask parliament for authorization to legislate by decree in order to carry out its programs; provisions for the automatic validation of the budget if parliament has not passed judgment within a certain time, or automatic validation of a text to which no vote of censure has been passed and for which the prime minister has guaranteed government responsibility.

Also imitated were the innovations of the 1958 constitution on the role of the head of state (Article 16: exceptional powers in case of serious crisis for the state). "Only East Cameroon," says Jean Buchmann, "has imitated such a regime in detail, but the new constitutions in the four states of the Entente have drawn from it the most important powers of the head of state (referendum, special powers) and added them to those the president already has. It is to be noted that the Gaullist constitution does not make the ministers formally responsible to the head of state, as they are to the Chambers, although in practice this has come to be the case in France. In this respect, the constitution of East Cameroon, in seeming to imply the double accountability, goes beyond its French model."[22]

The governmental structures of Congo and Somalia were largely inspired by the Belgian and Italian versions, respectively, of "a parliamentary regime along British lines."

The imitation of the parent country's institutions, then, has not led to the formal adoption of a parliamentary regime of the British and French type (which, in fact, no longer exist even in the parent countries). But there have certainly been imitations of important characteristics of the parent state constitutions in their real functioning.

From this starting point the African regimes began their development toward a purer form of presidentialism than the models allowed. The evolution continued until about 1963, with Nigeria and Ghana at opposite ends of the spectrum and with Congo-Kinshasa and the French-speaking states strung out in between. Liberia is an example of classic presidentialism, with origins in the United States' system. But, for the other states, Buchmann prefers to speak of a neo-presidentialism, a presidentialism rediscovered in a new context and owing almost nothing to imitation of the United States.

The new type of regime generally has the following characteristics: the head of government (often the head of state) has no political responsibility to parliament; the executive is vested in one person; the fate of the executive is often bound up with that of parliament, but the initiative in appealing to popular decision is reserved to the head of the executive.

This new kind of regime first appeared in Congo-Brazzaville in 1959 after eleven constitutional laws in a row (November 28, 1958, to December 7, 1959). But new constitutions were later to be established in 1961 and 1963 after the dismissal of President Youlou.

In Ghana the new model was adopted in 1960. Here are the chief characteristics of it according to the white book which accompanied the government's plan: "The head of state holds the executive power and is president of the republic, responsible to the people." Parliament is "the supreme legislative body, and is made up of the president of the republic and the National Assembly; the president of the republic has the right to veto legislation and to dissolve parliament." The president's position is thus much stronger than in the Congo. "The president of the republic is elected at each general election (the legislature having normally a five-year term) by a method which guarantees that he will normally be head of the party victorious in the general elections." There is a cabinet "named by the president of the republic from among members of parliament, to help him in exercising his functions."

Some months later, a second presidentialist wave swept over the fours states of the Entente, which on August 10, 1960, had announced their intention of adopting identical though separate constitutions. The central thrust in each was to establish the governmental and parliamentarian monopoly of a majority party.

The Ivory Coast constitution of November 3, 1960, itself influenced by the Gaullist constitution, served as prototype. The president is appointed by direct universal vote; his mandate expires after that of the deputies; he is sole holder of executive power and shares in the exercise of the legislative function. As for parliament, the scope of law is restricted (by limitations on the subjects that fall within its competence), as are the number and duration of its sessions; it must surrender its power in favor of the president under certain conditions (explicit delegation "for the carrying out of his program" and exceptional powers like those of article 16 in the French constitution). Finally, the president can at any time substitute a popular verdict via referendum for a vote of the assembly; he can do so, however, only with the consent of the committee of the assembly, a restriction which will be omitted from constitutions modeled on that of Ivory Coast. Some independence of powers for the assembly is kept since the assembly cannot be intimidated by the threat of dissolution. But such a counterbalance is very much a formality.

Dahomey, Niger, and Upper Volta adopted similar constitutions in November, 1960, followed by Congo-Brazzaville (March 2, 1961) and Mauritania (May 29, 1961). In all these instances, an important innovation strengthens the Ivory Coast solution:

the president can, on his own initiative and without restriction, submit to a referendum any subject "which he judges to require direct consultation of the people."

A further reinforcement of presidential power was the introduction of a right to dissolve the assembly, in the Central African Republic, Gabon, and Togo (constitutional provisions of late 1960 and early 1961). And in constitutional modifications of 1962 and 1963 in Gabon, the Central African Republic, and Chad, we observed a further increase in presidential prerogatives.

The constitutional amendment adopted in Gabon, May 31, 1963, removed ministers from the competence of the supreme court in case of high treason. Only the president of the republic falls within that court's competence henceforth; the ministers fall under the jurisdiction of the common law. The removal of their privilege was facilitated by a reduction of the assembly's prerogatives; by comparison, the president's powers as head of the executive were increased.

There is a further side to this constitutional evolution. In the Central African Republic a law of December 28, 1962, amended the constitution so as to establish a single party system. (This had not been done elsewhere in Africa up to that time, but Chad soon followed the new example.) In fact, on November 7, 1962, the Council of Ministers of the Central African Republic had already dissolved all political parties except the Movement for the Social Emancipation of Black Africa (MESAN). The new constitutional text stated: "The people exercises its sovereignty freely and democratically within a single national political party: The Movement for the Social Emancipation of Black Africa, MESAN." Formerly the constitution had read: "The parties and political groups vie for votes, exercise their activity freely, etc." (Article 2). Article 5 was similarly amended: "On the suggestion of the Directive Committee of MESAN, the national assembly can dismiss deputies who have seriously failed in their duty of representing the people." A further constitutional revision, November 19, 1963, extended the president's term from five to seven years.

However, second thoughts led to a reversal of direction: the countries which experienced revolutions in 1963 (Togo, Congo-

Brazzaville, and Dahomey) later adopted new constitutions which limit presidential powers.

The upheaval in Togo (the overthrow and assassination of Silvanus Olympio on January 13, 1963) followed on the establishment of a new party, the Togolese People's Rally (October 1, 1962). The new constitution promulgated by Mr. Grunitzky on May 11, 1963, reduced the president's term from seven to five years and provided for a vice-president to be elected by popular vote. The president is described as "holder, along with the members of government, of executive power." He is installed by the Supreme Court and takes his oath before the people who are "sole possessors of sovereignty." He can submit subjects for referendum, but only after official consultation and receiving the reasoned opinions of the presidents of the National Assembly and the Supreme Court. He has power to take exceptional measures in extreme cases, but only after consulting these same persons. In addition, the scope of law is somewhat broadened. The assembly can question the government's responsibility if the president refuses to modify or dissolve said government. The president can dissolve the assembly, but then there must be a new election of president and vice-president as well. In short, the constitution strengthens the assembly's position and aims to prevent the president of the republic from arrogating all power to himself, as President Sylvanus Olympio was blamed for doing.

In many respects the development of Congo-Brazzaville in 1963 followed a different course. The trouble was triggered there, too, by President Fulbert Youlou's announced intention of establishing a single party. A general strike followed on August 6, 1963, and on August 15 Abbé Youlou was dismissed. The new constitution (December, 1963) does away with presidential election by universal suffrage and provides for election by an electoral college made up of the deputies and the councils of the prefectures, subprefectures, and municipalities. The president can now be reelected only once. He determines national policy but "with the council of ministers." Furthermore, it is the government, under the prime minister's direction, which carries out the policy. The assembly can dismiss the government by a vote of censure, whereas the president can dissolve it only if there have been two crises within eighteen months. He can use his extraordinary powers only after official consultation with the prime minister, the president of the National Assembly, and the president of the Supreme Court; the National Assembly can terminate these exceptional powers by a two-thirds' vote.

In Dahomey, the government and the unions ran afoul of each other in September 1963. On October 28 the army took power under Colonel Soglo, and a new constitution was adopted by referendum on January 5, 1964. The new constitution was an amendment of a very president-oriented text presented by the government on Novembr 30, 1963; the unions had sharply criticized this earlier text. Henceforth "the people of Dahomey . . . reaffirm their fundamental opposition to any regime based on despotism and personal power." President and vice-president are elected along with the National Assembly. The vice-president is president of the council and chooses its members. No strict ministerial responsibility to parliament is provided for, but, at least in oral questions, the assembly can vote a resolution by a two-thirds' majority, and if the resolution is not applied, it can call for a decision by the president of the republic; if the assembly fails to win its case, the president goes to the people with a referendum. This constitution thus continues to be more presidentially oriented than the Togo and Congo-Brazzaville constitutions of 1963, although several provisions do limit the president's prerogatives. In Leo Hamon's interpretation, "These constitutions intend to avoid the monopolizing of power by one man and to force him into cooperation with other holders of power . . . . Development up to that time, on the contrary, had been more or less toward the concentration of effective power in one man's hands."[23]

The pace of constitutional change has slowed a great deal in recent years. However, there have been more and more military coups, which transform regimes in a different way. Let us once again note some significant steps in this development.

In Togo the most important coup d'état occurred in 1963; others were to follow. President Sylvanus Olympio was assassinated for refusing to reinstate in the Togolese army some Kabrai soldiers who had been demobilized from the French army. The reason for the president's refusal was, in fact, a desire to be independent of France. This first coup had been led by Sergeant-Major Bodjollé. Recalled from exile, Mr. Grunitzky, former head of government, succeeded in restoring order, although at the price of concessions to Sergeant-Major Bodjollé who was promoted to captain, then to commanding officer, before Grunitzky finally pensioned him off. Grunitzky then had to deal with Lieutenant-Colonel Eyadéma and was at last forced to resign under his threats on January 12, 1967. Another colonel, Kleber Dadjo, presided for a while over a Committee for National Reconciliation, but was soon eliminated by party schisms, and it was Lieutenant-Colonel Eyadéma who finally took power.

In Dahomey the chief event took place on December 22, 1965, with the seizure of power by Colonel Soglo, after it had proved impossible to unite the political leaders behind a program or a cabinet. Previously in 1963, as we have seen, Colonel Soglo had taken provisional control over the operations of the state, but had soon restored it to civil leaders after new elections. This time he decided to remain in power. He was however finally swept out in 1968. Civil power was restored under President Zinsou, but he in turn was removed in 1969. In 1970 there was a new return to civilian rule, but with the explicit backing of the army.

In the Central African Republic, a coup took place during the night of December 31, 1965. President David Dacho was put under house arrest, and Colonel Bokassa took power, proclaiming that "the bourgeois ways of the privileged classes are abolished," and expelling the Chinese Communists from the country.

Three days later (January 4, 1966), Lieutenant-Colonel Sangoulé Lamizana seized power in Upper Volta, practically against his will. The coup followed upon the discontent of civil servants against an austerity program decreed by President Maurice Yameogo whose popular prestige had just suffered a setback (especially after his divorce and remarriage to a very young girl, which aroused general criticism in a county whose elite is deeply Catholic). The unions called a strike on January 2. The president's first wife's sister organized a demonstration of young women at the technical and secondary schools. The president had to resign, and Lieutenant-Colonel Lamizana, pressured by mass enthusiasm, had to take power. He announced his intention of holding for only four years, after which he would restore it to a generally accepted administration and government. In 1970 he was still in power, though it is true that a constitutional revision is under way.

The coup which dismissed President Youlou at Brazzaville in August 1963, kept civilians in power: Mr. Lissouba and Mr. Massemba-Debat (the latter as president of the republic). In 1966 there was mutiny during the president's absence, because of punishment meted out to an officer of the parachute corps. In addition, there was distrust of the influence being exercised on public affairs by the so-called revolutionary youth. The government came to an agreement with the rebels, but nonetheless held its ground only thanks to a guard of Cuban soldiers who were engaged in military training of the Congolese. A new coup in 1969 again changed the balance of forces.

In Gabon there was a military coup in 1964, but it failed due to intervention by French airborne troops who kept President Mba in power.

A military coup also brought about the fall of King Mabutsa IV of Burundi. The king managed at first to resist a mutiny during the night of October 18, 1965, and had thirty-four soldiers and ten politicans shot, among them the president of the National Assembly, the first and second vice-presidents of the Senate, and the president of the Popular Party. After calm was restored, however, the king withdrew to Geneva; his nineteen-year-old son, Charles Mdizeye, obtained special powers from his father and then on his own authority took over the government, installing twenty-six-year-old Captain Michel Micombero at its head with the support of the Matutsi youth. Charles had himself enthroned as Ntaré V. But in November, while the king was paying an official visit to Congo-Kinshasa, Captain Micombero deposed him and proclaimed a republic.

A journey abroad was also the undoing of Nkrumah of Ghana. On February 24, 1966, while flying to Peking, he was deposed by Colonel Kotoka, who immediately deported the Chinese and

Soviet experts. The years preceding this event had been marked by a strong trend toward dictatorship. In January 1965 Nkrumah had eliminated the posts of assistant ministers, condemned to death certain persons acquitted in 1963, dissolved the Chamber of Representatives, and had new deputies appointed by the party without recourse to elections. He also imported guerilla fighters who were to be sent to Niger, Togo, and Ivory Coast. As a result, Nkrumah had been the object of several unsuccessful attempts at assassination.

After the coup, power fell into the hands of the National Council for Liberation, directed by General Ankrah, who promised to withdraw, when occasion offered, in favor of a regularly constituted government. He had to face a further military revolt, led by Lieutenant Aithu; during the disturbances that followed, General Kotoka was assassinated. General Ankrah retained his position but kept his promise, and a civilian regime was peacefully restored in 1969.

In Congo-Kinshasa, Tshombe was removed as head of government on October 14, 1965. Kasavubu then secured the establishment of a Kimba government, despite the reluctance of parliament. Soon there were rumors of a pro-Tshombe plot, and amid this troubled atmosphere Lieutenant-Colonel Joseph Désiré Mobutu decided that the army alone among national institutions enjoyed popular confidence. He dismissed the president of the republic by a simple letter and gave Colonel Mulamba the responsibility of forming a new government. He won approval of the coup from a docile National Assembly and had himself made president of the republic for five years.

What are the root causes of these various upheavals? In more than one case, we can point to heightened racial tensions, along with those peculiar circumstances of pluralist societies which we have already described. But there were also abuses and excesses by those in authority as they became intoxicated by the opportunities for enrichment and prestige which the new powers of independence brought. One example among many was the scandal given his people by Maurice Yameogo who spent public funds lavishly for a wedding trip to Brazil. Generally, younger men have then risen up who trusted military leaders as arbiters who would not take advantage of the situation; they incited the latter to take power.

In Ghana it was the totalitarian spirit that caused a reaction. Nkrumah gave himself the title *Osagyefo*, "Redeemer, Messiah," and even *Katamanko*, "the infallible one." He imprisoned or liquidated his opponents in parliament, dismissed judges who acquitted his enemies, loaded the country with debts, and pursued a mad policy of prestige-seeking.

There was also, in growing measure, a conflict between an older generation of leaders who often had good sense but who had gotten their education in the school of experience and had no degrees, and a young generation coming out of the great universities of the world and aspiring to leadership.

The army in these circumstances seemed to provide "the needed arbiter between clans or persons, the instrument of social justice, or even the direct interpreter of society's aspirations."[24] In the eyes of these young people, it was not because of political ambition that the military men took over power.

We must also observe that apart from Nkrumah whose rule had taken on too many dictatorial traits, the coups did not touch the more honored leaders. Their personalities continued to uphold the value of presidential regimes; this was especially true of Senghor, Houphouet-Boigny, Sekou Touré, and even Ahidjo, Dior Hamani, or Modibo Keita (though the last-named fell in 1969).

This fact underlines an important aspect of African presidentialism: strong personalities are needed to fill the larger place left to the executive. In other words, presidentialism is not synonymous with a strong and stable regime; the regime is strong and stable only if the person at the helm is strong and stable. We can even say that the African presidentialist regimes are regimes of personal power. This is not meant in the sense the expression had in France under de Gaulle, that is, a power exercised with too little participation by others. Personal power in our context means rather a power which depends very largely on the qualities of its possessor, a power with little institutional structure despite constitutional appearances.

Natural Regimes for Developing Countries?

Doubtless the situation is already changing in South America, where presidential preponderance means something halfway between personal power of the traditional kind and a depersonalized democratic power. The real bearer of presidential power, even in recent years, has been the great populist leader, personally prestigious but supported, above all, by the ardent enthusiasm of the masses. Such were Vargas, Kubitschek, Peron, and Odria. Such, in the beginning, was the recent Peruvian president, Belaunde Terry. Such in many respects is Fidel Castro. And, I would like to add, such were at one period many of those who later became full-blown dictators: Gómez in Colombia, Pérez Jiménez in Venezuela, Battista in pre-Castro Cuba.

The armies frequently play a role in Latin America: not the leadership role of other years when every captain could pull himself up into power, but a protective, usually conservative role in the interests of order, when civilians can no longer govern effectively and no individual has populist backing. There is an analogy here to the role of armies in Africa, but there are differences as well. The intervention of the army in Latin America is more clearly conservative, with a rather sharply defined social function over against the progressive forces that upset the balance. In Africa, on the contrary, the army intervenes rather to block clearly regressive abuses of power. We must add, however, that in Latin America, too, more than one military group is nationalist-progressivist in outlook, and some actions of the military spring from disgust at an impotent flock of politicians.

In short, the regimes that are "natural," in a way, to developing countries are fated to be occupied by strong personalities who enjoy either a solid traditional allegiance or a massive popular prestige. When such an individual is not at hand and the cliques take over with insignificant personalities at their head, the hour of the military is never very distant. The reason for this is a negative one: the lack of civilian leaders, rather than the desire to establish a military rule as such. Thus, after Peron's fall the armed forces made and, above all, unmade Argentinian governments; Frondizi himself was too changeable, too little of a populist leader, to hold presidential power in a stable fashion. In the same way, Jânio Quadros, then Joao Goulart (with his unpredictable politics) brought the Brazilian regime to the point where it was ripe for the military coup of 1964.

We spoke just now of regimes that are "natural" to the developing countries. There is no more typical case than Brazil, where the pendulum always swings back to a presidentialist regime after brief attempts at an unsuitable parliamentary (cabinet) regime. After the departure of Jânio Quadros, Vice-President Goulart received power only at the price of a lessening of that power in the form of a cabinet regime and the abandonment of election by popular vote. Less than two years later, a referendum restored the system of presidential election by popular vote. Then the military, which dismissed Goulart, abolished this kind of election, and Marshal Costa e Silva was chosen by Congress (the two chambers of parliament). But in 1968 there was talk again, even in the majority party, of returning to popular elections. The same talk will probably start up again after the present troubled period. At the present stage of development, is it possible to govern Brazil in any other way? Yet such government requires unusual personalities, and these are not always to be had on demand.

If such men are lacking, the regime is unstable or the military comes on the scene. We mentioned Argentina a moment ago. Here a new military coup d'état occurred on June 28, 1966, and unseated Arthur Ilia who was governing with the "popular radicals." General Ongania, who succeeded him, said in July 1967: "The political intentions of the government shall not be submitted to short- or long-term electoral supervision." He interpreted the Argentinian situation thus: "Argentinians were hungry for authority; that is why it was so easy to establish it." In 1970 General Ongania in turn had to surrender his power, but to other soldiers.

We can understand then why, in countries which have not for some years produced the kind of leader required by regimes congenial to them, there is a deep sense of political disappointment. Attempts to reconcile opposing groups—radicals and Peronists in Argentina; Lacerda, Kubitschek, and even Goulart in Brazil—do little to alleviate the disappointment. Disillusionment leads some to see no alternative but guerilla warfare. Yet this itself would have no chance of success if it did not lead to a new presidential regime with a prestigious leader at its head like the hero of Sierra Maestra.

THE ROLE
OF THE
SINGLE PARTY

Our description of political regimes has stressed the Third World's presidentialist tendency and the resultant fact that strong and stable government depends on a strong personality as president. It may be objected that there are single-party regimes in many countries of the Third World or at least in Africa: did not the single party appear, a few years ago, to be a more natural regime for Africa than a civilian or military presidential government? This view is widespread and was sustained, even demonstrated if you will, with great scholarship in the large volume edited by James S. Coleman and Carl R. Rosberg, Jr.: *Political Parties and National Integration in Tropical Africa.*[25]

The single party seemed natural in Africa because the nations were as yet so unintegrated. Since there was no national allegiance, a plurality of political groupings had to be carefully avoided, for under the circumstances these would only engender separatism. The single party seemed natural, too, in facing the urgent tasks of modernization. "In the immediate postcolonial period in many African states the dominant party seemed to be the national institution most capable of performing a variety of political functions."[26]

If natural to Africa after independence, the single-party system seemed no less natural, to many observers, for the other developing countries of Asia and Latin America. What is the value of these judgments?

The Facts in the Case

We must, first of all, make some observations on the present extent and limits of the single-party phenomenon.

The trend to a single party is by no means universal in the Third World. We leave China out of consideration here. In China, as in a number of people's democracies in Eastern Europe, an effort is made to keep up the appearances of a multiparty system, with the various parties (especially those of the middle class and the peasant class) being united in a single front; under this cover, a single-party system of a Leninist kind is in fact strictly maintained. The same is true of that other people's democracy of the Third World, Cuba. But the trend to a single party has hardly been manifested at all in Latin America or in India. In India, the Congress party has a dominant position and has never been dislodged from power at the federal level (though it has in many states of the Union), but it is not identifiable as a "dominant party" in the meaning this phrase has had in recent years in black Africa. In Africa, indeed, there has been a tendency to set up a single-party system. But even here distinctions must be drawn.

In North Africa, we would have to mention Egypt, Algeria, and Tunisia. But let us limit ourselves to black Africa. In the years before independence there were generally several parties, though the number was limited: six in Nigeria (the maximum), four in Ghana and Senegal, three in Sierra Leone, two in Guinea, Mali, Niger, Upper Volta, Dahomey, Mauritania, and Togo. Ivory Coast, however, already had in fact only one party, the African Democratic Rally (RDA). At the moment of independence, a plurality of parties was recognized by all constitutions, in the sense that all of them spoke of parties in the plural.

After independence, on the other hand, we observe that the

parties in power are generally annoyed by the presence of one or more opposition parties and try to get rid of them. Sometimes these are eliminated by force, sometimes they are persuaded into fusion. Thus there arise parties which for practical purposes are single parties. This is the situation in most of the West African countries (except for Sierra Leone and Nigeria) and in the countries of the East as well.

In Ghana, Niger, Dahomey, Togo, and Mauritania, the new situation was brought about by force. In Guinea and Mali the weaker parties were more easily absorbed by the stronger. In Senegal the Union of Senegalese Peoples (UPS) effected "a more or less equal merger."[27] In Upper Volta a coalition formula was adopted, and there was a return to a coalition formula in Dahomey and Togo after the coups of 1963.

The general process of concentration affected not only political parties but also social and professional organizations. The effort was made to have, along with the single party, a single youth organization more or less attached to the party. Similarly, organizations of women and labor unions were forced to amalgamate and, in several instances (as in Ghana), these were made dependent on the party.[28] The fusion of the labor unions into one was not always accomplished easily. The revolution in Dahomey (November 1962) was largely due to the attempt to dissolve the Dahomean Confederation of Christian Workers (CDTC).

The labor unions in this context are said to be "politicized." In fact we must distinguish two successive forms of politicization in the African labor movement down to the present time. In the beginning, the unions politicized themselves and, along with the political parties, played an important role in the days when independence was being won. Union claims and protests at that period paralleled the political claims and protests. The politicization of a later time is quite different. It is more forced than chosen; it tends to a moderating of union claims (even to the point of abandoning the right to strike) rather than to expressing their convergence upon political claims, as in the period of struggle for independence. Thus the political leaders generally make no concessions to the unions; they ask them not to continue with the kind of politicization characteristic of the earlier period, but to "be converted." In its extreme form, we are dealing with depoliticization rather than politicization, for the aim is to assure the domination and unhampered freedom of some body other than the union, namely the party. Pursuit of that goal must involve an effort to unify the unions into a single union closely linked with the political party. The aim is to win orderly cooperation in the developmental task undertaken by a state which is the monopoly of a single party.

Significance of the Single Party in Africa

To evaluate the development of single parties we must go back a bit and consider events of recent years in Africa.

In a true single-party system, a group of convinced and determined men claims to be the instrument of popular action without any need for elections, and it dominates the state in virtue of a right grounded in the nature, purposes, and knowledge which the party has. The party is thus self-legitimating, and there is no source of legitimacy beyond it. In principle, such a regime is oligarchic and collegial, not personalized. Corresponding political constitutions have a parliamentary character and exclude any properly presidential elements. Power is strong and centralized not because of a president, but because of the single party with its cohesiveness and discipline.

In many African countries where the trend to a single party is clear, the reality looks quite different from what has just been described. The presidential regime is to the fore, and the single party is only an aid to this.

The presidential type of regime has itself special characteristics in Africa which distinguish it from its Latin American counterpart, as we noted earlier. In the beginning, in fact, the African states generally established a preponderance not of presidential power as such, but of a parliamentary majority on the British model. In 1962 Jean Buchmann could see as one of the specific principles of black African presidentialism "the most perfect possible correspondence between the president and the parliamentary majority."[29] This principle was affirmed in Ghana (with its British tradition, even if a distorted one). It was affirmed also in the

French-speaking states of the Entente where the official aim was to give effective power to the majority party. In most cases, then, the president's power was constitutionally linked with that of the majority or "dominant" party.

A second stage followed quickly and brought presidential power in the full sense. The shift can be explained by doubts about the effective power of the dominant party, for the party was often too shaky. The president's powers were strengthened constitutionally and thus artificially, though they were still tied to the power of the dominant party. In adopting this solution, the nations were ratifying an existing situation. For often what mattered from the very beginning (even from before independence in several instances) was not so much the party, which was weak, but the man at the head of the party, who guided it rather than was guided by it.

The parliamentary system was rejected, then, because it cannot produce a stable government unless the majority in government is itself stable and well organized. In a word, it can be stable only if the head of government exercises an effective leadership over the party, apart from any constitutional provision. When they are unable to promise themselves such stability, nations try to secure it by strengthening the president. Thus, after first trusting in parliamentary representation and after next handing over the government to the parliamentary majority (the dominant party), they finally try to protect themselves against the consequences of insufficient organization in the dominant party itself, that is, against the lack of stability in the parliamentary majority. The juridical reality is now the primacy of one man (the president) elected to the supreme office. His power is now protected against the dominant party, because the latter is too weak a foundation on which to rest power.

But this one man will seek, in turn, to protect himself against opposition from within the party and from outside. He needs a party at his service, in order to exercise his power thoughout the country. Thus the third stage is reached: the president tries to make of the party (which he already supports more than it supports him) an instrument of his power. He will therefore tend to make of it the sole party, that is, to exclude all other parties, and even all other independent organizations, in order the better to exercise his own presidential power.

The single party which emerges from such a situation is, however, an instrument rather than an initiator. It is not a single-party regime as though power were truly in the hands of a party oligarchy. Rather there is a presidential regime in which the single party is a necessary but subordinate part. Another characteristic is that the effort is now made to turn the party, not into a limited group of "the pure and the strong," but into a vast gathering of the greatest possible part of the population. The single party in Africa tends to be the framework into which everything is to be put. The reality of the single party here is consequently quite different from what a Leninist system allows.

The relative positions of president and party are clearly evident if we examine the functioning of power in a country like Ivory Coast. Seydou Madani Sy summed it up when he wrote: "The single party in Ivory Coast neither governs nor legislates. It has the role of adviser through its higher committees and, above all, an informational role. The party basically explains to the people the decisions of its constitutional representatives and informs the representatives of the needs and desires of the people."[30] President Houphouet-Boigny has a distinguished personal position which ever since independence has allowed him to bypass the congress of his own party (the Democratic party of Ivory Coast: PDCI) in guiding the government. In fact, from 1960 to 1965 there was no party congress.

In 1961, it is true, Philippe Yacé, secretary-general of the party, stated: "More than ever the party must be the guide whose doctrines inspire responsible politicians." In practice, however, the party's program is indistinguishable from the government's, and the initiative is with the president of the republic. It was he, for example, who defined his government's program before the National Assembly on January 3, 1961, after his election to the presidency of the republic. Mr. Yacé was content to say to party militants at the time that the program thus outlined from the rostrum was the same in essential objectives as that of the PDCI.

The party's political committee is more an advisory than a deliberative body, and never acts alone to force a decision on the president. It cannot take it upon itself to discuss government projects. Instead, the president decides when it is opportune to consult the committee on a question being debated in the council of ministers. Consultation seems to be required, moreover, only on projects whose implementation among the people is a delicate matter. Thus in 1962 the president consulted the committee on a project for regulating proper names and instituting a registry office, and a project for forbidding dowries and regulating marriages. The committee, according to the communique, proceeded to a thorough examination of the subjects "because of their possible political repercussions." In every case the committee only offers advice, and the president can make what use of it he will.

In appearance the party designates parliamentary candidates for the ballot, as required by the election law of 1960. In fact, for the 1960 elections, the president himself weeded out the excessive number of candidates proposed by the subsections of the party. The communique of a conference of secretaries-general of the subsections said: "The secretaries-general of the PDCI unanimously vote, for the country's sake, full confidence in the president of the African Democratic Rally and in the political committee for drawing up the national roster of parliamentary candidates for November 17,1960." The president had the last word.

Furthermore, the elected assembly legislates directly in collaboration with the government and with no direct party intervention. The party, on the other hand, has the task of explaining delicate legislative matters to the membership. Seydou Madani Sy therefore rightly concludes, "Contrary to Mr. Duverger, for whom 'the existence of a single party in a country implies an absolute concentration of power in that party's favor,' we believe that there exists a single party in Ivory Coast because all power is in the hands of a national leader who is at the same time head of the executive."[31]

The kind of situation we have been describing is common in Africa. Most often the single party has only an instrumental function and, in fact, became the sole party precisely in order to be a better tool. We must advert, however, to situations which are partial exceptions to this generalization. For Guinea and Mali, we must speak with Seydou Madani Sy of "the cooperation of constitutional organs and party institutions" (in Guinea) and of "the subordination of constitutional organs to party institutions" (in Mali). These two countries were practically born with a one-party system and with constitutions of the people's democracy type, whereas elsewhere the single party was set up later to help in a system of presidential power.

In Mali, at least until the fall of Modibo Keita, the preeminence of the Sudanese Union African Democratic Rally seemed clear. "The party determines the government's political line and directs its daily action. The party is not satisfied to orient the government's action by the decisions and resolutions of its congress, but claims the right to share, in a day-by-day and effective way, in implementing congressional decisions through the party's political committee. Moreover the party names political commissions in whose hands political and administrative powers are fused."[32] The party has held several congresses since independence, the most noteworthy being that of 1962.

The political committee, ever since 1962, has contained six members of government but also twelve other members who in their majority could genuinely control government action; the real decisions have come from this political committee. Seydou Madani Sy concluded: "If it be still possible to speak of President Modibo Keita as leader because of qualities which the militants acknowledge and respect, we must nevertheless insist that in Mali collective direction is a reality. Like his predecessor, Mamadoy Koné (who died in 1956), Modibo Keita is a leader subject to regular control by the political committee, and the latter through its weekly meetings intends really to share power with him."[33]

The same principles hold for Guinea and were expressed by Sekou Touré: "If you do not grasp the important fact that behind the state there is a higher reality, the party, you cannot understand the political value of these provisions of the Guinean constitution [the provisions on party power]. Because the party has the function of directing the nation's life, it has at its disposal all of the nation's powers; political, judicial, administrative, economic and technical power is in the hands of the Democratic Party of Guinea." In fact, there are two parallel hierarchies which Sekou

Touré wanted to keep distinct, but there is also close cooperation between them. Perhaps we must go further and say that we are closer here to the Ivory Coast model. For the political committee is an instrument of the head of the executive; twelve of its fifteen members (in 1962) are "directly dependent in one or other way on the president of the republic," nine being cabinet members, two others regional governors, the twelfth an ambassador, and all appointed by the president.[34]

"It is probable," says Seydou Madani Sy, "that a Guinean president forced into a minority by Congress would lose his post as secretary-general and as head of government." But it is improbable, he adds, that he would ever be in a minority since he has such means of controlling the political committee and the party itself. Successive congresses of the PDG have passed without comment the resolutions proposed to it by the secretary-general of the party, who is also the president of the republic. And this tendency has only grown stronger.

"Since the seventh congress of the PDG (1963), the national political committee seems reduced to ratifying decisions prepared or even already adopted by a five-man executive committee made up of the secretary-general, the presidents of the technical committees, and the permanent secretary."[35] The technical commissions themselves work under the control of the secretary-general, Sekou Touré. The identification of party and president is not total in Guinea, as it is in Ivory Coast, but it is quite extensive. The Guinean example shows much less of a departure than the Malian from the general scheme of a presidential regime with a subordinate single party. Mali is really the only exception.

For and Against the Single Party

We must then, not be misled by appearances nor confuse the existent regimes in Africa with single-party governments in the strict sense. Nonetheless, the institution of a single party which is the instrument of a power concentrated in the hands of the executive, is a notable characteristic of most current African governments. Is such a "monocracy" viable? Does it meet the needs of the developing countries? Or does it mean that the apparatus of state is strengthening its own position without any genuine concern for the people as a whole? These questions are suggested by the recurring coups d'état in Africa. They have been raised recently in W. A. Lewis' *Politics in West Africa*;[36] until then, analysts had usually been ready to find numerous justifications for the presidential system and the single party.

In their *Political Parties and National Integration*,[37] for example, the Americans, James S. Coleman and Carl R. Rosberg, piled up arguments in favor of the single-party system. The tendency to it is universal, they claimed. It is also deep-rooted, being related to a series of factors. The political situation at the time of independence is the first: leaders at this time inherited "the full autocratic power exercised until then by colonial governments which had recognized no constitutional limits to their action."[38] A second factor is that the nations have as yet achieved little integration. There is no national allegiance to restrain separatist tendencies; opposition groups therefore cannot fail to be suspect to the government, either because they have had close ties with the former colonial power, or because they are supported by tribal or regional ethnic feeling, or because they are associated with foreign governments or movements. A final argument: leaders must confront difficult tasks of modernization; hopes and aspirations are high, and there would soon be deep frustration if results were not quickly forthcoming.

The single party, in these circumstances, seemed to be "the national institution most capable of performing a variety of political functions."[39] It alone was able to interrelate and coordinate varying interests, to recruit political personnel effectively, to bring about the necessary "political socialization" (that is, to substitute a new national allegiance for previous loyalties), and to bring about a minimum degree of "political communication" (since adequate means of mass communication did not exist). In a word, the single party was the providential instrument of national integration. The authors do not deny that a multiparty system might have accomplished the same purposes, but they claim that at the moment of independence the dominant party appeared on the scene as the national institution that could do the job.

The authors also have the impression that African tradition

was moving in the direction of a single-party system of "pragmatic-pluralist complexion." The heritage of centralized and authoritarian colonial administration likewise favored the same kind of solution. In addition, party structures had already been deeply influenced by socialist and Communist example; think, for instance, of the African Democratic Rally.

A final element in the picture: the politically oriented class of "educated" and "developed" people feels a special vocation to govern. What is being expressed here is the important idea that an apparatus of state first came into existence and then naturally found for itself the task of motivating that larger society from which this limited social class, this elite of movers, had become detached.

All these arguments and factors do constitute an explanation of the regimes that in fact took over in newly independent Africa. In attacking the single party in his 1965 book, Lewis does not weaken that explanation, but he does raise another question which deserves no less attention: If the single party is an understandable phenomenon, is it a good solution to the problems? If it is not, must not other ways be sought, even if in a first stage of development circumstances may have necessitated what was in fact a bad solution, namely the single party?

Lewis does not call in question some of the ambitions of the single party: national integration, rapid and effective development. He does question whether the system has succeeded in its purposes. First of all, it does not really guarantee the representation of all the people; in fact, in a pluralist society there is rather the danger that a single party will serve the interests of one ethnic group or of one particular region at the expense of the others. Or else opposition and conflict will arise within the single party, and then nothing will have been gained by the system. Instead of alleviating tensions, the single party would be more likely to deepen and sharpen them. In brief, the single-party system would really work only in countries where the population is homogeneous and uniformly poor; Lewis instances Tanganyika (now Tanzania). But in such a situation, he adds, there is really no need of parties at all, except for the political education of the citizenry. (This is precisely one of the functions which a single party frequently fulfills). Wherever society is pluralist and heterogeneous, the single party is out of place and more likely to worsen the situation than to better it. A single-party system really supposes the problem of national integration to have alrady been solved.

In all this we can see that Lewis is thinking of the single party as a political framework (such as it generally is in Africa), rather than of the single party in the Leninist mold. But he no less strongly rejects the Leninist scheme for Africa, on the grounds that in Africa there is no class conflict to justify a Leninist solution.

Lewis believes that the single party as found in Africa sprang in fact from an unwarranted application of the Marxist scheme or at least from the unthinking application of a European political scheme appropriate to a society divided along class lines. In such a situation there is a kind of war going on between a party which governs and prevails, and an opposition which objects, between the Ins and the Outs. It is a violent struggle, even if somewhat moderated in the European political systems. European parliamentary democracy is only what its name says; it is not full-blown democracy. Yet this rather undemocratic system, unadapted to the realities of African life, was imported into Africa. With it, and just as imprudently, were imported the regulations (grown liberal with time) on press and sedition. The danger is that the opposition will abuse such rights and that it will then inevitably be suppressed. Once again, why impose on Africa the least democratic aspects of a political regime suited to a society in class conflict? In Africa the natural solution should rather be sought along the lines of federal pluralism, or at least in some form of decentralized power that is adapted to a pluralist society. The government should be a coalition of representatives from the various sectors of the population. No more Ins and Outs, but only Ins. Genuine democracy, and African democracy in particular, arises from unanimous consent reached by discussion by all concerned, with no minority having to bow to a majority and no group being forced into opposition in the European fashion.

Lewis' case is well argued, and his judgment seems irrefutable. But we think that not all of his conclusions are equally valid.

First of all, we cannot speak as assuredly as he does of the absence of social classes in Africa, for they are now in the process of being formed. But let us pass over that point, since African party systems up to the present time have not really relied on class conflict. It seems to us, however, that the divisions within traditional pluralist society are just as tenacious as class distinctions. Yet Lewis seems to suppose the contrary when he proposes a decentralized democracy with a coalition government and no majority decisions imposed on minorities. Lewis is right in proposing that situation as an ideal, but we ought not overlook the difficulty of bringing it to pass.

Lewis is also right in attacking the single-party tendency to bypass, unwisely, the inherent pluralism of African societies. Violence is done to reality by such action, and there is bound to be a reaction. But Lewis' criticism is valid only for the abuses involved in the establishment and implementation of the single party. It is not valid against the open single party which some statesmen, such as Julius Nyerere, want to set up. We can also ask whether Lewis' single but decentralized political organization, in which all sectors of the pluralist society would have their rights and no minority would be oppressed, is so different from the open single party. Such a party would be as open as possible, and closed only to those who do not respect the basic rules of democratic action, whether in domestic or in foreign affairs.

The goal sought by a single-party system is the limitation of tribal, group, and other kinds of opposition. That task remains a real one. It is necessary to assure the representation of such opposing groups and to do justice to their divergent interests and opinions, while at the same time avoiding fragmentation; what is needed, therefore, is a limiting national framework within which all discussion is possible and outside of which there is no likelihood of national integration or cooperation between groups. Once again we think Lewis does not do justice to the deep divisions within an ethnically plural society in claiming that such divisions are not the same as those of a class society. If we really take these divisive factors into account, we see the necessity of limiting or moderating their expression. This cannot be done (and here Lewis is quite right) without giving all groups maximum participation. Some types of single-party systems would probably meet these needs, and some multiparty systems certainly would not.

It seems to us, finally, that Lewis overestimates the effective role of the single party as such. We have stressed the fact that in Africa we are dealing rather with presidential regimes in which the single party plays a subordinate role. Some of the defects which Lewis attributes to the single party are also, and perhaps even more, the faults of regimes in which presidential power is strengthened without limitation, thus opening the door to abuses. The need, then, is rather to limit presidential power without destroying it, than to eliminate every form of single party. In fact, an open single party could be the means of moderating presidential power in greater measure than is done at present. In a sense, the issue here, as formerly in the old European absolutist regimes, is the creation of parliaments which will control but not supplant the presidential power. Such parliaments will be the more effective, the more all group interests are represented in an active and cooperative way, within a framework of rules of actions.

In short, whether it is put under the rubric of single party or not, the problem of necessary unity and necessary diversity (if only to make unity more tolerable) will continue to be urgent in the nations struggling for integration. In these nations the difficulties of national unification are intensified rather than eased by efforts at development (since such efforts impose sacrifices now on one group, now on another). The single party as hitherto found (whatever be said of its theory) has ignored national diversity too much for the unity it seeks to be genuinely tolerable.

UNDERDEVELOPMENT:

NATURAL OR

ECONOMIC?

What are the causes of the political situations which we have reviewed? The observations we have been making have already suggested this question in various ways. A brief recapitulation will make this clear.

We began by looking at the Third World states as they appear on the international scene, looking at them from the outside as it were; we then looked more closely at the characteristic traits of their political regimes. From the former viewpoint we found these nations eager for international status and activity (the more so perhaps, the weaker they are), attaching high importance to world recognition in international organizations, and carrying on considerable activity at this level in the interests first of decolonization, then of development. At the same time we saw them to be very isolated, bereft of firm backing from the great powers except, at times, for the ambiguous support of their former parent-states. They are consequently bent on uniting with each other, even if this means sacrificing many political ambitions.

On the domestic scene, we met states whose national integration is threatened by civil troubles with manifold roots. These nations are usually organized under presidential regimes which are solid and stable as long as they have at their head strong personalities with traditionalist or populist backing, but weak and subject to military coups when such leaders are lacking. Such political situations may seem aberrant or abnormal if one's viewpoint is that of the pluralist, liberal, and relatively depersonalized constitutional regimes of the West, or the single-party regimes found in Communist countries. It is better not to try to pass judgment. But at least the Third World countries are politically in a special category, since regimes that seem natural and spontaneous to them are not elsewhere natural or spontaneous. Such regimes raise a question for us, and this question we must now try to answer. Why, among the Third World nations, do we find such a situation at the international level? Why such political regimes with their ups and downs?

The cause? "Underdevelopment, of course," many will say. But "underdevelopment" is a neutral and abstract term. What is behind it? Two quite divergent explanations are offered.

For some, underdevelopment signifies a kind of dark damnation. It is the Nazareth out of which no good can come, but only wretchedness, corrupt political regimes, international demagogy, and deceit. For others, on the contrary, underdevelopment is a passing state of poverty, and escape from it is easy once the rich nations decide on it and either offer sufficient help or pay a just price for products bought from Third World countries. Or else the nations will escape from underdevelopment simply through a strong political regime and planning.

In this chapter we shall dwell on these two explanations and conclude that we cannot be satisfied with them.

Races, Resources, Climates

According to the first explanation, underdevelopment means that peoples or even whole continents are simply incapable of engendering any other kind of political life and thus destined to endure presidential regimes, personal dictatorships, the ceaseless maneuverings of civilian presidents, and, from time to time, military coups. Confronted with such an explanation, we must look briefly at the case for inferiorities inherent in the Third World countries, whether the reason for them be race or lack of resources.

On the subject of race, Yves Lacoste, a qualified observer of the Third World, collected a number of current opinions. "It has often been pointed out that apart from Japan the peoples of the developed countries belong to the white race and that the colored peoples are to be found in the underdeveloped countries. The development of nations of the white race is then often explained by qualities inherent in white men: industry, ability, energy, enterprise, etc. Some authors have even drawn up lists of deficiencies proper to other races."[40] Development and white race coincide, then, as do underdevelopment and colored races. Yet anthropologists and ethnologists all note the surprising constitutional homogeneity of the present human race, that is, homo sapiens, the human race that occupies the earth now that the others have vanished. This is the unqualified conclusion reached by research on race since the Second World War under the egis of UNESCO.

A great deal might be said, of course, on the supposed equivalence of development and skin color. A journalist writing on Peru once described the difficulty of defining the South American Indian. What is an Indian? He quoted from a United Nations report: "The fact that an individual is an Indian depends largely on whether he himself, his family, his relations, and the relevant authorities consider him to be one." A "subtle and subjective" definition, indeed, as the journalist noted. But he cites an instance from Peruvian life which favors just such a definition. "At Pamacochas, at the end of road being built by the Sacsahuayman battalion to link Chachapoyas, capital of the Amazonas district, with the rich agricultural region of Rioja, there is a community of Indians with whiter skin than many of the half-breeds of Lima's middle class. White Indians? They exist because in colonial times a revolt broke out in the region, and the natives massacred all the male Spaniards (Basques) and took their wives. The result of this Peruvian rape of the Sabines was individuals with predominantly European features. But these people still live in a community very like the old Incan *ayllus*, hardly touched by any degeneration of the old communal system. They still use the ancient sledge, an ox-drawn, leather-covered stretcher, which their wheelless ancestors of four hundred years ago used for hauling. They still live in earthen houses with high-pitched roofs of straw."

"To be an Indian," he concludes, "means to belong to the most disinherited economic and social class."[41] We could, in addition, give many examples of small homogeneous white communities, of varying origins, which have undergone no development; for example, the Slavic group installed in Northern Argentina since the First World War, which is completely underdeveloped and has even greatly regressed in relation to the mother community back in Europe. A good half at least of the South American population belongs to the white race and can nevertheless be regarded as underdeveloped.

On the other hand, the single case of Japan is enough to overturn the racist thesis. This nation "developed" hardly fifty years later than many European countries. It has long been said that Japan imitates and does not create. But even that is no longer true today. Rare in any case are the nations which did not first spend a long time in imitation. For decades the Americans of the United States were imitators or, at best, discoverers of practical applications.

But the racial argument can be carried a step further. Some claim that, whatever be the case with skin color, underdevelopment is correlative to the "nature" or national temperament of the peoples in question. But, here again, in almost every case facts belie the thesis. It often takes only a transplantation or migration for peoples hitherto passive and seemingly incapable of development to become suddenly active and dynamic, once they escape their original setting. Think of the many Chinese, Indians, and Arabs in Southern Asia, Africa, and Latin America; of the importance of Levantine groups in West African commerce; of the Southern Italians, Greeks, and Levantines transplanted to the United States or South America. It was Italians from South Italy who built the industries of Sao Paolo in Brazil. "And the Andalusians played a similar role when sent to Northern Spain, while the Northern Spaniards did the same in the South."[42]

Thus, although entire groups, with or without a common skin color, remain in fact untouched by development, there is no proof that they do not have the same cultural plasticity which in others has allowed the transformation we call development. Anthropologists are unanimous: there are cultural differences and specializations, but there are no inherent incapacities founded on race.

The problem of comparing racial aptitudes has been attacked anew in a seemingly more scientific way thanks to psychological testing of individuals from various races. Babies, if possible, or at least young children are tested to establish whether children of one race react less well to testing than those of another: to aptitude tests, IQ tests, etc.

The validity of such comparisons is questionable, however, and has in fact been questioned. Generally the comparison is between the dominant race and the dominated race within the same geographical area. But such comparisons can be regarded as significant only if one fails to realize how much social factors influence the manifestation of aptitudes. The results will always differ, for example, even between members of the same race if children from a higher social class are compared with those from the lower, poorer, more illiterate classes. The differences, in a word, are probably not due to the racial factor at all.[43]

Nor must we forget that the tests have been devised by Europeans and Americans, and are a function of their milieu and culture. This alone is enough to explain why individuals from some underdeveloped countries, faced with such tests, are immediately nonplussed, give wrong answers, and receive poor marks. In a book on the professional formation of African youth, Mr. R. Durand reports that at Dakar some years ago a test was given to children of the same age and school level. The results differed a good deal from race to race: the Europeans came out first, the Lebanese were a little behind, and the half-breeds, the black Catholics, and the black Muslims brought up the rear. But the test dealt with technological data quite familiar to European children and quite unfamiliar to the others. The difference thus had nothing to do with race or religion, and most probably depended only on the degree to which each group had been assimilated to the European culture which the tests reflected. The European or Europeanized children alone were fully at home with the objects presented: bicycles, electrical equipment, household appliances.

To prove anything about racial differences from testing, we would need fully transcultural tests for aptitude or intelligence. But to construct such a test would be like trying to square the circle, since every factor by which we can judge aptitude or intelligence involves a cultural context.

In any event, where the degree of acculturation is the same and the samples are large enough to be statistically valid, no substantial differences are observable.

Let us turn next to the matter of natural resources in the developing countries. The earth is less adaptable than men are, and some thinkers find here the reason for the devastating course of underdevelopment.

Here it is difficult indeed not to be disturbed by the facts: the underdeveloped part of the world coincides almost wholly with the tropical and subtropical zone. Underdevelopment extends as far as the Mediterranean regions of North Africa and Europe, and these also mark the limits of the arid subtropical world.

It is also true, however, that brilliant civilizations once emerged in the tropical zone: the Mayas and Aztecs of Central America, the Incas of Peru, the Benin civilizations of Africa. We may think, too, of the ruins of Angkor, the Taj Mahal, etc. We must recall, above all, that all the Mid-Eastern civilizations, from which the Western was born, arose in unpropitious places; the same was true of Roman civilization in the disinherited South of Italy.

But the problem remains, for there is a technological gulf between all those civilizations, however brilliant, and development as we understand it today. What, then, is the real situation at the present time?

A first important point is that the poverty of the Third World in resources for energy and minerals is by no means sure. The Third World, on the contrary, ranks high among oil producers: the Mid-East, South America, Indonesia, and now North Africa. The same is true of hydroelectric capacity for Africa and Brazil. Minerals, too, are well represented: copper, uranium, bauxite, etc. Some of the world's most important iron deposits are in the Third World: Mauritania, Gabon, and Brazil. India and China show good possibilities for coal.

For agriculture a prognosis is more difficult. We could legitimately figure that agronomic research will someday allow as rational and productive a use of land in the tropics as in the temperate zones. All that is needed would be research along different lines than in the temperate climates. But a big question remains: what would be the cost of irrigating dry lands, improving equatorial soil, and effectively combating erosion and soil decomposition?

In the past, endemic tropical diseases were an even more serious obstacle than the difficulties already mentioned. But this obstacle appears surmountable almost everywhere today. In Africa the eradication of some of the most fearful of these diseases (sleeping sickness, yellow fever), and the conquest of others has begun. Researchers in tropical medicine claim that even malaria in a country like Africa can be wiped out at an acceptable cost, provided the attack on it is well organized.

There remains, in some instances, the obstacle of climate, especially of heat. Even a man well nourished and protected against disease will admit that tropical climates are oppressive and offer little stimulus, especially for intellectual work. At times even the native of tropical countries will compare tropical and temperate climates in the same way as men from the temperate zone. Yet this obstacle, too, cannot be said to be insurmountable. Climatic control may, in the more or less distant future, play the same role in tropical lands as the heating which is indispensable in the temperate countries. The question is primarily one of cost: can effective climatic control be provided on a large scale at a reasonable cost?

It is true, of course, that the Third World is not everywhere the same. To say that one or other continent has rather good resources is not to say the same of every country on the continent. On closer inspection, some prove to be truly disinherited, and prospects for developing natural resources there are poor. This holds, for example, for parts of the savannah zones in Africa. It is possible, of course, to object and point to cases where a lack of natural resources has not prevented a rather remarkable economic development. Switzerland has reached a high living standard on a poor natural foundation (except for hydroelectric resources). But Switzerland had the good fortune to be close to several rich and large neighbors. This is not the case with the countries of interior Africa, which are cut off from the ocean and where population is sparse and transporation costs prohibitive.

In short, it would be an oversimplification to reject wholly the objections drawn from the "natural" situation of certain countries. But neither may we generalize these objections. On the contrary we are justified in saying that, taking the Third World as a whole, the obstacles are probably not insurmountable.

In drawing an accurate picture we must also take into account that what seems possible today was not necessarily possible yesterday, before certain kinds of scientific, technological, and medical progress had been made. What kind of economic growth was possible on the West African coast, for example, before yellow fever was eliminated along with some other dread diseases that regularly decimated the population? A further question which comes to mind is whether the order in which scientific discoveries have been made, with their application first to the now developed countries, was an inevitable one. Is it possible to conceive that discoveries facilitating development in tropical regions could have been made before those which made development possible in the temperate zones? The question is probably unanswerable. But we can at least maintain that if the order of discovery was not wholly illogical, then the peoples in certain climates were condemned to await their turn and to reach the goal later.

A final point must be raised. Are we to count among the natural factors of underdevelopment the contemporary demographic fact, namely, the rapidly increasing populations so often mentioned in this context?

An elementary distinction is needed if we are to take account of the real history of population. While not being completely universal (since there are limited areas where growth is slow, and vast regions where density is insufficient and even ridiculously low), the phenomenon of population growth in many developing countries (an average annual rate of 2 percent to 3 percent) is undoubtedly an aggravating circumstance. It is one more difficulty in the way of successful development. But we must immediately add that the phenomenon is recent. It is by no means "natural," but rather the result of initial economic changes in the developing countries and of exposure to the medical technology and hygiene of the more advanced nations.

As for the past, we may suggest that in many instances the absence of population growth meant the lack of stimulus for economic development. Under certain conditions a growth at least equal to that of nineteenth-century Europe is a favorable stimulus for development. Yet growth at such a rate (1 percent or 1.5 percent annually) seems not to have occurred in the past of most countries today regarded as underdeveloped.

In summary: whether we look to color or race, to physical or demographic resources, we are not led to share the pessimism of those who see the underdeveloped countries as burdened with a hopeless "natural" curse.

Poverty

It is just as simplistic, we must admit, to see in underdevelopment only a passing economic state of poverty, from which the underdeveloped countries can emerge as soon as the wealthy nations are willing to pay a just price for the products of the underdeveloped countries. In this view, the precarious political situation of these countries and the international tensions between developed and underdeveloped nations would disappear along with poverty.

Unlike the pessimists spoken of above, believers in this formula take a purely economic viewpoint, conceive of underdevelopment as poverty, and write it off much too easily. We must remark, first of all, that poverty as such can engender very disparate political regimes. But further, and above all, if we speak only of poverty, we are far from accounting satisfactorily for the situation in the Third World. To speak of poverty is immediately to be drawn into other aspects of underdevelopment.

By poverty is generally meant the low level of national revenue, and reference is immediately made to the great disparities between developed and underdeveloped countries. But we must note, first of all, that there are three, not two, large categories of countries: developed countries with a per capita revenue of $1900 to $3500 (Common Market countries, United States, and Canada), the countries of Latin America with a per capita revenue of $300 to $500, and the countries of Africa and Asia (except for Japan) with a per capita revenue of $100 to $200.

Secondly, we must not pass too quickly over the fact that these figures are themselves open to serious criticism. The national bookkeeping of developing countries includes many dubious statistical evaluations. More importantly, the bookkeeping of developing countries and that of developed countries are hard to compare; more accurate account would have to be taken of such things as consumption of home-produced goods, or services, which are itemized well enough in developed countries, but not in the developing ones.

In any case, it is more important still to observe that these figures give only averages. Inequality of revenue is much more marked in the developing countries than in the developed ones. Roughly 80 percent of the people in Latin America receive only 40 percent of distributed revenue; in Asia, where the situation is less serious, they receive 55 percent.

We must look, then, more at the startling social inequality than at an average poverty stated in unqualified numbers. This point is highly important. We must also avoid imposing on other societies interpretive schemata suited to our own. The inequality of distribution we have referred to points to an even more fundamental inequality, alluded to in a UN report not long ago: "In less developed countries the most striking disparity is between the 'modern' economy sector and the 'traditional' economy sector. The difference coincides partially with the difference between a market economy and a subsistence economy, but only partially, since a traditional economy can also produce for a market. It coincides partially, but again only partially, with the difference between the urban and rural sectors. The modern sector is primarily urban, and the traditional primarily rural, but there also exists an increasingly important middle group: unskilled and underemployed workers who have lost their ties to the land and come to the cities, but have not been absorbed by the modern economy. Very often the difference we speak of corresponds to ethnic differences. It may also be due to regional differences in the hinterlands." In brief: poverty is one thing, social inequality another and more significant thing. In connection with the unequal distribution of revenue, we find an inequality of sectors, and this represents a genuine inequality of societies within the bosom of a society apparently one.

Furthermore, "social" indicators ought to be allowed no less importance than purely economic ones such as national revenue. For we are dealing here with figures which translate a people's life expectancy, infant mortality, illiteracy, amount of schooling, consumption of proteins, and medical services. Several of these indicators only confirm the economic indicators of poverty; they bring to the surface aspects of poverty which are more eloquent than simple revenue figures. Some of these social indicators say even more, especially the degree of literacy and schooling. Behind the numbers rises up the absence of written communication in very large strata of the population, or the almost complete absence of a modern school system (which is not the same as a complete absence of any systematic education of the young). The differences, then, are only superficially quantitative; they are really qualitative. We are dealing with distinct societies within society.

Behind the question of poverty, then, which would perhaps be easily answered if it were no more than that, lies the question of divergent societies, for which a solution is perhaps harder to find. In still other terms, our real subject is not so much "underdevelopment." "Underdevelopment" is an abstraction, pointing to quantitative economic facts and missing the qualitative element, pointing also to "natural" factors which do not have the significance often given to them. Our real subject is different societies: underdeveloped societies, if you will, but in any case societies. Behind the political regimes examined earlier, behind the primarily political news that reaches us from the Third World, there are, in the final analysis, "underdeveloped societies."

But here distinctions are immediately called for, and we shall deal with them in ensuing chapters.

We have to do, first, with societies that have remained "on the fringe of development," because their institutions and value systems are very different from those of developed countries. We shall have to describe these sociological aspects of underdevelopment.

These societies are, at the same time, shaken by such economic transformations as have already reached them. We shall therefore have to observe the brutal social processes that agitate these societies (migrations; urbanization; evolution of the kinship system, the family, and the condition of women; birth of new social groups).

Thirdly, these societies are not only underdeveloped; they have also already entered the modern age, because there is present in them a yearning after development, largely due to cultural contacts during the colonial period. The desire is articulated by a rather small elite and implemented by the newly established state. The decisive role of the state calls for analysis, as does the role of planning and of the numerous means by which the state sets about refashioning society: agrarian reform, reform of family law, educational policy, community development, etc.

After such an analysis we shall look at the basic difficulties and contradictions which the process of reform must face. Finally we shall return to our starting point by reconstructing in summary and synthetic fashion the domestic and international political situations, with which we began our observations. In a conclusion we shall try to estimate what the future has in store.

"TRADITIONAL"

SOCIETIES AND

DEVELOPMENT

Underdeveloped *societies?* The term refers to societies which, when the Western societies took up the challenge of industrialism, remained in a condition, a manner of life, and an economy, which were once known in Europe but are now regarded by Europeans as archaic.

Some observers, indeed, will say that what we have here is simply societies blocked in their development by an event originating outside of them but penetrating deep into the heart of their existence: colonization. Let this question remain open for the moment. Later on we shall have to examine the social effects of colonization and to evaluate its real role. But, anticipating the results of that examination and evaluation, we can here turn to the original structure of the societies which have remained on the fringe of recent European development. We will take up the question of colonization when we ask again why certain "traditional" civilizations remained such in many respects.

"Traditional" Societies

The expression "traditional societies" is a popular one for describing the social foundations of underdevelopment. What does it mean?

The term can be given a narrow sense: a society in which the principle of tradition holds sway. Its institutions are understood to be permanent and are obliged to adhere to an ancestral model. Social rules, too, are inherited, and all social life faces toward a past which is to be reproduced and preserved. We shall see that these are, in fact, some of the characteristics of the societies we are dealing with.

But we prefer to use the term "traditional societies" to describe societies which seem old to us, in comparison with the modernity engendered by the industrial revolution. We know that before its recent rapid development in the last two or three centuries Europe too had such societies. We can even discover traces of them in our own not too distant past; for example, the kinship and cousinship systems in Brittany remind us of the extended family system. The latter is far removed from the limited conjugal (husband-wife) society which replaced it, but traces of the earlier system were to be found until quite recently.

The history of a large nation like China is very instructive in this respect. Contacts with the West were infrequent and quite limited before the second half of the nineteenth century. We do not find in China anything like the slave trade which may have weakened a number of African societies before the colonization of the nineteenth century. Yet for centuries, down to its encounter with the West and even long after it, China with its extraordinary human and natural resources, with its brilliant political flowerings across the millennia, led an economic existence marked by no progress (in the sense of economic development) and by no industrial revolution or anything like it. The same was true of Japan.

Europe lived for a long time in the same fixity or stagnation. It was aware of no difference in development between itself and any of the exotic civilizations it encountered. Early travellers saw no radical difference between their own European cultures and the Asiatic cultures they visited. Bertrand de Jouvenel notes: "They did not comment that the farmer was worse off than in Europe; and, until the sixteenth century at any rate, they thought the splendor of foreign cities superior to their own. The material differences which strike us today must then be presumed recent."

The most likely hypothesis is that independently of and, in any case, before colonization most peoples of the world lived in the same kind of political, social, and economic condition, from which Europe alone was to emerge.

These traditional societies had a genuine and durable balance. But the very conditions which guaranteed the balance also prevented the desire for development and all that goes with it. Such societies, then, were following another path. In a sense, they had made a different choice; they were caught up in a different, coherent, and satisfying structure; and they maintained it with no thought of deviating from it.

We can rightly remark that this earlier balance is nowhere to be found today. It has everywhere been disturbed either by colonization in the narrow sense, or by contact with foreign monetary economies and the international market, or simply by the use of imported scientific medical techniques which were enough to change a hitherto stable population. Everywhere, except in rare and isolated instances, the traditional economies have been undermined, or, as people like to say, we find "dual economies." "Some writers will apply the term 'underdevelopment' only to economies thus unbalanced by outside influences and unable to respond to these influences by adaptation."[44]

Today, at any rate, traditional societies that are not subject to distortion or imbalance cannot be found. In other words, underdevelopment is a relative thing, and our contemporary problem is caused by contacts between societies, cultures, and economies. This is not to say that traditional societies have been wiped out. If the disturbed balance of former times has not yet disappeared and made way for a restructuring and a new balance, this is surely due, at least in part, to the durability of the traditional societies and their habits, customs, and value systems. The very fact that colonization is often said to have involved the superposition of an alien society and economy on a native society and economy shows that the original structure continued to exist. It is then very important to take the latter into consideration in studying the factors of underdevelopment.

We will speak of "traditional societies" here in the broad sense described. Ethnologists would frown on this usage. In South America, for example, they would perhaps be willing to apply the term only to those Indian tribes which have remained almost completely free of contacts with European cultures. The rest of South American society is, for them, European. As a matter of fact, however, the European element in South America dates from the static age of European culture, from Europe in the predevelopmental period. Such European elements too, then, are "traditional." This is true in particular of all the feudalism brought to South America by Portuguese and Spanish colonists. They themselves knew no other way of life, no other model for social and political relations, and they inevitably brought it with them, just as others, later on, would inevitably bring with them the political systems of parliamentary democracy.

We need not hesitate, then, to include such "traditional" factors in our examination of the characteristics of underdeveloped societies.

Causality of Sociological Factors

We must immediately face up to an important question. Can we allow the structures of the traditional societies a properly causal function? Are they a cause of what we call underdevelopment, or simply an accompaniment of it?

It must be recognized that in speaking of social factors in underdevelopment we always begin by simply noting the difference between the social institutions of contemporary developed countries and those of underdeveloped countries with their traditional character. Such notations are still only descriptive.

What are the observable differences? A UN report of 1961 on the social situation of the world notes the following: "In countries with a high level of economic development, the family is generally smaller, more mobile, stripped of any productive economic function and of various other functions now taken over by public services in the area of teaching, administration, police, and social security. It continues to be a consumer unit and establishes psychological bonds and bonds of sentiment that are all the stronger now that other functions have been reduced or altogether eliminated."

The report continues: "Larger institutions based on real or presumed blood relationships, such as classes or tribes with their varied political, social, and economic functions, disappear at this level of economic development. They are replaced by a complex, independent or state-controlled network of institutions based on factors such as profession, amusement preferences, place or residence, sex or age group, and political affiliation." The report simply lists differences and changes. The establishment of a difference does not prove that one or other characteristic of traditional society is an obstacle to development or a "cause of underdevelopment."

"It is practically impossible in this area," says the same report, "to reach the kind of scientific verification that a laboratory experiment yields, such as would allow us to determine in a decisive way which of these institutional factors exercises real influence on economic development and how important the influence is, and which of them have only a superficial impact." There is a great danger, it adds, "of basing judgment on ethnocentric preoccupations."

We observed above that the colonist brings with him what he knows from his own experience. Similarly, anyone observing an underdeveloped society today compares it with his own experience, and may too readily regard the difference as a cause. "Since most of the economically developed countries," says the UN report, "are European or of European origin, all manifestations of European culture from clothing to political and religious institutions will be automatically linked to economic development."

If one adopts such a viewpoint, the danger is that the most obvious yet least important manifestations will be taken as key factors in economic development. People in developed countries are not the only ones to make this mistake. Their presence often leads people of the underdeveloped countries into the same error. Thus "the Pacific islanders hoped to reach the degree of prosperity they had observed among the military personnel stationed in the islands during the Second World War and so therefore they destroyed their ritual masks and costumes, arranged their houses like a military camp, and paraded with sticks for guns. They may have grasped in a general way the need of institutional reform, but they had no idea of how to go about it."

There is no close relationship between such cultural elements and economic development. The latter is compatible with widely varying institutions. "Institutions exist for noneconomic reasons, and such factors as social justice and the dignity, equality, and liberty of individuals will decide whether or not change is desirable. It is perhaps normal to believe that the regime most desirable for noneconomic reasons will naturally be the most favorable for economic development as well. All things being equal, however, it may well be that a socially desirable institution will be economically more effective simply because it has popular backing and encourages people to share in economic effort. It is observable, on the other hand, that, in industry at least, economic production can reach very high levels under a system of forced labor in which individual morale counts for almost nothing and is placed by terror or analogous methods in the hands of the state."

There has in fact been economic development under varying systems and regimes. The comparison just made looks, it is true, to institutions that are all modern, even if different among themselves, and not to traditional as over against modern institutions. But there is an example which is quite instructive for our purpose: Japan, a country which has been able to develop, or at least to begin to develop, without throwing over all its political, religious, and social institutions.

The day indeed came for Japan, after the Second World War, when the traditional structure of the family was somewhat weakened, but this fact alone does not mean that its continued preservation even today is impossible. What is sure is that, having held up for the last seventy years, the family has given Japanese economic development some special characteristics. These include, on the one hand, a very high rate of investment, consumption limits favored by a very strong family structure, a taste for saving which is tied up with the permanence of the family structure through the generations; and, on the other hand, a rather authoritarian, although private, system of production (the same degree of authoritarianism has been achieved elsewhere only by state force or by an extremely tense social climate). Yet no one disputes the results reached by the Japanese.

For the future, of course, the question is whether when it reaches a certain level, development does not require to be stimulated by consumption much more than by production or saving, and whether it does not suppose a society in which men are all freer and more independent than in traditional societies. The example of the Japanese family does not by itself settle all disputes, for many other features of Japanese society have had to make way for economic development.

Thus we must surely be very cautious in asserting a causal connection between cultural elements of traditional society and the fact of underdevelopment. It is no less true that we have difficulty in imagining modern economic development without some social obstacles being removed. We must try to determine at least some of these obstacles while avoiding unjustified extrapolations.

In what areas are such obstacles to be met? It would seem that they can be found in the landownership systems, family and village institutions, caste and archaic class systems, traditional political institutions, and finally mentalities and value systems as well as traditional religions. The following chapters will deal with these subjects.

In this series of possible obstacles the land systems and the familial and village institutions seem to touch most closely on economic mechanisms. In fact, however, all the areas mentioned are interconnected, and we make distinctions solely for ease in presentation. A chief characteristic of traditional societies, one much stressed in ethnology, is the high degree of integration between the various constitutive elements of these societies, their structural coherence. Ethnologists and anthropologists insist therefore on the brutal and generalized disorders which an attack on an apparently limited aspect can excite. If then, in the ensuing chapters, we are to treat distinct aspects in succession, we must also bear in mind that all of them form a single whole: that mentalities or value systems do not exist apart from institutions, that political institutions are not strictly separable from land and family law, and that we cannot encounter religions apart from value systems.

MAN AND THE EARTH:
THE VILLAGE

Let us look first at land systems and village organizations. Not, let us repeat, that these institutions can be isolated from others, but they do have a more obvious economic bearing, and our concern is with the relationship of institutions to economic development.

Is not development the better use and exploitation of natural resources? Among natural resources the most widespread is the agricultural resource, the land itself. It is well known, however, that the use and development of agricultural resources depend on the juridical systems by which men have, in various ways for different societies, stabilized their relationship to the land: in a word, land systems.

The village for its part has a decisive role in economic exchange and in the division of labor.

We shall speak here of land systems, not just of property systems. For, as we currently understand the term "property" in our economic and mental context, property in the strict sense is not always to be found in traditional societies. On the other hand, we acknowledge in our own countries varying kinds of relationship to land, varying kinds of "tenure" which are not reducible to ownership, for example, tenancy and rent with payment in kind. Traditional societies show a similar variety of tenure systems. In practice we find two great primary land systems: systems of ownership and systems of unstable tenure. The former tend to be over-rigid, the latter over-flexible and excessively undefined.

Ownership Systems

In this system there is property in the fullest sense, but the property is divided into a small number of very large holdings with a few owners. In between such large estates there are often numerous tiny holdings in the hands of a large number of individuals.

The large estate or feudal domain requires a large number of people to be attached to the lord's land, but without any ownership interest; these people are rather themselves part of the estate. The land and the men go together. This does not mean that they are transferred together. In fact, the large estates are really not transferred or, rather, they are not alienated. They are an inheritance which each owner's son will inherit in his turn. The land is hardly a business property at all. There is, consequently, a notable fixity of property in such a system, and this is one of the first manifestations of a weak economic sense.

At the same time, the countryman's links are not only to the master's land but to his person as well, so that the relation is not an economic one pure and simple. We do not find here a simple exchange of economic values. The farmer, a quasi serf, works with his family on the master's land, owing him a certain number of days' work; in exchange he receives the use of a small parcel of land from which to derive his own sustenance. He does not always receive payment in money, but he does always receive, at least in principle, an invisible return which is traditionally part of the system: the master's protection. Such a payment is clearly less and less valuable once the modern state is established. But even where it had greater value, the value could not be called economic. What is missing, then, in such a system is sufficient incentive to increase production: not only does the farmer not have property, but he has not even any kind of right based on property. When all is said and done, he does not even have that ownership of his own labor which in the salary system is the basis for reward proportioned to labor.

Sometimes there is a system of payment in kind, instead of payment by work. But the small renter who pays in kind is hardly different from the farmer who pays by his work. He too has hardly any incentive to increase his efforts at production. At times he keeps only 20 percent of his produce for himself and owes 80 percent to the owner. He would still owe him 80 percent of any supplementary produce gotten by extra effort. This is enough to discourage such effort; the man keeps his production level high enough only to gain subsistence for himself. We say nothing of the fact that the very small size of his rented section hardly leaves room for extra effort anyway.

This last named factor—the small size of the piece of land—also comes into play, and always with the same result, for the proprietor of the tiny estate.

The large proprietor is often not stimulated to progress. He can indeed more easily be stimulated, and is so at times. In fact, today we must often distinguish, in speaking of large estates, between estates following the unchanging traditional way of using the land and estates put under modern agricultural methods with consequent higher yields. On the latter kind of estates, workers begin to receive salaries in the proper sense. They are indeed often exploited, but at least the economic exploitation begins to be recognized for what it is in these modern and improved conditions, whereas it is not yet so recognized in traditional situations where relations are not primarily economic ones.

Many proprietors, however, do not yet choose the new way or have not yet done so. They live in a society of large agrarian landowners, within which prestige values have more weight than market values. In addition, the absence of other roads to rapid enrichment means that there is as yet no rivalry for wealth.

Such owners make use of a quasi-servile work force. It is difficult to stimulate such workers to increased production, and men are often driven to contribute their labor by an army of overseers, bailiffs, and private police. Even under such constraints, which of course tend to undermine the patron-client relation proper to the system, the owners do not obtain any notable economic results.

The situation would change if the large landowner would sell land to men able to buy it and profit by it, that is, if the land became truly a commercial property, a means of production rather than of prestige. Or if the large landowner modified his relationship to his work force and began to acknowledge and honor the economic value of work. But of course such changes would change the very system, characteristic of which is not simply the large scale of possessions, but even more the fixity, the quasi inalienability, and the uneconomic character of property. Property in such a system is by nature more feudal than capitalist.

We have just been describing the traits of the land system which is, in fact, still widespread in a whole area of South America. We find traces of it in Asia as well, especially in India, and it is still represented in some few sections of Africa where politico-social systems analogous to feudalism have flourished, for example, in various principalities and kingdoms of the East African lake zone. But South America is today the typical example.

Indian South America, indeed, still shows some even more archaic kinds of communal ownership. These antedate the Portuguese and Spanish colonizers and derive from pre-Columbian civilizations. But such communal properties have now been suppressed except in some limited areas, usually the less productive ones of the Andes: the Peruvian, Bolivian, and Ecuadorian high plateaus. The private estate system is much more widespread on the continent as a whole.

Here are some statistics to show how important the system was fifteen years ago, before the first agrarian reforms. Agricultural estates of more that twenty-five hundred acres covered 65 percent of the arable land and represented 1.5 percent of the property units. Properties of less than fifty acres, on the other hand, constituted 73 percent of the property units but only 3.7 percent of the land under cultivation. On large estates 90 percent of all rural South Americans lived either as laborers or tenants. Agrarian reforms have been under way for fifteen years, but they are slow and the situation has shown little improvement.

Systems of Unstable Tenure

Private estate systems account for only a part of the undeveloped countries today. There are other systems of a more archaic kind in which property is much less monopolized, but also less clearly determined. Property titles in any strict sense are not to be found, and, for rather different reasons than in the system just examined, the stimulus to development is also lacking.

In ancient China a traditional saying had it that "all the land under heaven belongs to the emperor." This did not mean that the emperor was the sole real owner of the land, as though he were a feudal lord. It would have been more exact to say (and this holds for most of the systems we are now to speak of) that the land belongs to everybody. Everyone has a right to the earth. The right is not equal for all but proportionate to the rank of each, for ancient Chinese society was markedly hierarchic. There were thus various rights of partial and temporary appropriation on the basis of everyone's right to the earth. Maspero wrote on this subject: "The right everyone has is not a right of eminent domain, different from each one's right of occupation." This means that the only concrete rights were multiple rights of occupation, and that such rights did not of themselves constitute a true and complete right of ownership.

In China it is only from a relatively recent period—the eighth century of our era—that men gradually abandoned these earlier systems and established ownerships of a more stable and determined nature, which slowly became land ownerships of a feudal type. The same process took place in early India, with the same movement from a poorly defined land ownership to a stricter ownership but of a feudal kind.

The situation in which the earth belongs at bottom to everyone may seem a happy and just situation. In fact, however, it involves an immobility and inalienability which takes from the land any possibility of use for genuinely economic production. This is why many in the past have been so critical of such a situation. Marx, following Colbert, wrote: "The absence of land ownership is the key to Eastern political and religious history." In particular, Marx saw in it the source of Asiatic despotism.

Perhaps we need not speak with Marx of an "absence" of ownership. But in any case the economic right of ownership of land was not distinguished from the religious meaning of the earth and from the rights and duties of various individuals within a strongly hierarchic political society.

Africa is today the favorite breeding ground of such systems. Appropriation still has a clearly religious and traditional character, well expressed in a Nigerian chieftain's reply to the question of ownership: "I consider the earth to belong to a huge family. Many of its members are dead, a few are alive, and a huge number is not yet born." In this view, the rights of men living today are relative. The only complete and total right belongs to the whole great family in which many are dead and very many not yet born. Men now alive have partial rights, primarily rights of usage, and these are relatively impermanent.

In regard to Africa we hear people speak at times of "communal ownership," but distinctions are needed here. The community does in some degree have communal possessions, but the community uses very little in a communal way. In fact, ownership and economic activity have little direct connection. Economic activity is usually carried on in a more limited, almost individual framework or at least in the framework of a limited kinship group that is much narrower than the formally proprietary community.

We can go further and say that the community itself does not strictly exercise true possession, if by "community" we mean the living men who make up the group today. The possessing community is more than these men; it extends into past and future and into the religious sphere. Georges Balandier wrote: "In African civilization real possession of the earth is always attributed to religious powers, not to social groups or chieftains or sovereigns." Such a trait clearly distinguishes this system from a purely feudal system of ownership, for in the latter we deal only with men, chieftains indeed, and sovereigns, lords, and masters, but in every case only men. In Africa, on the contrary, man's relationship to the earth is neither purely economic (once again: usage is not always, in fact it is even rarely, to be found at the same level as ownership) nor primarily political (like the feudal relationship).

In order to acquire a more accurate understanding of the situation, let us consider the chief characteristics of the system as explained by L. Thoré in his investigation of land law in Upper Volta. We must avoid generalizing, but at least we find here certain characteristics which are frequently repeated, even if with variations.

The prime characteristic is the superposition of various rights, none of which correspond exactly to ownership as we know it in, for example, the French civil code. Each right, unlike our right of ownership, is limited by higher rights and even by lesser ones. On the one hand, then, there are graduated rights of eminent domain, and on the other rights of more or less permanent usage.

Rights of eminent domain, even more than the estate rights of a feudal type, strengthen the inalienability of property, for they mean that property cannot pass from the clan or even from the village. We are dealing here with native land rather than property or even with sovereignty rather than ownership. Consequently ownership rights here are very strong but economically very weak, for a right of ownership, however strong, which is not also a right to dispose of what is owned, is economically a very weak right.

This anomalous situation emerges most clearly when the land is under the control of a "land head" who is not the current village head: a person, therefore, who represents earlier occupiers of the lands and witnesses to this older occupation even when a new population has long since been installed by migration or conquest. He is there to testify that the land does not belong to men in an unlimited way but that rather the men belong to the land. "As descendent of an ancient occupier of the land, he intercedes for men with the supernatural powers which are connected with this land."[45] His function is generally more religious and juridical than economic, but he is also overseer of the lands not appropriated by the village.

Subordinate to the rights of eminent domain, there are rights of usage which are vested in collectivities: the clan, the village, the family. In practice, the head of the group exercises these rights by parceling out the land for the use of various families; he can withdaw these grants under certain conditions and can intervene to confirm an occupation which would otherwise be very unstable. If there is anywhere anything like our right of ownership, it is this right exercised for the benefit of the collectivity, which is also a right to divide property among members of the group.

But we must note that this right has nothing to do with collective ownership. The right of appropriation here is collective in the sense that it concerns a group, but it is in practice vested in the natural head of the group, the head of the family or clan. The rights of the person thus vested with the function of collective distribution are limited only by the fact that he is but the representative of a more or less extended community. As representative of a family or clan, he must avoid using the property at his whim.

We must add that the right being exercised here is one of simple ownership. In addition there are various rights of cultivating the lands in question. These are clearly the most important of all rights for those who have to live off the land, but they are only rights, more or less stable, of using the land, and are never as definitive as our rights of ownership.

Such rights of usage are vested in individuals or in family heads who direct the usage. The family in question may be a patriarchal family with a grandfather still at its head; but even in Africa it may also be a more limited kind of family: man-wife or man-wives. Through the head of the family the small family group has cultivation rights to a piece of land which is part of the land collectively appropriated (as we saw above) by the larger family or clan and placed under the final authority of the land head.

There are, however, also lands which are apparently without a master. "A third essential trait of the property structure in Upper Volta is the existence in many areas of lands not yet definitively appropriated. That is, they have not yet been cleared or, if cleared, have not been claimed by a definite individual or family."[46] We might think that such lands would belong purely and simply to the land head, who could pass them on at will. Not so. Rather, clearing and cultivation will establish a right of usage over them and thus a right of appropriation in favor of the larger group to which the laborer belongs.

Let us return to the person who holds the land in order to cultivate it, the one who makes use of it. It can be said that he never owns it in a strict sense. But in Upper Volta usage rights themselves show a great variety, reducible to four main kinds.

In the first place, a peasant can have a permanent right of usage. Such a right is vested in every user by a group, clan or family whose head has the right of collective appropriation. For Upper Volta as a whole this type of tenure, involving a permanent right of usage, accounts for 54 percent of the cultivated land.

A second possibility is that the peasant has a permanent right of usage, not because he belongs to a family, but because he has cleared and now cultivates a free and vacant section of land. Such tenure applies to 14 percent of the cultivated ground. The peasant can, thirdly, have a right of usage which he has inherited from a cultivator who himself had it from someone with powers of collective appropriation. If in a given family there is too little land and in another too much, it may be that someone in the latter family has inherited a right of usage deriving ultimately from the former family. Such an inherited right is more or less permanent, since it is very difficult for someone who holds the right of appropriation to claim back land that has been used by two or three generations of a family. Such tenure is less frequent and accounts for 6 percent of the cultivated area.

In the fourth place, the right of usage may simply be borrowed. The holder of a permanent right of usage or of the right of collective appropriation lends the right of usage to a plot of ground. This kind of tenure is much more impermanent and applies to 26 percent of the cultivated land in Upper Volta. We must note that such loans are not real leases subject to payment. The borrower makes a return, but there is no strict equivalence. Gifts are made at harvest time, and services may be provided which recall the client's relation to his patron, but in no case is the return a real rental price. It is never fixed, always small, often varies from year to year, and is frequently renegotiated. The corresponding right of usage is thus quite impermanent.

Another characteristic of the property situation in this region (we find it in many other areas as well) is that the rights over trees are distinct from the right to the land where the trees grow. A person is therefore not always owner both of the land and of the trees; or, rather, ownership of the land does not necessarily include ownership of the trees. The reason for this special treatment is the high economic value of a number of fruit-bearing trees (Upper Volta has baobabs, orange, lemon, and mango trees, among others). There is also, of course, the value trees have as firewood in deforested areas with a dense population.

The law on the appropriation of trees differs rather widely from one region to another and even at times from village to village, and according to the species of tree. These variations seem to be a function chiefly of such factors as the supply of the trees in question and the degree of cooperation and understanding between groups making up the community. There is an instance reported of concurrent rights to the same tree, where the situation ends in comedy. The case occurs not in black Africa but in Tripolitania. "There is record of a single olive tree at Garian, Tripolitania, that had sixty owners, fifteen of them from Benghazi. The pruning of the tree raised insoluble problems, and the tree therefore remained unpruned and unproductive."[47]

In Upper Volta a further distinction is maintained between the right to build and the right of appropriation of the plot on which the building is set.

From the viewpoint of agriculture and modern economic development, the disadvantages of these systems are serious. First of all, such property systems make it difficult for land to change hands. The land is basically inalienable and ought not pass from the possession of a given group of people. The outsider will not be able to receive land, and will therefore often be a craftsman or a smith, but not a farmer like everyone else; or he will receive it only with a less permanent title than if he were a member of the group. Eminent domain, on the other hand, is never extinguished and can be claimed long after a piece of land has been yielded up by modern legal procedures. The latter cannot, in the eyes of the traditional system, have the absolute power to alienate which we claim for them. The result is endless litigation about the possession and use of countless plots of ground. The cities of Africa today often run into this formidable barrier to rational urban development.

A second disadvantage is that the cultivator is not so clearly master of his land as the property-owning peasant of Europe. In varying measure his right is provisional. We often come across instances today of elders granting some land, often the least attractive, to enterprising young people who manage to make it productive by modern methods, and then suddenly claiming a right to the produce on the ground that they had not granted full appropriation. The young get discouraged.

A third disadvantage is that the system hardly favors the stepping up of production. Increased production supposes an investment of capital in soil improvement: removal of stones, irrigation, fertilizing, etc., and this over a period of years. But such investment is discouraged by a land system which does not easily allow permanent occupation.

The situation here is doubtless less discouraging than under the estate system. We do not find society here divided into a few great landowners and a mass of men who have no personal ties to the land. On the contrary all members of the clan or village are on almost the same footing. But all are confronted with the power of the collectivity, clan or village, which limits the individual's hold on the land and makes it uncertain. Ultimately they are even confronted with ancestral power embodied in the person of the land head. The land is only in a partial and limited way a productive property; still less is it available for economic transactions. There is also the fact that the land is often left to produce by itself, with little artificial intervention by men, since this is considered an assault on the land; but this is another matter, going beyond the simple question of property systems.

All these systems are viable enough where the people stay

put and the population is numerically stable. They become problematic as soon as people become more mobile and population begins to increase.

In conclusion, we must observe that the collective character as such of land rights is not usually the real obstacle. The obstacle is rather the uncertainty of the user's right and the lack of stimulus when the farmer has little opportunity to profit by his own efforts at increased production.

The Village and Its Economic Function

After the land system, the village is the most characteristic socio-economic institution in traditional society. From one point of view, traditional civilizations show no reality more solid than the village. Thus, to say that Upper Volta is a republic with so many square miles of area, so many inhabitants, etc., is to say little that is significant. To say that it has seven thousand villages is to get to the heart of the matter. To say that India has five-hundred thousand villages is likewise to say the essential thing about India.

Village is distinct from city. The latter because of its size is a place for much freer and more diversified exchange. Size alone is of course not the decisive factor: the traditional world has some very large villages with up to ten or twenty thousand inhabitants, but they remain no less rigidly organized communities.

The village is the place of important economic cooperation, for example, between age groups. Such cooperation can be a factor in progress. But we must immediately add: do not allow the village an exaggerated importance as a place for economic cooperation. The study cited above on the Upper Volta land system observes: "Extended families or clans form extremely coherent social units, the more so as they assert their indentity by mutual opposition. The group often has priority over the individual and, as such, is irreducible to some larger whole, for example, the village. Social structure and the forms of production are not directly correlated, and it is probable that in many instances it would be more difficult to get several families to cooperate in a collective form of production (at the village level, for instance) than it would be to get separate individuals so to cooperate."[48]

In such situations it may be said that the village is too extended a social universe to allow close economic cooperation; what really matters are the large families, and between them distrust and jealousy rather than cooperation are the rule. At the same time the village is too narrow a social universe to produce independent individuals who might cooperate with each other once they see a common economic interest. The groups within the village are thrown together too much, and ancient quarrels and hatreds often remain too much alive among them for them ever to cooperate.

In brief, the village is usually too small a unit, too closed in on itself, too filled with parochial spirit, for development to get very far with the village as its base. Its size, especially, does not permit any very specialized division of labor.

In the nineteenth century Karl Marx was already vividly aware of this narrowness in the Indian villages which others were proposing as ideal social models. He wrote, "Those idyllic republics, the villages of India, which spend their energies jealously defending their borders against the neighboring village, still exist in their ancient form in the Northwest provinces of India where English sovereignty is of recent date. It would be impossible to imagine a more solid foundation for stagnant Asiatic despotism. Despite all that the British have done to turn the country into a second Ireland, Europeanization has proved impossible without the breakup of these stereotyped archaic forms."

The village has been an institution of great value for the survival of mankind through difficult periods. It met the essential needs of protection and even of economic subsistence, but it did not foster progress. In the past, however, it was necessary to choose between the more urgent needs of protection and subsistence, on the one hand, and, on the other, a developmental function which could be accepted only once security and subsistence had been assured.

FAMILY, CASTE,

POLITICAL

INSTITUTIONS

Many problems of development have to do with the space—social and geographical—within which economic activity is carried on. In several of the property systems we have discussed, we are dealing with small, land-holding communities which cannot alienate the land but only enjoy the use of it. Such a right of usage would certainly make an individual's efforts worthwhile if he could exercise it without a sufficiently large social and geographical space. A more or less collective, socialist system might arise in such circumstances. This is what happened, for example, in the Incan civilization of South America. But generally the communities are too small, and the plots of lands do not change hands at all or not often enough. We shall find, among other traits, this same characteristic of narrowness when we look at several other institutions of traditional society: the family, the caste or class system, the political institutions.

Family

Let us look first at traditional family institutions. The very power they have had for preserving the race has also been the reason why they have hindered development. Paradoxically we can speak of constricted social space when dealing with families which are broad, "extended," patriarchal, and therefore very large by comparison with the restricted family of father, mother, and children, with which we are familiar today.

The difference between the two types of family is really in the functions of the familial unit. The traditional extended family may be said to have served all purposes: it was an effective, productive, and consumptive unit, the almost exclusive place of education, a means of social security and old age assistance, to say nothing of its being the unit of religious worship, etc. In brief, it was a rather self-sufficient society. The conjugal family, on the contrary, assumes few of those functions. It is still indeed a consumer unit, but only partially, since the young have their own access to youth-directed consumer goods; only rarely (on the family farm) is the family a production unit. It is far from able to provide education, powerless to take care of the elderly, etc. From all these points of view the modern family can be regarded as retrograde.

But the limited family is accompanied by the deepening of many other social relations. The traditional extended family, on the contrary, is an enclosed circle and, in the modern period, has become at times a suit of cumbersome armor. It limits the horizon. It reduces economic life to subsistence and the consumption of home-produced goods. It is difficult to link large families together in productive activity, and even more so in large-scale investment. What has been accomplished in the past in the areas of production and investment has been accomplished by imperial intervention, not by associations of families.

Thus the limitations inherent in the traditional family system are many. Even apart from the fact that the patriarchal system means the rule of the elderly (since a man remains a dependent son into his forties), the traditional family system impedes initiative and innovation, and this in the very measure in which it is adapted to its conservative function. Furthermore the system allows almost no individual differences in revenue, one of the most notable elements in all developed economic systems whether of free competition or of the current socialist types.

After these apparently severe criticisms, there is room for many qualifications, and we tend to generalize too quickly on the basis of our experience at home. We have already referred to the persistence of the traditional Japanese family during a long period of economic development. That kind of family allowed for limitation on spending. It gave business an organizational model, for business in Japan is modeled on the family, with the head of the firm being a quasi father to his quasi sons who are associated in a very stable way with the business. This characteristic was of great value during the transition from rural to urban life. The business head often recruited and attached his close associates to himself by outright adoption. The large families with their ramifications were moreover the financial backers of the very large trusts, the *zaibatsu* (at a period when such strong confidence would perhaps not have been placed in men who were not kin). On this point, Europe of course offers parallels in the family business of the first generation of modern industry.

It remains true, however, when all qualifications have been made, that the family could not continue to be the almost exclusive focus of economic relations between men. Broader social spaces were needed, which meant the automatic limitation of the family's importance.

Caste Regimes and Archaic Class Systems

The village and the extended family are a source of tradition-bound rigidity and fixity incompatible with the social flexibility that has generally marked the evolutionary movement we call development. Often the whole of a society has been organized in the same rigid way, for example, into castes. This observation holds first of all for that most visible and real of social spaces, the village. But it also holds for society as a whole, in the measure in which all the constitutive villages are organized in a caste system.

Each caste is bound to set occupations, strictly limited to members of the caste. The caste also has a religious meaning, in that each group of men has a definite place in a religious interpretive system. In India, people of one caste wear a different garb from those of other castes. Distinctive signs are multiplied because the distinction between castes bears on the whole of social life and is at work in all encounters between men; in the case of the untouchables, the harijans, other castes must avoid all proximity.

Essential to caste distinctions is their definitive, irreversible character. A person is born into a caste and belongs to it until death. It is easy to imagine how such a system kills aspirations for social betterment. The segregation of economic and professional activities, for its part, prevents the kind of mobility and adaptation which development requires.

The caste system reached its perfection, if we may so put it, in traditional India, and the system is only slowly giving way in modern India. But in many other traditional societies we find comparable, even if more limited, phenomena. Think for example of the smiths or the minstrel-clowns (*griots*) in African villages; here too a social classification is determined definitely and irreversibly at birth, and a destination of the individual to set kinds of work (which are not necessarily of an inferior kind).

In this context we must mention slavery too. We refer to domestic slavery—the "house slaves" of Africa—which did not necessarily have a racial or political cause but derived rather from a caste system.

In the feudalism imported into Latin America at a fairly recent point in its history, we find a number of parallel traits, though in class rather than in caste form. Here again people belong in a fixed way to groups that have no communication with each other: the great feudal landowners and their stewards, on the one side, and the farmers and peons on the other.

Observers like to speak of the absence of any middle class in Latin American society. This may indeed be said to be the central issue, but in using the term "middle class" we must be clear on what we mean. What is missing in Latin America is not a particular class called "middle," itself fixed within a system of unalterable classes. What is missing is the social mobility, the possibility of rising higher, the presence of which is generally indicated by the existence of a middle class. What strikes us in the older Latin American societies is how closed in the landown-ing oligarchies and the mercantile bourgeosie are. The young, even if qualified by studies and degrees, do not enter easily into these groups. The old system of rigid classification is meant to last forever to those within it, and it resists the modification of social functions. Yet this is what is most wanted by men who see new possibilities. It is natural to many that no one should leave his class or disturb the established balance. The traditional class system of Latin America is, of course, less rigid than the Indian caste system, but not much less. And here again religious justifications have not always been lacking.

Political Institutions

Political institutions do not exist outside the totality we have been describing. Sometimes, indeed, they simply fuse with fam-ily, clan, or village institutions, the political entity being the village or a small group of villages. In such cases, political authority derives from domestic authority and is almost identical with it, as in the Roman clan (*gens*) where in the early days the family head had power over life and death, that is, political power. Sometimes, political institutions are distinguished by being more comprehensive, but, in passing to this larger scale (which can reach the level of kingdom or empire), we do not see any change in the bonds between men. We see only that the system in force at the family and village level is transposed into a vertical series of overlapping familial relations, right up to the emperor who is father of his people. Such was the Japanese emperor as he still existed, in theory at least, down to 1945. The emperor exer-cises his role as head and father directly only toward his vassals, the lesser lords; the latter in turn have the same relationship to petty lords, and so on, down to village and family heads.

The differences between these types of political institution come down, essentially, to the extension of the authority exercised. In some cases political authority is limited in extent (the village heads, as in the Bamiléké country of Cameroon) or even extremely limited (as in "anarchic" societies where there is no real political power outside power within the family). In other cases political authority has a much wider scope (for example, the feudal king-doms of Buganda and Burundi or the Mossi empire in Upper Volta, where the chief was set over a limited number of vassals who in turn were feudal heads of groups of villages).

Further real differences, even if less important, are observable in the forms of government. Sometimes the systems are surpris-ingly democratic in that councils of all kinds and even assemblies of all family heads play an important role. (In such societies there is nothing analogous to our absolute monarchies of divine right, which are really a quite modern phenomenon.) Sometimes the systems are more authoritarian, especially when conquest has played a significant role in the establishment of power over peoples forced into dependency.

The defects of all these systems when it comes to development lie not so much in the forms of government as in size and in the nature of the political bonds.

The size is generally small and does not allow for the deploy-ment and mobility which are typical of development. In Europe the administrative unification of large nations was one of the major factors in development. In a country like Germany, where unification was delayed, the beginnings of economic development forced a rapid political development. The customs union or *Zoll-verein* was the first thing organized and it in turn helped bring about the final step, political unification. In traditional countries on the contrary, even where they may have been extensive king-doms or empires, the political organization was loose and had no real administrative network. The large geographical areas under one head were internally united only by the sporadic and inadequate communications between a feudal lord and his vassals. Nowhere do we see anything like the administrative centralization which the king of France effected in the seventeenth and eighteenth centuries.

The difficulty arising from size is related to the difficulty arising from the nature of the political bonds. In traditional society these bonds continue to be personal. The feudal relationship is typical here: it consisted of a personal exchange of protection by a strong overlord and various services from his dependents (statutory labor, etc.), which in principle were intended to help the overlord secure the means of protecting his servants. The local lord, the petty chieftain, knew his men personally: those whom he protected and those who could help him with strength of arm and weapon (the knights). Between great lords and little lords the same kind of relationship existed. This is why in the great political entities of the past there were always personal relationships in a vertical series and no impersonal horizontal administrative relationships. But the personal relations considerably limited the economic relations, for these suppose greater impersonality; they suppose the contract according to which buying and selling is done with no respect for persons. In the feudal system, on the contrary, the other man was never considered simply as the bearer of one or other economic value, as producer of this goods or supplier of that service.

Traditional political institutions, finally, expressly aimed at protection (initially against outsiders) and justice (security within the society). They were not established to promote economic well-being. Even if it often intervened to raise levies and secure forced labor, the state—if the term be appropriate—remained economically neutral and did not intervene in economic progress. Still less were the political institutions concerned with promoting the various conditions (for example, scientific and technical progress) which would help in economic development. Even in cases of stronger intervention—for example, the control of irrigation of large areas in pharaonic Egypt—the basic issue was still distribution and justice rather than the promotion of development as such.

We can, indeed, see that such systems would not be totally unadapted to promoting development (consider the role of the Meiji empire in Japan, and the empire of Bismarck's Germany) and consequently we cannot condemn all use of such systems for purposes of development. But in fact there is no future for this line of thought, because it is in their political institutions that the traditional societies have been most shaken through their contacts with other societies, for example, through colonization. Political institutions are not among the most perduring elements of these societies. Some political elements do remain, however, and these must be taken into account. They can be used, but only after undergoing a radical reinterpretation. The traditional political structures, founded as they were on personal relationships, have by their nature been oriented to protection and justice, not to development.

MENTALITIES

AND

VALUE SYSTEMS

The traditional institutions described in the preceding chapters have corresponding mentalities and value systems. These, too, seem to be an obstacle to development. We shall be taking the term "mentality" in a fairly broad sense here and using it as synonymous with attitudes and behaviors.

Are mentalities or institutions more decisive in a society? The question can be debated at length and with subtle arguments, but we shall simply take a stand on the essential point. Mentalities, attitudes, and behaviors are clearly related to institutions. However, institutions as such seem to us to involve a kind of inner necessity: nothing in them suggests that they might outlive their usefulness. The ones we have described seemed to be, and at times still seem to be, the only means men have of surviving in a hostile environment or—what amounts to the same thing—in an underdeveloped economic environment. The strictest of restraints and the most traditionalist of hierarchies were justified as long as human life had to be assured in these conditions, that is, in relatively small groups. There was always fear that the small groups might be fragmented; and fragmentation would bring insecurity, destitution, and danger of death to the individuals of the group. At the same time, given such an institutional framework, the possibility of openings toward an economy of investment and of progress by risk-taking hardly existed. We can speak therefore of a social vicious circle, analogous to the economic vicious circle which so many studies of underdevelopment stress (the vicious circle of absurdly small investment and wretched returns).

However we cannot be satisfied with such observations on institutions. For it is a fact that some societies have broken out of the impasse and found ways of protecting life without having to retain small compact groups or the hierarchic traditional closed institutions that had formerly seemed essential to survival. We must ask, then, whether there are not at work, in traditional societies, other factors besides the limitations imposed by basic needs. These other factors would be mentalities, thought structures, value systems.

We understand a mentality to be, in some measure at least, a choice or preference, even if the choice or preference be not entirely conscious or not conscious for all members of the group. Some of the reflections of Claude Lévi-Strauss point in this direction. In certain of his books Lévi-Strauss has indeed insisted in an extreme fashion on the role of colonization, to the point of seeming to see in colonized society nothing but the opposite of the dynamic initiative shown by other societies. Elsewhere, however, he stresses the considerable differences in mentality between traditional societies and developed societies, and sees this difference as the result of a real choice. "The passivity and indifference which have struck observers may manifest a trauma due to contacts and not to an original condition. Nonetheless we cannot insist too much that such noncompetitiveness does not result simply from outside influences or from previous passive conditioning, but from a deliberate choice based on a conception of relations between man and world and between man and man.

"How deeply rooted attitudes quite different from those of

the West may be, we see rather drolly expressed in a recent observation on the Gahukukama of New Guinea. These natives learned soccer from the missionaries, but instead of seeking victory by one or other team, they increase the number of teams until the total of wins and losses is perfectly balanced. The game ends not as with us but only when all are assured that there is no loser."

Lévi-Strauss supposes throughout his work that one behavior is as good as another. He raises no value questions but only shows the inner coherence of diverse structures and mentalities. But, if we may trust some of his expressions, the diversity itself supposes a deliberate choice of outlook, and there is, in any event, a real discontinuity between the mentalities.

We must, of course, not exaggerate the discontinuity. If we did, we would make it impossible to understand any evolution. But we can at least admit, with Lévi-Strauss, that mentalities and firmly structured value systems exist in the background or as the substructures of many institutions, and that in the last analysis mentalities explain the institutions in large measure, because the latter embody a kind of choice and preference. A new basic choice can then come along to shake an institution that seemed until now destined for permanence and bound to continue by the force of its own inner logic.

Even if one does not go along wholly with these conclusions, one will doubtless agree at least that we can derive a better understanding of the obstacles to development by observing how these obstacles are mirrored in mentalities and value systems. It is important for us, therefore, to determine accurately some of the basic and widely distributed mental characteristics of the traditional societies. We are interested, of course, in those characteristics which seem to be connected with continuing underdevelopment or which at least hinder developmental breakthroughs.

Since we are dealing essentially with economic development, we shall look primarily to mental traits which are especially related to economic life. First, we shall take up a very basic trait: the "principle of conformity." Then we shall move on to characteristic attitudes relative to nature, to time and history, to money, and, finally, to other men.

A General Characteristic: The Principle of Conformity

Modern industrial civilizations are founded on effort, individual and group competition, a will to power, and, at the very least, a desire for freedom which opens men's minds to possible, even if dimly glimpsed, futures. Traditional societies, on the contrary, are built essentially on conformity. (We do not say "conformism," for the "ism" would refer to the value system of a society which had already undergone a change.)

The conformity we speak of is really twofold: conformity to nature and conformity to an established society. But the two are not unrelated to each other. Let us try to recapture the reasoning of men in traditional societies. Our attempt will doubtless be an oversimplification, but it can be of some help in understanding. Man in traditional society has the feeling that only in order does he find his own security, even his liberty. He finds the image, or even the reality, of such order in external nature. "Cosmos" was the old Greek word for "order," but the cosmos was also external nature. Such a man thus thinks of himself as a fragment of nature or life. To become truly a man is to rise to the level of that pre-given ordered whole: nature as a whole, generally conceived as a living whole.

He cannot indeed be so united to cosmic nature as to be identified with it. But he approaches such identification by integration into a social order which has a stability and permanence modeled on the cosmic order. This social order is considered as itself closely bound up with the order of external nature.

In the vitalistic philosophy of the African Bantu, things are pretty much as we have just described them. Men seek to share in the one life that moves in things and animals and men. They are thus linked to their own origin and rise to the level proper to the whole.

The outcome of such an attitude is that stability and integration are themselves values, that the primary social law is balance, and that the chief danger is imbalance. Each person has his determined place. Various groups have their places relative to each other; the result is the caste system. "Among the Sudanese," Griaule says, "nothing is left to chance; everything is classified, from celestial powers down to refuse." Among the Bantu, "the universe is regarded as a hierarchy of powers ranging from divine power through human, animal, and vegetable powers, down to material and mineral powers."[49]

Hierarchy, too, is itself a value, in the sense that man must adapt himself to the other elements and to the whole. In society he must take and keep his place. He "has a place relative to his contemporaries, to the dead, to the ancestors, and to a world system" (G. Balandier). The whole orientation of the typical African "urges him to be in harmony not only with his own society but with the universe as well, much more than to oppose this society or this universe" (Balandier).

We can speak here of submission, provided we recognize that it is not a servile submission nor the submission of a man to another human being who represents nothing more than himself. The submission has rather a metaphysical and religious character; it is submission to a will greater than man's.

Some observers have thought that the colonial experience, so unusual for men of traditional societies, involved for them a transfer of this metaphysical submission to the colonizer with his extraordinary technological powers. In this view the Aztecs and Incas saw in the Spanish colonizer something like the white god of their mythologies who had vanished and was to return. Mannoni, writing on the psychology of colonization, believed that he had found among the Malagasy a similar transfer to the colonizer of the feeling of dependence and submission. He attempted a psychoanalytic interpretation which is open to question but has some suggestions worth noting.

"The point I have tried to bring out is that the Malagasy in course of colonization transfers to his colonizer feelings of dependence, the prototype of which is to be found in the affective bond between father and son. In the European these attachments are usually sublimated or liquidated in the course of growth, but in the Malagasy they persist without any marked change and are preserved in the structure of society and the cult of the dead."[50] Thus they could also be transferred to the colonizer, who came from outside and was strange to them.

Whatever be the case with such transfers under colonialism

and with their interpretation, the role of a dependence and submission which is not interhuman but metaphysical and religious, is great in many traditional mentalities. We must take it into account in any explanation of underdevelopment. A whole conception of reality is involved here. In the following sections we shall really only be observing some particular elements within this fundamental attitude.

Attitude toward Nature

Traditional cosmologies all set high value on respect for external nature, which is regarded as inviolable. We mentioned this point in passing when dealing with land systems. In the developing countries, on the contrary, man's attitude toward nature is spontaneously one of domination and conquest, a determination to transform it. Modern society represents a collective effort to master nature. "Development implies an unconditional priority of culture over nature; but outside of industrial society such a priority is hardly ever admitted" (Lévi-Strauss).

Undoubtedly, the discontinuity between the realms of culture and nature "is universally recognized, and no society, however humble, fails to grant an eminent value to civilizing acts, since by their discovery and use man has been distinguished from the animal. But among the so-called primitive peoples the idea of 'nature' is always ambiguous: nature is preculture and even subculture, but it is also, and before all else, the terrain where man can help to establish contact with his ancestors, the spirits, and the gods. Thus the idea of nature has a 'supernatural' component, and the supernatural is as unquestionably superior to culture as nature is inferior to it" (Lévi-Strauss). Nature thus understood (with its supernatural component) cannot be treated as a mere resource or instrument or material.

As a result, we find much resistance to the instrumental use of nature and especially of the earth. This we have already seen in passing. For example, the earth is a "mother," and when they are offered certain agricultural techniques, many traditional societies will refuse "to wound their mother, the earth."

The traditional mentality which thus retains an age-old opposition of nature and culture, often transfers the opposition to the relation between the sexes. Woman is more on the side of nature, man of culture; that is, man is able to take possession of nature, to transform it, to do violence to it. The result is a rather rigid division of labor between the sexes, and this fact is, of course, economically important. Lévi-Strauss speaks here of a "homology between the nature-culture and female-male contrasts, in virtue of which women find reserved to them any activities regarded as belonging to nature (gardening, for example) or as bringing the artisan into direct contact with natural products or objects (handmade pottery, weaving, plaiting). Men, on the other hand, tend to take over the same kind of activities or even the identical ones mentioned, whenever the activities require the intervention of culture in the form of tools or machines of any complexity." The same activity which women engage in (for example, simple modeling with clay) becomes man's work as soon as it becomes more technical or demands the use of more complex tools and instruments.

The foregoing does not mean that in all traditional societies we find an identical division of labor between the sexes; it does mean that the same principle generally determines the division. In any event, the rigid division of labor between the sexes is an obstacle to the flexibility which economic development seems to require.

Attitude toward Time

The contrast between traditional societies and developed industrial societies becomes even clearer when we look at attitudes toward time and change. Such attitudes are important, of course, because the very nature of progress is at stake.

There are numerous testimonies to the difference in attitudes to time. Alioune Diop, president of the African Cultural Society, could write: "The ideas of progress and revolution are specific to the European mind. Neither China nor the black world would give the same value as Europe does to ceaseless improvement.

They are astounded and baffled by the instability in human relations, esthetics, and philosophy, which accompanies a society
in permanent and restless change."

In regard to Vietnam, Paul Mus used almost the same terms
to contrast the Confucian and European outlooks. He insists especially that "the outlook fashioned by Confucianism is essentially
cyclical. The whole thrust of such an attitude to time is to see,
not evolution, progress, and advance, but periodicity as the law
of the universe. In this cultural framework, stability and conformity are valued as long as a system seems to have fate on its side."

So long as it is not breached, this attitudinal system can handle
any problem; it is a self-contained world. But if any change is
introduced, the crisis is all-embracing. Then the effort is made
to start all over again—but in a cyclic fashion. It is impossible
to speak, in this context, of a process of continuous progress
as we Westerners know it (even if we call it "revolution").

Robert Montagne has said the same thing about Islam. "Islam
always tends to unite in rejecting us with scorn despite the perfection of our technology and in refusing our humanist ideal. For
we do not regard the transitory world as a mere passing caprice
of the divine mind. Islam does not believe in history or accept
its law."

The interpretation of time and history is the subject of lively
discussion today, and we would surely be wrong in saying that
traditional societies are societies without a history. Wherever men
exist there is, in the last analysis, some kind of history and testimonies to the fact. But, according to Lévi-Strauss, there are
civilizations which close their eyes to history. Then "the ideal
is to enter into oneself, since no one ever reenters his mother's
womb," as a proverb among the Hovedu of South Africa puts
it. We cannot physically return to the maternal womb, but we
can do our best to return into ourselves, to lock ourselves up
in a ready made tradition and not go out from it. Such an attitude
is diametrically opposed to the conception of time which marks
industrial societies, for the latter seek to be open to the always
and wholly new future.

Apart from this general result, the traditional attitude to time
has repercussions for the economy in particular, for it does not

sit well with foresight, programming, and planning. This is not to say that the men of traditional societies live wholly in the present moment and take no thought for the future. But this kind of forethought cannot be identified with foresight in the full sense of the term.

Pierre Bourdieu noted the difference in a study of traditional society in Algeria. "Can forethought be validly identified, in basis and goal, with foresight? Is putting aside reserves a real confronting of the future, a carrying of the assault against it, or is it a simple gesture of defense, a preparation for a siege?" He answers: "Forethought usually bears only on consumer goods. But this is not whole of what foresight means. For, what is used as consumer goods is at times economically undifferentiated and can become at the user's will a means of production. For example, grain, if used as seed, would allow better harvests. In fact, however, either unpredictable climatic conditions or habit keep the traditional peasant from seeking this better yield. He sees no real advantage in it. Future production is therefore sacrificed to future consumption, possible goods to actual goods, foresight to forethought."[51]

Whatever be the ultimate roots of the two outlooks, the distinction between them is important, for the motivation is different. The motive of forethought is of the traditional type; usually it is a matter of conforming to models bestowed by a tradition. Tradition obliges a man to more or less solemn ritual feasts which depend on his position in the family or group and are unavoidable if he is to measure up to his rank and duties. Therefore he needs food reserves, for daily use of course, but also such as will enhance his personal or family reputation and prestige.

In its method foresight is, on the contrary, explicitly rational, unlike forethought which springs chiefly from custom. Foresight looks to the future insofar as it is beyond our grasp, intangible, not directly bound up with present circumstances, and insofar as it can be consciously and deliberately brought to pass. The traditional mind, on the other hand, is aware of the future but stops at those aspects of it which are linked to the present by relatively simple experience or familial custom; there is nothing speculative about the mental processes here.

"Forethought is distinct from foresight because in the former anticipation grows logically out of the present situation and has nothing to do with an external plan to be followed. Forethought does not regard the future as the goal sought through action, but apprehends it as a 'what-is-to-come' which is concretely united to the present in accordance with earlier experience. Modern economy, on the contrary, in which the distance between the beginning and the end of a production process is or may be quite great, supposes a goal which lies beyond experience and beyond all observed statistical links; the goal is, in a way, abstract. By the same token, a modern economy supposes the construction of this abstract future, with rational calculation supplying what experience cannot. We need not postulate in men of traditional societies a fundamentally different kind of logic from that of modern societies, but we can impute to them a different value system and a different choice of attitude toward time.

"Traditional civilization has no ambition to take hold of the future and of chance, but tries rather to give these the least hold on itself." Defense against the future, not attack upon it, is the important thing. "The fear of objective disorder which can shake or destroy the established order of things leads men methodically to obviate all unusual situations; to maintain, at the cost of diminished aspirations, a situation that can be mastered by customary means; to reduce the unknown, when it suddenly appears, to the already known; to give old solutions to new problems. Traditionalism may be called the characteristic trait of societies which choose not to engage in the struggle with nature but attempt instead to keep an ordered balance by reducing their activities until they are such as their slender means of acting upon the world will allow."[52]

We can sum up these important remarks by saying that the principle of maximizing security is a major characteristic of traditional societies, especially in their evaluation of the relation between past, present, and future.

Attitude toward Money

Characteristic attitudes toward money derive from attitudes toward time. In industrial civilizations time is truly money, but money is also time; more accurately, money is the future. By the same token, money in the proper sense is too abstract and future an asset, offering satisfactions too distant for it to be correctly understood in traditional societies. "Correctly:" that is, as modern societies or developed industrial societies understand money. More often, people in traditional societies will think of money only as a means of exchange which can quickly be transformed into a real value. Or, on the contrary, money may be considered as a specific good in itself, with an absolute value; then it has a quite different meaning than in modern society where it is the only possession which has no inherent value of its own.

In many cases indeed people today are not wholly estranged from the idea of barter, although between barter (merchandise for money) and monetary exchange (which passes through the undifferentiated, homogeneous, and universal mediation of money) there is a radical difference of mentality and attitude.

In this matter we shall again quote from Bourdieu's remarks on Algeria: "Monetary exchange is to barter what accumulation from capital use is to storing up. When dealing with objects exchanged, we grasp directly and concretely the use to be made of them, for such is inscribed in the object itself just as much as its weight, taste, or color are. But when dealing with money, such a direct and concrete grasp is impossible; any future use indicated by money in itself is distant, imaginary, indeterminate. Money, the indirect asset par excellence, is not in itself the source of any satisfaction. This is the point of the story about the Egyptian peasant who died out in the desert beside the sheepskin full of gold coins which he had just discovered."[53]

Money has existed, of course, in most civilizations: metal pieces in various shapes (iron bars, crescents, etc.) or shells (for example, the African cowries from the Indian Ocean) or cattle (goats, oxen, horses), all used for exchange of some kind. Most often, however, these monies are specifically intended for a determined use; they are assets whose value is not wholly separable from their specific qualities. In any case, their value is not universalized to the point where they can serve in any exchange whatsoever.

Such money—cowries or cattle in Africa—will serve, for example, to indemnify the parents of the girl a man is going to marry.

Sometimes it may serve this use exclusively. That is, there may be markets in which some other kind of money may be used, but this particular kind of money never moves outside the circuit of exchange between families on the occasion of marriages.

The modern function and use of money are entirely different. Yet it often happens that when modern money is introduced into a traditional culture, it loses the functions it has for us. In its new context the money may be reserved exclusively for a special use, even though the money may be francs or pounds sterling. For example, the money may be set aside for the payment of taxes or for buying one or two particular commodities (loincloths, bicycles, etc.) and nothing else.

W. Arthur Lewis remarks in his *Theory of Economic Growth*[54] that "new monetary revenues seem often badly used by Western standards." This is not surprising, since this money could not be spent as it is by Westerners. In particular, it will often be used less to buy new goods different in kind from those already possessed than to buy a larger number of the same goods: more drink, women, clothing.

There will likewise be a tendency to treat modern money as an asset for immediate consumption, not as a value to be stored up for more remote use. This practice gives us the impression of a wastefulness that would not occur in a barter system. "Goods exchanged in barter, according to equivalences established by tradition, carry their potential use with them. They show openly their proper value which is based on their immediately useful qualities, and do not depend, as money does, on external and perhaps unusual conditions."[55]

For modern money to be used in keeping with its own nature, there would have to be a wide market, merchants, varied products, etc. For the objects met with in barter to serve their purpose, they need only be seen in their immediately ascertainable qualities. "Consequently, it is much easier to use stores of commodities in a rational, reasonable way, than to spend a salary over a month's time or to establish a rational hierarchy of needs and expenditures."[56]

At a still more elementary level, money may at times be taken as a specific good with its value in itself, suitable for no other use but to be stored up. This is why we meet instances of vast accumulations, especially of metals in the Mid-East and India, and of flocks in East Africa.

Thus traditional society largely lacks a conception of money as a universal medium of exchange (not a specific possession with its own inherent value) and as a perduring asset. Yet such an understanding of money is manifestly part of every economically developed society and every kind of economic development. The difficulty of getting accustomed to such a new conception of money is thus an obstacle which traditional mentalities put in the way of economic development.

Enterprise and Solidarity

Looking further into our subject, we find that economists like to stress the absence of the enterprising spirit in traditional civilizations. All that we have seen thus far of traditional mentalities and traditional value systems would make us anticipate precisely such a lack.

"Attachment to traditional values and rigidity of social structures prevent the spirit of enterprise from spreading. They block the emergence of a class whose role is to discover combinations of production factors which would draw upon the specific nature of the country."[57] Such a class could be entrepreneurs not only in the private sector but also in the no less demanding public sector.

It is a fact, however, that in some Latin American countries especially, the enterprising spirit seems not at all lacking; the same is true of some parts of India and West Africa. But the spirit of enterprise in these instances is directed to purely commercial ventures and to investment in home businesses which are very limited in their productivity. People avoid getting involved in a long and indirect productive process which is spread out over several years. If the enterprising outlook is present in a broad sense of the term, it is accompanied by the conviction that profit must be quick and short-term.

Chronic inflation in a number of countries, especially countries of Latin America, obliges people to maintain the value of goods already possessed and thus plays a role in the whole question. But we do not know whether outside the rather perduring climate of inflation the speculative spirit (which now is usually only an instinct for conservation) would be automatically transformed into a true spirit of enterprise. Such a transformation is by no means certain in view of the mentality which forms the global context.

We need not further insist on this lack of enterprise. It is sufficiently brought out in economic works on the subject. But at times the analyses of enterprise which are made in such books seem quite insufficient. The reason is that the authors see no value except in an individualism which, it is argued, must replace the pronounced spirit of collective solidarity that supposedly is typical of peoples in the underdeveloped countries. In brief, the spirit of enterprise calls for individualism; individualism is missing because of the existing sense of solidarity; therefore, observers often say, there is too much solidarity.

Yet it is at least as necessary to see in underdeveloped societies a serious lack of the spirit of solidarity and mutual confidence, which are the conditions of any undertaking, individual or collective.

For example, economic progress requires a division of labor. This phrase seems to express the idea of separating off, yet it really implies, beyond all else, cooperation of one or other kind. The more detailed the division of labor, the greater and more demanding the cooperation. We may go further and say that cooperation is the law of all modern economic activity. This holds for all forms of company, all partnerships, etc. It holds, on a more technical level, for any enterprise, capitalist or socialist. It holds, too, for the establishment of that confidence on which the functioning of the broad market or of interconnected markets depends. Finally, the functioning of every credit system depends on these same elements of mutual confidence, and the word credit itself expresses this idea.

The attitude of confidence, so necessary for a modern economy, is often missing, however, in the traditional mentality. Or rather, there exist very strong solidarities, much stronger than those we have in any modern society, but they function at the level of units which are too small for development: large families, villages, clans. Beyond these units, on the other hand, between men of different families or ethnic groups, between distinct clans, there is often only distrust and no real obligations based on solidarity.

Thus the stronger the solidarity at a certain level and within limited dimensions, the more likely it is to be weak, infrequent, and difficult to establish at a wider level; at wider levels, men are really strangers to each other.

All this is true not only of Africa, Asia, and Latin America, but also of many areas of Europe, especially in the South, where solidarity at times does not extend beyond the family. A situation of this kind has been described by the American sociologist, Edward Banfield, who writes of a small section of Southern Italy; he calls it "amoral familiarism."[58] The phrase refers to a withdrawal of the family into itself, admitting no kind of obligation to anyone outside the family. As soon as an individual in the village ventures on some new business which requires cooperation from others, his neighbors are bent only on finding out what plan he has for trickng them. Thus, each person lives within his own more or less extended family and acknowledges no moral obligation outside of it.

Despite varying circumstances, analogous situations occur in all civilizations in which the tribe, clan, or family is the basis for societal organization. The spirit of solidarity is often weak at the level of the wider community in proportion as it is strong at the level of the small, integrated unit.

Pierre Bourdieu, whom we have already quoted, observed "the essential difference between mutual help, on the one hand, which links those individuals connected by real or fictive blood relations and which is encouraged and praised by tradition, and, on the other hand, cooperation or collective work for more distant and abstract goals.

"In the case of mutual help, the group exists prior to the communal achievement of a communal task, even if the latter may be the occasion for stirring to new life the sentiments in which the community is grounded. In the case of cooperation, the group exists only by virtue of the future goal which is cooperatively planned and sought, so that once the goal is reached as specified in the contact which is the group's unifying principle, the group ceases to exist along with the grounding contractual bond. Thus nothing is more illusory than to regard traditions of solidarity as preparing Algerian peasants to adapt to cooperative or collectivist structures. Perhaps the agricultural workers in the great colonial zones, now disposessed of their lands and traditions, are more disposed to such structures than the small scattered landowners of other areas."[59] The same observation might be made of the village communities of black Africa and of the ancient communities of the Andean altiplano in Latin America, for example, in Peru.

In short, solidarity of the traditional type is perhaps not the springboard for modern economic development that it is sometimes thought to be. But if the traditional communities are not such a springboard, it is not for lack of individualism but for lack of that broader solidarity which can develop among men less restricted by the immediate ties of family or neighborhood.

The absence of this larger social solidarity, even where local solidarities are present, seems to be as heavy a handicap as the absence of the spirit of individual enterprise. Observers in the liberal economic tradition have stressed the latter too exclusively.

TRADITIONAL RELIGIONS

AND

UNDERDEVELOPMENT

Now that we have seen the influence of mentalities, attitudes, and value systems, we must turn our attention to the role played in underdeveloped societies by the religions typical of them. What significance do these religions have for underdevelopment, and, correlatively, for development?

Some observers see their role as, on the whole, a baleful one. Others make distinctions. Still others consider them to be, in the last analysis, without influence one way or the other.

Before attempting a general answer, we shall look at some particular instances. Since we cannot examine all forms of traditional religion (for example, the animist religions or the great Asiatic religions) we shall limit outselves to Latin American Catholicism and to Islam. In dealing with the latter we shall present in summary fashion the contemporary discussions on Islam's role relative to underdevelopment.

Traditional Catholicism in Latin America

At first sight, no doubt, traditional Latin American Catholicism seems quite unfavorable to economic development, and quite likely to increase stagnation and underdevelopment. We must distinguish, however, between two basic attitudes of Latin American Catholicism, both of which seem unpropitious to economic progress. One attitude is more typical of the lower social classes, the other of the upper.

Among the people one can observe a simplistic kind of providentialism (to which not every faith in a divine providence is to be reduced). In the providentialist outlook of popular Latin American Catholicism, man addresses God "that God may help him bear up under the material difficulties of earthly life. Prayer and sacrifice are offered to God to win good weather for crops, healing for animals or cherished human beings, or social success, for example, in love affairs."[60]

Such motivations correspond to what can be called "the biological or cosmological function of religion . . . . Beyond any doubt, given the unsure circumstances in which many people in Latin America used to live and still live today, many devotions and practices still spring from such motivations."[61]

In extreme and properly superstitious cases, God is considered a being of the natural world, though more powerful than the others. His action and man's make one whole, complementing or opposing each other; often they can be substituted the one for the other. Such religious conceptions clearly do not lead to a changed moral life and an individual ethic; neither do they foster social change. Men count on God as a powerful instrument, but God rarely questions man or challenges him.

This conception of God, be it noted, is different from that proper to Islam. In Islam God's action is not so much the complement of man's as it is the only real action, with man's being only the occasion for God's. The simplistic conception of providence to which we now refer is, however, no less unfavorable than some Islamic views to initiative and development.

The conception we have been discussing is especially typical, we said, of the poorest classes in South America, of men living in insecurity. The upper classes, on the other hand, being free of daily worry about their livelihood, are more open to the motivation of "eternal life." This motivation is less naively providentialist, but, if it be of a "dualist" kind, it is not less unfavorable to development. And dualism is very common in Latin America. Thus the religion of the more fortunate levels of the population also lacks the ethical or moral quality we are looking for.

This time, "the things of earth have no relation to those of heaven. Christians whose sole motivation is the things of heaven belong to the educated and better off classes, and they can easily be insensitive to social justice. Consequently they make the Church seem disincarnate and careless of injustice, and this in turn alienates the suffering masses from the Church."[62] Such a firm and strong faith in another world does not prevent a man from investing his capital abroad, from living in complete idleness, and from treating peasants as serfs. If a priest, bishop, or even a Catholic layman proposes social reform in the name of religion, he is sure to be misunderstood and treated as a socialist, a communist, etc.

Still speaking of Latin America but going beyond Catholicism proper, we must note the existence of other religious motivations which, psychologically, are closely connected with the loss of cultural roots. "Many individuals look to religion for peace of soul, tranquillity of mind, a cure for the anxiety in which the contemporary world imprisons the individual. This motivation is common in all social classes and especially in the marginal populations of the large industrial cities. This is why sects and spiritualism are so successful.

"In the sect, in the small spiritualist group, in the Afro-Brazilian cults, uprooted people who are not yet integrated into the city's life find the atmosphere of brotherhood and protection which they need: protection of spirits, of saints, of God; protection against the evil eye, diseases, bad luck. The Catholic Church has traditionally played an important part in psychological integration. Today, however, the immense size of administrative units, the ritualism caused in many parishes by the lack of priests, and a somewhat authoritarian conception of the priesthood, all prevent the Church from successfully effecting such integration any longer, while other religious denominations are especially well adapted for doing so."[63]

Under pressure of these unsatisfied needs, men often abandon Catholicism in Latin America. But the substitutes for traditional Catholicism, the Afro-Brazilian cults, the macumba, or the numerous sects, are clearly no better able to develop a moral awareness that is open to initiative and development.

The foregoing picture would have to be modified, of course, for some sectors of Latin American Catholicism. At least it must be said that in some sectors a serious effort at renewal has been underway for several decades. What used to be true, then, is often less true today. We often find a very positive attitude not only to development but to social and even revolutionary change. But all this holds only for small groups. It is not yet clear that the transformation can be spread and completed quickly enough.

A religion like Latin American Catholicism has a trump card, however: it is not alone in the world. Revitalizing influences can reach it and have in fact reached it through contacts with other forms of Catholicism in other countries, especially in Europe, where the mentality is less alien to the attitudes which make for development.

Discussions on Islam

Islam is more isolated and, for many observers, raises even more serious problems. Whether that be so or not, the importance of the Third World Islamic nations invites us to discuss them in some detail and to advert to current discussions on the subject. The problem of Islam's relation to economic development has aroused great interest, not least among French-speaking economists.

A few years back, Jacques Austruy edited *Islam et développement économique*. The Institute of Applied Economic Sciences, under Francois Perroux's direction, also devoted two successive series of studies to the subject. These were published in the Institute's *Cahiers* as "Islam, l'économie et la technique" (October 1960) and "Archaïsme et modernisme dans l'Islam, contemporaine" (December, 1961). We shall be referring above all to these studies.

The authors of these essays are all anxious for progress in the Muslim countries and will not permit indifference in the face of a problem which concerns so many human beings. One writer remarks: "Islam is ambivalent: it seeks to reconcile the irreconcilable, for it can survive only by transcending itself, yet it cannot transcend itself without denying itself. This is the drama of Islam, and no nation can be indifferent to it" (J. Poirier).

In addition, the writers often show deep sympathy for the Muslim countries and even for Islam's religious values. They are almost shocked at the idea that the Islamic religion might be an obstacle to economic development. They are thus disposed to gather up every indication that Islam and the requirements of development are compatible. But we must look a bit more closely at their analyses and try to determine what conclusions their discussions warrant.

One further preliminary remark, however: the specialist in Islamic problems is quick to point out the vagueness of the term "Islam." He wants us to distinguish between the great geographic sectors, or at least between Arabic Islam and black Islam. In black Africa, according to J. C. Froelich, Islam cannot be called a factor in underdevelopment, because it is of too recent origin there to have such an influence. Besides, the roots of Islam in black Africa are for the most part not deep. Every man in black Africa follows his own native customs. Consequently the blacks are today perhaps more affected than any other Muslims by the reform of Islam. This is because they have not experienced, as others have, the long closure of the "gates of effort," to use an ancient Muslim phrase.

Islamic tradition claims, not without historical foundation, that after Mohammed's death, for a period of at least some centuries (according to the early writers), the "gates of effort" were closed. Authors of the late nineteenth century, the ones called "reformist," are regarded as having opened these gates, that is, as having abandoned in some measure the fatalism typical of Islam. Black Africans were probably but little touched by the "closure;" by the same token they are freer to accept the reformist interpretation. Analogous remarks could doubtless be made of Malayan, Indonesian, and even Pakistani Islam. Most of the current discussion concerns Arabic Islam, which is considered to be the most faithful to tradition and which is, in any event, closest to the origins of Islam.

Arabic Islam seems to many to be an obvious factor in underdevelopment and an obstacle, in the fullest sense, to development. It could even wholly prevent any effective development. What is the value of this judgment?

Some deny it outright. A common view is that underdevelopment in Muslim countries is in no way the fault of Islam, as is too often supposed. The famous fatalism comes not from Islam but from an archaic economic situation which could not but engender such an outlook. Consider the parallel situation in traditional rural economies from which there is no escape but in resigned waiting and fatalism.

G. de Bernis writes in this vein. "The illiterate peasant with no tool except a plow drawn by a starved camel knows from the long experience of successive generations, as kept alive in oral tradition, that one can sow only if autumn rains fall. He waits for the rain, which does not depend on him at all. If it falls, he scrapes at the earth and sows; if it does not fall, he does not sow. Why throw away his meager resources in wasted seed? Suppose he did sow, even though no autumn rains had fallen? He knows that then, if the spring rains come, he will have a fine harvest; if they do not come, he will have none. What else can he do then but wait helplessly upon events he cannot control? He is wholly in nature's hands, and nature acknowledges no mastery by men. It would take less than this to make a fatalist." In such conditions, the idea of making an extra effort can only be missing.

Such a situation, typical of traditional rural civilizations, is intensified by the disjointedness of underdeveloped economies, that is, by the lack of any connection between modern economic sectors and traditional agriculture, such as might be the starting point for progress throughout the economy. The disjointedness only aggravates the feeling of helplessness and of dependence on foreign economies. Islam, then, does show a religious fatalism, but its cause is not properly religious nor is the fatalism peculiar to

Islam. In regard to the famous *mektub*—"It is written"—de Bernis remarks: "One would have to be wholly ignorant of the religions of the past and of past stages of living religions to see in this something specific to Islam." All religions, in this view, have experienced the equivalent of a fatalistic period, without themselves being the origin of the mood.

The second argument against Islam's being an obstacle to development is that as soon as environmental factors become more favorable, Islam does not put any hindrance in the way of development. Among other examples de Bernis mentions some Muslim families of Ktatis in Tunisia which have developed rapidly: "These families were and remain Muslim. Islam has never shown itself an obstacle to this change. It has not even had to become more flexible. No rule of social morality or constitutive principle of Muslim thought has been weakened. A genuine social transformation has shown no incompatibility with Islam. This example, among others, shows how the fatalism springing from economic-social structures is dismantled along with the structures."

De Bernis does not deny, of course, the existence of difficulties arising from some traditions and traits of the Muslim outlook. But he has in reserve a third argument: such traditions do not come from the Koran itself but are pre-Islamic. This holds, for example, for all that concerns the nomadic life, the condition of women, and the law governing property. De Bernis alludes here to the absence of land titles for some kinds of property and to the existence of collective holdings or mortmain, which are obstacles to mobilizing land as a productive asset. The Koran is not responsible for these obstacles, since they date from much earlier times.

Nor is the Koran responsible for the fatalism. According to de Bernis, the call to action can be quite explicit at times in the Koran. As an example he quotes the saying, "God makes no change in a group's circumstances if the members do not try to change them." This text he says is known throughout the whole Maghreb and the Mid-East; in the era of national struggle it was recited by all at the beginning of every gathering. The call to action even takes an extreme form in a saying attributed to the Prophet: "If man's will reaches for a goal beyond even the heavenly throne, he will surely not fail to reach it."

The situation is no less favorable if we look at several specific points in the Koran. According to M. Hamidullah, "for the Koran earthly goods are not something to be contemned but are the very basis of human society . . . . God himself has given man the means to well-being, and man may not scorn the Lord's gift." The Koran, he adds, favors commerce, for this is closely connected with pilgrimages. It also shows itself in various ways to be concerned for the circulation and redistribution of the national wealth: by its inheritance laws, its law for the state budget, its prohibition of certain testamentary legacies, its prohibition of interest on certain loans and of games of chance.

What of the condemnation of lending at interest? According to Hamidullah, the interest condemned by the Koran must be carefully distinguished from profit, which is entirely legitimate. Or again, we must distinguish between productive and non-productive borrowing. We can "envisage the abolition of interest for nonproductive loans by friendly societies and cooperatives, along with some government aid, at least in the first phase. Productive loans to commerce and industry would form a different category."

Not all specialists in Koranic exegesis would be quite so optimistic. But, no matter; some scholars do not bother themselves with so many details and simply put forward a still more radical view. According to them, if the Islamic world remained passive while economic development was getting underway in the West, this was because the forms of development available at the time were not suited to the Islamic mind. But this mind is not unfavorable, it is on the contrary eminently favorable, to a different form of development, examples of which are known today. Development in the eighteenth and nineteenth centuries was individualistic; today, however, we know of development in a communal or collective form. Islam is little suited to the former but perfectly in harmony with the latter. Islam and the Koran were handicaps in an age of individualistic development; they will be advantages of the first order in the age of communal development.

Some of de Bernis' views move in this direction. "If Islam

has precepts incompatible with capitalism, the same is not true with regard to other modern economic systems which push development." Or, to quote Jacques Austruy: "All the possible ways of development are not equally in keeping with Islam's vocation. It is important to choose among existing modes of production the one which suits Islam's aspirations and specific dynamics."

A way of development suitable to Islam did not arise in the past, and this is enough to explain why the Islamic countries have taken no part as yet in the economic advances which Europe experienced. But "there are no major barriers to adapting juridico-social and technological structures to the needs of economic development in Islam, provided that the adaptations themselves are acceptable to the Islamic mind."

The discussion here turns once again to the well-known Koranic prohibition of loans at interest. If this prohibition (it is argued) makes savings unavailable for private enterprise, the same is not true for public enterprises, and these after all are the only ones that matter in countries where there are no private entrepreneurs. "We know," says G. de Bernis, "that the underdeveloped countries lack entrepreneurs (we are constantly being told this in the literature) and that profit-motivated investments are not what is needed for an effective developmental policy. The prohibition of usury will allow the lack of private entrepreneurs to be compensated for in other ways." He adds, "Recourse to public intervention and to the mobilization of capital by public borrowing, taxes, partial use of bank deposits, continuous, regular, and controlled increase of paper money, these remain fully possible. In addition, the very conception of ownership in Islam makes such measures easier, just as expropriation for the common good can be justified by a tacit mandate from the rightful owner. The prohibition of lending at interest, by cutting off all other possibilities, has the advantage of directing us toward effective measures."

Jacques Austruy notes that Islam found incompatible the individualism of capitalist enterprise. But it is not opposed to collective risk. "The fear of risk which prevented the development of economic growth in Islam was due to the fact that the risks imposed by the capitalist system as a means to success were individual risks. The weak sense of the individual among Muslims seems to have hindered the establishment of capitalism, as much as any anachronistic precepts of the Koran did. But things are different in the modern world, for we now have experience of collective ventures."

The aspect of Islam that is regarded as most favorable to development today is thus the feeling for the collectivity, the idea of the community of believers which transcends political frontiers. "This special sense of the collectivity, so characteristic of Islam, can today motivate economic progress if it is adequately utilized, whereas it could only be a restraint on development in a society where progress and individualism went together." The idea of the collectivity which transcends national boundaries immediately helps create the large dimensions needed by a modern economy. Even the "lay theocracy" aspect of Islam is, according to Austruy, an advantage for Islamic countries in an age of great ideological blocs.

In short, thanks to the ban on usury, to the Koranic limitations on private ownership and its sanction of collective ownership (pre-Islamic in origin), and to the principle of the solidarity of the community of believers, Islam in its purest form would seem to be a priviliged factor in development along communal lines, although it was an obstacle to development on individualist and capitalist lines.

Such a thesis undoubtedly does highlight some contemporary possibilities open to Islam. But it runs into serious criticism too. We can ask, first of all, why Islam, so favorable to "communal" development, has not engendered such development of its own accord in Muslim lands, without waiting for the idea to be suggested from outside. Furthermore, many sociologists would surely question the view that wholly new forms of communal or collective development have arisen today which are radically opposed to yesterday's individualist or capitalist forms. There are indeed large differences between the industrial revolution of nineteenth century Western Europe and, for example, the transformation of Soviet economy since the five-year plans began. Enterprise financed by the state has there accomplished what was formerly done by private capital, and the difference is important. But does this mean that initiative and risk, even at the individual level, do not play an essential role in all development, even in the kind we might call communal? This is the key point. Did not such initiative and risk play a great part in the careers of the businessmen who built the Soviet economy? We think that they did, and that economic creation, whatever be the general framework of property law within which it occurs, follows the same rules in every case.

There are standpoints from which it is not indifferent whether all capital be private or be more or less controlled by organs of the body social. But the use of capital always depends on initiative and always involves risks, and many of these risks are taken in the last analysis by individuals, not by groups. The most important distinction to be made in this area is, it seems, not so much between socialism and capitalism or individual and community. The fundamental distinction is rather between traditional routine, whether of individuals or communities, and dynamic action, which can only be both individual and collective. If development at bottom involves the passage from a traditional and static civilization to a civilization which accepts movement, a degree of risk, and social change, then we do not resolve all problems by appealing to the traditional community spirit of Islam. This spirit is rather the obstacle in Islam or at least in a large part of contemporary Islam.

It is not enough here to reread history, even the history of Islam's first centuries when, as the chroniclers recognized, there was a notable adaptability, flexibility, and expansionist quality. We must rather ask whether the adaptability is there today and whether the "gates of effort" have indeed been reopened.

In this light, the real situation remains complicated. For example, a Lebanese Muslim village may adapt no less well to a new agricultural technique than the neighboring Christian village. But we can only be amazed at the subtle and difficult exegeses which the teachers of Egypt and Tunisia must go through to accept reforms requested by the public authorities in matters of fasting, marriage, or the condition of women. In other matters, the public authorities have had to go against well-grounded traditions which were backed by the religious authorities. An evolution is certainly taking place, and we doubtless ought not to speak of a radical incompatibility of Islam and development. But the evolution is slow and must overcome strong resistance.

Islam is here like Latin American Catholicism. We can always contrast a particular form of a religion or the face it shows in this or that community of men, with the same religion's purest and richest aspirations as these are manifested elsewhere or in books. The contrast enables us to see possibilities of development everywhere. But it does not prevent the particular form from appearing to be an obstacle to development and a factor in stagnation.

The General Situation

We have been approaching the general problem through particular cases. What broad conclusions are justified? The following remarks are based on *The Theory of Economic Growth*, by W. Arthur Lewis.

In the first place, it seems impossible to deny that there are connections between traditional forms of religion and underdevelopment. But it is equally impossible to generalize. "Some religions are involved more comprehensively than others. First, growth requires that people should be willing to give their minds to ways of increasing productivity, whether because they desire goods, or because they would value additional leisure. Some religions do teach that salvation can be reached through the discipline of hard and conscientious work, and do elevate the pursuit of efficiency into a moral virtue. Some forms of Christianity also lay emphasis upon the virtues of thrift and productive investment. But most religions also teach that it is better to give the mind to spiritual contemplation than to the ceaseless search for ways of increasing income or reducing cost; and practically all religions discourage the desire for material things."[64]

A second aspect of development according to Lewis is the inclination to experiment. Religions show varying degrees of openness to the desire for knowledge and experience, and the variety must be respected. "Very few religions share this attitude [willingness to experiment] to the nature of the universe. Much technological progress springs from an attitude that everything in this world is here for the convenience of man, and can be altered by man in his own interest. This is quite compatible with those religions which put man in the center of the universe, but it is not compatible with religions in which man is merely one manifestation of the spirit of God and a minor manifestation, at that."[65]

There is a further series of factors which can help or hinder progress. Economic progress, says Lewis, "also involves the growth of impersonal economic relationships, in which people do business with other people irrespective of kinship, nationality, or creed."[66] But if there are xenophobic religions, there are others which urge the extension of relationships between men without exception.

Finally, religions are generally conservative of social institutions and in favor of the status quo. "If a society is based on slavery, religion teaches the slaves to be obedient; but equally if the society is used to a high level of vertical mobility, the priests will be in the forefront in denouncing efforts to restrict opportunity."[67]

On the other hand, if religions are habitually conservative in their structures, almost all of them have their prophets, and in every age there are innovative groups, orthodox or heretical, operating in the religious and social spheres. "Periods of rapid social change are often associated with religious ferment whether we think of the rise of capitalism in Europe or of contemporary events in Africa, and if we are assessing the role of religion we must take account of the reforming zeal of the new religion just as much as of the resistance offered by the old."[68]

In short, Lewis concludes, "some religious codes are more compatible with economic growth than others. If a religion lays stress upon material values, upon work, upon thrift and productive investment, upon honesty in commercial relations, upon experimentation and risk bearing, and upon equality of opportunity, it will be helpful to growth, whereas in so far as it is hostile to these things, it tends to inhibit growth. Of course, the code may not be fully effective; people do not always act in accordance with the religion they profess. Priests are expected to be more strict in behavior . . . . Priests apart, people tend to ignore religious precepts which conflict with economic interests. However, religious teaching is often strong enough to prevent people from doing what it would clearly be in their interests to do, e.g., from killing sacred cows or removing sanctified oppressors."[69]

This being the case, another question is raised by the relative flexibility of those religions which do not in fact permanently hinder economic progress when it begins, or which even at times reach the point of encouraging it. We have already met the question in dealing with Islam. Is it the religion or is it rather the economic and social situation which is the real obstacle? Muslim fatalism, we saw, might be only the natural reaction of the peasant who is habituated to an unfavorable, hostile, and uncertain climate. René Gendarme writes: "Passive submission to the decrees of providence in the least details of life seems much more closely connected with the material impossibility of taking hold of the future, with the extreme harshness or instability of the climate, with the unreliability of methods. Religious precepts or the influence of an ecclesiastical philosophy can indeed restrict economic development in some ways. Numerous examples of such restrictions have been gathered, such as the Hindu opposition to eating beef or to the use of the Ganges for irrigation, the Chinese fear of angering the earth spirits by building railroads, and the opposition of some Iranians to the telephone because the Koran does not mention it. But such opposition, however significant, has but a very secondary influence as compared with that passivity toward the economic life of which we have spoken, a passivity which justifies the self-concept of the members of such societies."[70]

Lewis refers to the same viewpoint, namely that religion neither hinders nor helps development. "If the religious doctrines of the day are incompatible with certain changes, this is merely because the underlying economic and social conditions are not yet ready for such changes. When these conditions are ready, the change will be effected, and the religious teaching will be adapted to support the new *status quo*."[71] But Lewis himself does not share this view, and answers it with arguments that seem well-grounded. "In the first place, even if it were true that religious doctrines always give way to economic interests, it would still not follow that they do not restrict change, for they might both slow down the rate of change, and also distort its effects."[72] It may also happen that doctrines are indeed finally modified, "but in the meantime they can hold up change for many decades or even centuries."[73]

"More fundamentally," says Lewis secondly, "we cannot accept the conclusion that it is always economic change which causes religious change, and never religious change that causes economic or social change. It is not true that if economic interest and religious doctrines conflict, the economic interest will always win. The Hindu cow has remained sacred for centuries, although this is plainly contrary to economic interests. Or, to take another example, the failure of Spain to seize and exploit the economic opportunities presented by the discovery of the New World can not be explained satisfactorily without taking into account religious beliefs and attitudes which hindered Spain in her competition with other countries. It is possible for a nation to stifle its economic growth by adopting passionately and intolerantly religious doctrines of a kind which are incompatible with growth. Or it is possible, conversely, for conversion to a new faith to be the spark which sets off economic growth."[74]

We have thus shown, at any rate, how much the absence of economic development is connected with a cultural totality, and with mentalities even more than with institutions. The problem of development is certainly not purely economic; it is also social, institutional, and cultural. Development is a matter of mentality; it is even a religious problem. It is this complexity that makes development so difficult in practice.

SOCIAL UPHEAVAL:

POPULATION

AND MIGRATION

We must now add that the societies which we have been trying to describe in their major aspects are not intact. We have already noted in passing that the traditional political institutions have been deeply affected. The same can be said of the other areas we have considered. The description of the current social substructure of the developing countries must therefore be carried a step further. We are dealing with societies which have already been deeply shaken, changed, thrown into imbalance. Our discussion of all that goes under the name of colonialism will bring us back to this radical change. But we are also led to it by way of a set of changes which are chiefly economic in character.

We must, in fact, be careful to recognize that the underdevelopment or lack of development of which we are speaking is to be found in regions already marked by substantial economic changes. If we wish to distinguish the two terms "development" and "economic change," the former signifies, in principle, a conscious, voluntary, organized, and integrated process, while the latter signifies any sort of change, even one that is forced and uncontrolled, affecting primarily an economy but also thereby the society of the country.

Among the economic changes which have affected underdeveloped societies during the last hundred years, not all have been the result of chance encounters. In more recent times at least there has been more than one deliberate economic policy emanating from colonial governments or from native groups of producers. But these cannot be called policies of development.

On the other hand, some economic changes have already occurred almost everywhere, even if very unevenly, and nowhere are we any longer confronted with the so-called traditional societies in their fresh and "natural" state. The changes are, in addition, of such long standing that we are now forced to describe them with the help of historical documents rather than by observation of contemporary events.

Developing societies, it is usually said, have been unbalanced, shaken, even thrown into confusion, and not simply transformed, by the economic changes in question. Observers allude to an abnormal situation which can explain a great deal else, for example, the current political situations, the inadequate functioning of various regimes, the awkward international activity of the developing countries. It does indeed seem that we must use the language of upheaval and characterize numerous aspects of the current social situation as not simply new and different from the old traditional society but as even pathological. We could give examples of a whole range of psychological aberrations from people in these brutally transformed societies. But even if we restrict ourselves to more expressly sociological realities, we cannot but carry away the same impression of pathological aberration.

Beginning with the most external elements, we shall consider first the demographic aspect, and then the effects of transplantation of populations. In a later chapter we shall turn to urbanization and its profound effects.

Population Growth and Its Social Consequences

Demography is concerned chiefly with the quantitative characteristics of societies and of their futures. But these are important,
for, as we shall immediately see, the quantitative aspect soon
involves the qualitative.

Demographic effects are not really the very first ones caused
by economic changes in the developing countries. Nonetheless
we shall speak of them first, precisely because they are quantitative
and therefore ought to be first considered.

Some figures will be helpful, but they shall also be few, since
the data are widely known, even through the popular press. First,
let us look at an example—Japan—from a period between the
age of modern development and the contemporary changes in
the developing countries. During the whole Tokugawa period
(the long feudal age of Japan, approximately 1600 to 1850), the
population seems to have remained at about 30 million. Birth
rate and death rate were equally high. The high death rate was
due to inadequate sanitary conditions, fairly frequent famines,
epidemics, earthquakes, and floods, to say nothing of infanticide
and abortion. From 1868 on, however, early efforts at economic
change brought improvements in sanitation, diet, and medicine,
and these brought the death rate down almost within a few years.
But more than half a century would pass before the birth rate,
too, began to decline in 1924 (well before the laws favoring contraception and abortion, which were passed after the Second
World War). Meanwhile, the population had risen to seventy
million, as compared with the thirty million of the mid-nineteenth
century, and it has not stopped growing ever since.

If we turn now to present-day underdeveloped countries, we
observe again a very rapid growth. In Africa, in the ten years
from 1920 to 1930, the increase was 11.3 percent; from 1930
to 1940, 12.1 percent; from 1940 to 1950, 17 percent; from 1950
to 1960, 23.3 percent. In this last decade (1950-1960), black Africa
almost matched the growth rate of North Africa, where it had
been rapidly increasing over a somewhat longer period.

In Central America, the increases have been as follows: 1920-

1930, 13.3 percent, a rather small rate, as in Africa at the same period; 1930-1940, 20.6 percent; 1940-1950, 24.4 percent; and 1950-1960, 29.4 percent, an extremely high rate for a large section of the world.

South America shows certain differences from Central America. Growth has indeed been great but the high rates were reached as early as the 1920-1930 decade and have not been surpassed by much since then. Expansion thus occurred sooner, but today the rate of growth is still less than in Central America: 1920-1930, 23 percent; 1930-1940, 20 percent; 1940-1950, 23.3 percent; 1950-1960, 26.1 percent.

In Asia the growth has been slower, but the recent period shows almost the same rates as elsewhere: 1920-1930, 11 percent; 1930-1940, 13 percent; 1940-1950, 14.4 percent; 1950-1960, 21 percent. If we look for variations within the continent, we find that in Southeast Asia (the Middle East) the acceleration is very recent. The ten-year gowth rate was 9.3 percent between 1920 and 1930, but today it is the highest in all Asia: 28.3 percent.

In comparison with all these figures, the rates for Europe (excluding the USSR) were: 1920-1930, 8.2 percent; 1930-1940, 7 percent; 1940-1950, 3.7 percent.

The mechanism controlling these developments is also widely known. The essential factor is that the death rate declines rapidly while the birth rate remains at its traditionally high level (as in Japan, mentioned earlier). Thus, the birth rates during the 1950-1960 period were still forty-seven per thousand for Africa, forty-two for Central and South America, and forty for Asia (as against nineteen for Europe, for example). But the death rates, without equalling those of Europe or North America, were nonetheless considerably lowered: twenty-five per thousand for Africa, fifteen and nineteen for Central and South America respectively, and twenty-two for Asia.

The rates are only eleven per thousand for Europe and nine per thousand for North America. A gap still remains, but it has been much reduced.

Europe experienced a similar population growth, especially in the nineteenth century. The lowered death rate was, once again, the essential factor in growth, at least before a lowered birth rate began to offset it. It is important, however, to keep in mind some fundamental differences between what is happening today in the developing countries and what happened in Europe at the time of the first industrial revolution.

There is first of all the difference in rates. Once the population growth began, the population of Europe was markedly increased, but at a rate of not much more than 1 percent during the nineteenth century. In the Third World today the growth is at least 2 percent, and sometimes 3 percent, and this over an already long period.

There are some exceptions. Thus in South America the populations of Argentina and Uruguay are almost stationary. In Africa, too, there are limited areas where populations were recently still decreasing, for example the North of Cameroon, the Central African Republic, and Gabon, but a reversal is taking place even in these areas and will probably lead to rates comparable to those of the rest of the underdeveloped world.

The difference between 1 percent and 2 percent or 3 percent is very great. It is enough to cause the "population problem" so much discussed nowadays, especially in countries where land is lacking and in the island countries more than elsewhere, including that island amid the desert which is the Nile valley, the productive part of Egypt.

A second difference lies in the relation between economic change and population growth. In both cases there is a link between the two. In both cases, too, industrialization in the full sense does not precede; it follows. But there is an important difference between the two cases, which affects the underdeveloped countries today: the introduction of hygiene and some medical advances have preceded any real growth in production and have been enough to trigger population growth by a rapid reduction of the death rate. It is much easier to import and broadcast a few vaccines and medicines, it is easier even to suppress or eradicate some great tropical diseases, than to create the capital or develop the skill for setting the economy in motion. Yet this last is needed if a rapidly growing population is to be fed.

Population growth has not, of course, preceded all economic

change. Hygienic progress, after all, results from modification of commercial exchange and from the appearance on the markets of various foreign products, to say nothing of the action of colonial administrators. But the Third World's population growth has indeed preceded any real progress in production and especially in the production of agricultural foodstuffs.

In Europe, especially in the first countries to experience the industrial revolution, the situation was quite different. Population growth preceded advanced industrialization and any important raise in living standards. But it did not antedate all progress in production, especially in agricultural production. It was not medical progress (most vaccines, including Jenner's, were not yet discovered) nor the spread of modern hygiene that allowed population growth in eighteenth-century England. The economy, and especially the agricultural economy, was the first thing to change. More abundant and better food was responsible, in part, for the initial lowering of the death rate.

The drama of the underdeveloped countries today, therefore, is not simply due to a rate of population increase that is higher than in nineteenth-century Europe. It is due rather to the cause of the increase being at least partially different. The Third World increase is still independent of any economic advance in the full sense.

For the purposes of this book we must go on to indicate the social effects of the population growth. The most important are the effects on institutions of the changing average age of populations, and these effects are numerous. We see an extraordinary proportional increase in the number of young people. Population growth is, after all, due primarily to lower infant mortality, the rates of which often used to be almost unbelievably high. Today, those under twenty form more than half the population in most developing nations; in some countries, Venezuela, for example, this holds for those under seventeen.

The result of this proportional increase of the young is, first of all, an unemployment problem. Traditionally, of course, the young have always been both underemployed and employed, since in many traditional occupations very young people and even children had a place. But the problem becomes quite a different one in cities, if industry is slow to grow and furnish jobs.

A second result is an educational problem. The problem is already difficult if it is a matter of quickly schooling a hitherto illiterate population. But it is doubled or tripled in difficulty when the young form such an abnormally large part of the total population.

A third result is a problem of authority throughout society, from family to village and the highest levels of clan structure and political life. Traditional systems were grounded in the authority of the elders. But even if government by elders does not wholly depend on their being in the majority, it does risk being seriously challenged once there is a high proportion of young people and especially once these become young adults.

Changing population ratios affect government by elders in another way too. The elders become older still, for along with a decrease in infant mortality, there is an increase in longevity. The elders, who not too long ago were usually only middle-aged men, now really become old men, sometimes very old, and lack the flexibility that formerly could be found in gerontocracies. Their power is thus not necessarily undermined in principle, but it may be undermined in practice.

We are dealing here with an area in which situations change quite quickly. Even without going into the possible political effects of a drastic population reduction (such as Japan is experiencing), we must note that next to the very young, the middle-aged will be very numerous. Other things being equal, this will be a source of strength for the developing countries. But the problem of unemployment will become even more serious than it now is, if modern economic activities are not soon developed.

The New Migrations

Along with the rapid expansion of population and the inversion of the age pyramid, the geographical placement of populations has also been affected by economic change.

Traditional populations experienced migrations, of course, but these were quite different from the migrations of today. The movements of peoples were formerly large scale, like those, for example, of barbarian times in Europe (the Franks or the Huns). The whole tribe, group, or clan moved as a unit. It often did so under hostile pressure from other groups.

Africa, too, offers fairly recent examples of such large-scale migrations: that of the Baoulés who came to Ivory Coast from areas now in Ghana; or the Zulu migrations of the nineteenth century, from a northern part of Bantu Africa along the Eastern coast to South Africa. In these cases, the migration involved a whole traditional group which carried with it all its social equipment, its leaders, its social classes and its customs. The group settled down again elsewhere in the traditional way, even to the very shape of the village, the measurements of which were carefully marked out again.

In the migrations caused by economic (and political) circumstances, however, we are dealing with something quite different, and they are a deeply traumatic experience for the peoples caught up in them. These new migrations have rarely been due to hostile pressure; they began in the colonial period when an overall public order held sway: *pax gallica, pax brittanica*, etc. Above all, these migrations rarely involved traditional groups en bloc, but only individuals or parts of families who gathered together from various quarters.

There were indeed cases in which large-scale transfers of a single ethnic group were attempted. A large number of Mossi from Yatenga were transferred to the Niger delta (now Mali) in the great colonial undertaking called the Niger Project. But the undertaking suffered from numerous defects. Individual Mossi but not complete Mossi villages were moved, so that the expatriates were deprived of essential elements of social structure to which they were used; the political mechanism was thrown out of gear by the absence of the chiefs; the family was disoriented by the absence of essential members, especially the old people; customs and rites could no longer be observed. The result was many social traumas that made the experiment an unfortunate one We say nothing here about the economic miscalculations.

Most of the time, however, the migrations were not organized, as in the Mossi affair, nor were they organic. It was not a whole society but isolated members of families (isolated though traditionally not isolatable) that set out. The cause might be levies of forced labor (such as occurred in French Africa as late as 1950) or jobs which promised salaries in money (plantations, mines) or population pressure in bush areas which could no longer feed so many people. This kind of untraditional and unorganic migration occurs when the Indians come down to Lima from the Andean plateau, when the wretched peasants of Northeastern Brazil come to the shantytowns of Rio or São Paulo, when the Gabonese or Central Africans go to work in the lumber camps, or when the Mossi go off to the mines or plantations of Ghana or Ivory Coast: in short, when Africans of almost every nation leave home to seek work in the sisal or cocoa or coffee plantations, etc.

The effects in the place of departure and the place of arrival are different. In their new location men find nothing of the social universe familiar to them. By any accounting there is now no social structure save that of economic exploitation—perhaps a few bars, no kind of organized leisure. In addition, societies without women are formed. This is most often dictated by the fact that the plantation or mine is located in new and hitherto unpeopled areas; there is no humanized social world there. Add the fact that men used to living in a narrow social framework of extended family and village in which everything else is foreign or even hostile, are now forced to live with "foreigners" in the promiscuity of camps; this is a wholly new experience for them. In linguistically fragmented areas, these men have no common language. Imagine then the degree of social trauma, aggravated at times by a brutal geographic and climatic disorientation, as when, for example, the Indians from the Andes come to the lowlying coastal areas or the equally lowlying hot regions of interior Amazonia.

Back at the original home the effects are just as serious. The departure of the young and active males accentuates the female element in the population. The increased proportion of old men leads to both the strengthening and the deterioration of government by elders. There is the disturbance of the customs which regulate relations between various social groups in the village.

An American writer, Peter B. Hammond, did a careful study of the Mossi migration from Yatenga to the Niger delta.[75] In this case at least, he finds, there was a genuine ethnic homogeneity. The move was within the same climatic zone (the African savannahs) and the same geographical environment. Adaptation to a diet of rice (a new product in an irrigated area) was not difficult for a people used to millet. Finally, economic if not financial conditions were fairly favorable. Each family received a house, cattle, a cart, and a piece of land proportionate in size to the number of active workers accompanying the head of the family. Modern methods of cultivating rice and cotton were introduced, and there was a provision that if the peasant cultivated his land for ten years without getting into debt, he would be authorized to reside permanently on the land initially loaned to him.

Despite these various favorable factors, social adaptation in the narrow sense was very difficult, and especially adaptation in matters of social organization. Attempts were made in the new surroundings to recreate the forms of Mossi organization and to reproduce, among other things, the strictly ordered layout of houses within the village. The attempts failed. The reason was that although the group as a whole was ethnically homogeneous enough, in fact ideally so in comparison with plantations or camps, the transfer had not involved whole clans and bloodgroups in their integrity but fragments foreign to each other.

In addition, the traditional political organization, very strong in Mossi country, was missing, along with the vertical series of heads, especially the land heads. No one carried out the functions of these important heads, especially not the colorless individuals whom the colonial administration had put in charge of the whole enterprise. The traditional clan organization, with its obedience to the elders, could no longer function, since most of the elders had stayed back in the home territory. Marriages depended on the elders and became impossible or difficult in the Niger Project. On the other hand, the young who had been born or raised in the Niger Project could not understand why they should defer to distant people—uncles or grandparents, clan members—who had stayed in the home country, whom they had never seen, and who had no significance for them. Thus conflict arose between the generations.

In brief, the migration led to a land and a milieu which, despite all efforts, received only superficially the imprint of the social organization of the men who were to make the land bear fruit. The strong bond between land and society was broken, as were social bonds, because it was not a whole society or whole class that had been transferred, but only fragments of a society which traditionally was integrated.

Such an example prepares us to understand another migration of infinitely greater extent, the one bringing men to the cities of the Third World. To the urbanization of the developing countries we must now turn.

URBANIZATION

IN THE

THIRD WORLD

Urbanization represents the most notable and spectacular change that has come upon the peoples and societies of the developing nations. In several respects the change repeats what happened not too long ago in Europe and North America. There, too, the cities grew up in the wake of the industrial revolution. But the differences between the two cases are important, and it is these that we must stress.

Extent of Urban Development in the Third World

Before discussing the contemporary situation in the Third World, let us try to relate urbanization there to the history of urban life on the various continents.

Less than two hundred years ago, in 1800, urbanization in Europe was hardly greater than in Asia. If an urban population means a city of more than a hundred thousand inhabitants, then .6 percent of Asia's population was urban as compared with 2.9 percent of Europe's. Asia at the time had two-thirds of the world's city dwellers. During the nineteenth century, however, urbanization speeded up greatly in Europe under the pressure of the industrial revolution. It went on much less rapidly in Asia which was economically backward. In 1900 urban population was only 2.1 percent in Asia, but 11.9 percent in Europe. Asia now had only one quarter of the world's city dwellers. From 1900 on, however, the movement became more rapid in Asia than in Europe. In 1950 Europe had 19.9 percent of its people in cities, less than twice as many as in 1900. In Asia, on the contrary, the figure was 7.5 percent or almost four times as much as in 1900. In 1950 we find a third of the world's city dwellers in Asia, or 105 million as against 19.4 million in 1900.

Against this background, some figures and geographical facts will help us evaluate the current importance of urbanization in the Third World. Cities of more than a hundred thousand inhabitants are a sure sign of advanced urbanization. Such cities number 125 in Latin America: 88 in South America (32 in Brazil) and 37 in Central America (22 in Mexico).

Such large cities are numerous in Africa as well, 72 in all, the highest figures being 14 for the Arab Republic, 11 for South Africa, and 5 for Algeria.

Now these two figures, 125 for Latin America and 72 for Africa, are really high. We need only compare them with the figures for a country of comparable population: The United States has 175 such cities. The difference is unimportant since the United States has an incomparably higher level of economic development.

In Asia, cities of over a hundred thousand inhabitants number 469. But Japan alone, which is not an underdeveloped country, has 124 of them. This leaves 345 for the rest of Asia, the largest numbers being 103 for mainland China (according to somewhat dated statistics); 111 for India; 22 for Indonesia; 16 for Pakistan; 11 for the Philippines; 11 for Korea; 9 for Turkey. Alongside these figures we can set the following: for the United Kingdom,

56, although it is a highly urbanized country; 45 for Federal Germany; 39 for France. When thinking of France, recall that Brazil with its 32 is not far behind.

If we pass on to cities of over a million inhabitants. then (omitting Japan's 6) Asia has 14 in China, 7 in India, 2 in Indonesia, 2 in Korea, and one each in Iran, Singapore, Pakistan, Philippines, Thailand, and Turkey, or 31 in all. Africa has far fewer, but it does have some: Alexandria and Cairo in the United Arab Republic, and Johannesburg in South Africa. Latin America has the rather high number of 9: Buenos Aires, Rio, São Paulo, Bogota, Lima, Montevideo, Havana, Mexico City, and Santiago. Over against these 9, the United States has 14, the United Kingdom 4, and Federal Germany 3.

Even if we go on to the gigantic metropolises (over three million inhabitants), the underdeveloped countries are not so badly off. If the United States has 5, South America has 4: Brazil has 2 of them (Rio and São Paulo); the others are Mexico City and Buenos Aires, the former with about three million inhabitants, the latter with seven million. In Africa only Cairo has more than three million. But in Asia we find 3 great Chinese cities—(Shanghai, Peking, and Tien-tsin)—and 2 Indian cities—(Calcutta and Bombay). England, France, and Germany, on the contrary, have only one each.

These figures are enough to show that urbanization in the Third World hardly lags behind urbanization in the developed world. Within the Third World itself, Latin America is first, but Africa is not negligible with its 72 cities of over a hundred thousand inhabitants.

From a study already somewhat dated, we can derive another measure of urbanization, and the result confirms what we have already seen. In 1955, 18 percent of the people of South America and 12 percent of those in Central America lived in cities of over one hundred thousand inhabitants. Corresponding figures were: 21 percent for Europe, 18 percent for the USSR, 29 percent for the United States and Canada. In Asia the percentage was a less high but nonetheless striking 8 percent; in Africa it was 5 percent. The comparison yields almost the same results if we look at the population in cities of over twenty thousand inhabitants: 25 percent in South America and 21 percent in Central America, as against 31 percent in the USSR, 35 percent in Western Europe, and 42 percent in the United States and Canada; 13 percent in Asia and 9 percent in Africa.

Unemployment

The extent of urbanization in the Third World is not matched by its economic growth. Urbanization there is not wholly the result—far from it, in fact—of new job possibilities. Such a connection is fully true only of the strictly industrial cities, and these are rather few; it is especially true of the population centers created by the mining industry. In general, the rate of industrialization lags very far behind the rate of urbanization (by industrialization is meant the percentage of a country's active people that is employed in industry).

Thus we can point to same rate of urbanization (30 percent—33 percent) for a whole series of underdeveloped countries: Egypt, Chile, Mexico, Puerto Rico, and Venezuela; and for a whole series of developed countries: Finland, France, Sweden, Switzerland, and Canada. Yet the rate of industrialization for the first group has been only 10 percent, while for the second it has been 24 percent.

Apart from industrialization, other factors have been at work in urban growth, such as the attraction of commercial activity and the establishment of modern administrative bureaucracies (as in the African countries once they became independent). But even with these factors we are far from accounting for all urbanization in the developing countries.

Economic change is indeed the root of the phenomenon, but this is because it produces other effects besides new job possibilities. Such broad economic changes as the entrance into a modern monetary economy have played their part. Even more important has been contact with the products of the industrialized nations, for this has drawn men toward the cities, especially the commercial cities (and, among these, especially the ports), which are seen as the place for access to new consumer goods.

But we must also note that push factors (pushing men from the countryside) have played and still play a greater role than pull factors (drawing men into the cities). Among the former are the low standard of living in rural areas, which is itself at times the result of developments unfavorable to rural people in the Third World; population pressure, wherever land is scarce or poorly distributed; lack of food, associated with population pressure and leading at times to famine (for example, in Northeastern Brazil or in the Puno area of the Peruvian Andes).

It is of prime importance to observe that the introduction of new consumer products and new life styles into cities in contact with the world abroad creates a difference of level and an imbalance between city and countryside on a scale not known in nineteenth-century Europe despite all its industrialization and urbanization. The reason for the difference is that there is no comparison between the consumer goods and life style offered by the nineteenth-century European city and those offered today by a mid-twentieth-century African city. The imbalance, which is both a pull and a push factor, in turn leads to much more rapid urbanization.

We may add, finally, another effect of the population growth described above. There are proportionately many more young people, and they are naturally much readier to move. They above all have invaded the cities in large numbers.

On the whole, then, it is by changes in consumption rather than in production, that economic development has thus far brought urbanization in its train in the developing countries.

The Social Situation in the Cities

We can foresee the social consequences of such a sharp contrast between rapid urbanization and lagging economic development.

First of all, there is a much more anomalous population profile for the cities than for the developing countries as a whole. There is an abnormal predominance of young adults over older people, but also (at least in the first phase of urbanization) over children as well. (We leave aside any question of a possible difference in fertility between country and city, for such a difference would hardly be found in the first phase anyway.) It is the young adults above all, who migrate to the cities. Often enough, of course, they return to their native countryside, if, for example, they have saved a certain amount of capital. But even if they do not stay in the cities and do not start a family there, they are replaced by other adults, and the proportion of such adults in the city tends to be maintained. Thus we can estimate that the percentage of active people from fifteen to fifty-nine years old has been much higher for cities than for the country as a whole in most of the Third World nations.

The disproportionately high number of young adults in the cities might seem an economic advantage. But in fact the problem is more complex, since there is still a close, symbiotic relation between countryside and city. Those who live in the city must support a good part of their family who still live in the country, or send them funds, or provide for the upkeep of newcomers to the city; the income of this urban population is thus heavily burdened by numerous obligations. When urbanization and a slow rate of industrialization go together, the urban population of young adults bears the heaviest part of the burden created by the economically unproductive people of the countryside.

Part of the anomalous population profile is the clear preponderance of men over women in the cities. Whereas in most cities of the developed countries of Europe and North America there is a slight preponderance of women, the opposite is almost always true of the developing countries.

Some figures will bring home the contrast. In France the number of men for every hundred women is 86 in cities and 94 in rural areas. Women are in the majority in the countryside but still more in the cities. In the Low Countries, there are 96 men for every hundred women in the cities, 104 in the country. Everywhere the same disparity is found. In the United States there are 94 men in the cities for every hundred women, 106 in the rural areas. In Latin America the proportions are similar.

Ceylon, on the contrary, has 128 men for every hundred women in the cities, 104 in the country; India, 116 and 104; Malaysia,

118 and 110; Pakistan, 138 and 108; Union of South Africa, 119 and 93.

The results of such a situation are numerous, at least where the disparity is extreme: instability of the family and, often, commercialization of sex and development of prostitution. But, on the other hand, her very rarity gives the woman a chance to reverse her traditional role as inferior.

Wretched living conditions are a second serious consequence of urbanization in the Third World. Rapid exodus from the countryside and rapid arrival in the city, combined with the economic instability of the city (since it cannot furnish enough steady employment), all cause wretched housing conditions, and we see the rise of the *bidonville* ("tin can city") or shantytown.

The term *bidonville* came into use about thirty years ago, at a time when the new urbanization was getting underway in various parts of the world. Other names are also in use, especially in Latin American countries: at Recife, *mucambos* ("palm-frond huts"); at Rio, *favelas* ("native plants"); at Caracas, *ranchitos* ("little ranches"); at Santiago, *callampas* ("mushrooms"); at Buenos Aires, *villas-miserias* ("hunger towns"). Each name signifies some aspect of the reality: *bidonville* refers to the material used for dwellings; *callampa* to the speed with which they spread; *villas-miserias* to their wretchedness.

More scientific terms have an analogous import; in Latin America people speak of "marginal populations" and even, in the abstract, of "marginality." This characterization is, in fact, one of the most penetrating, for we are dealing here not with true structured cities but with unstable and temporary urban grafts, understood to be such by their inhabitants, and in this respect "marginal" or "on the fringe."

There is usually a simple juxtaposition in space of a city proper, commercial and residential, and a collection of shantytowns. Sometimes the two interpenetrate as at Rio, where the *favelas* cling to the hills above the residential sections, on ground left open because its steepness made building difficult. At other times there is a clear distinction between the city proper as a whole and the shantytowns as a whole. In any event, there is little communication and even few means of transportation between the two.

Here or there, in the first phase of urbanization, the new population had huddled together in hovels at the center of the old city. It is only in a second phase that new contingents of immigrants stop at the outskirts, all the more since the surplus population send the price of lodging up even in the hovels of the city center. The new graft onto the city is thus often marginal in the sense of geographically peripheral. It is all the more marginal in that it often takes place in areas where construction is impossible: the steep slopes at Rio, the swamps at Bangkok or Recife, areas exposed to the flooding of large rivers as at Baghdad, often even dumping grounds. In other cases, settlement on the periphery is the easier because the ground is too dry for cultivation, as with the *cerros* ("backbones") of Lima, and has no water supply, so that it is claimed by no one or else the owner doesn't bother with it. The occupant takes over as a squatter, or pays a minimal rent to the owner; sometimes better organized groups obtain governmental recognition of their right to occupy the ground. The occupation at times takes on the look of an invasion. There are instances in which building materials have been trucked in at night by a whole group, and by dawn all the barracks of a new quarter are up and occupied, even to babies in their cribs; expulsion is impossible.

At Rio, and in several cities of Asia, the peripheral areas involved are very narrow and cramped. Then the inner city becomes overpopulated—and people move quite simply to the city streets. Others move to the few vacant spots on river banks or in swamps or live on boats in the harbors, streams, and canals.

The collections of people of which we are speaking are marginal in still another way, in that there is but a very small degree of administrative organization that touches them. Where spontaneous organizations or associations do spring up, they are often expelled by the police as trouble spots. This happened in several *favelas* at Rio during the revolution of 1964.

There are even instances of shantytowns being built outside a city's administrative limits, even outside all municipal boundaries. No authority is responsible for public services here: sewerage, lighting, roads; and for a long time no one takes any charge of them. Such administrative marginality aggravates the conditions already described.

Of course, individuals do not generally stay in the circumstances they fell into on first coming to the city. The encampment, which is what the shantytown is, gradually becomes a better dwelling place when the migrants settle down or receive some help. But the effort to improve the living quarters is hampered by the fact that the dwellers themselves do not regard their city or shantytown as a permanent place of residence; it lacks too many elements of social organization, official and unofficial, for it to have the drawing power of a city. It is often vain to hope for improvement at that spot. A final aspect of marginality is that the unpromising living conditions in the shantytown keep the new city dweller from having his family come after him to the city.

People in a Latin American shantytown were asked what they considered their most urgent needs, the ones they would like to see met before all others? The inhabitants answered in the following order: a police station, stores, a telephone. The police station was to overcome the lack of protection, especially at night, in an area without administration or genuine social organization. The telephone was for summoning an ambulance at need; the people did not think of asking for a hospital because they were so aware of the provisional nature of their settlement. Stores, finally, were in order to avoid the higher prices of commodities carted in by merchants from the nearby city. In short, the shantytown people were looking for means to a minimum of social integration and of communication with the city, but they did not dream of more than this minimum, so conscious were they of the precarious character of their settlement. On the other hand, low incomes in a city with too few jobs made it difficult to find another kind of city dwelling, for this would demand some small resources.

Absence of Social Norms

The broad context we have sketched out explains some more general sociological characteristics of Third World urbanization. "The practical absence of social norms," as the authors of one collection of essays put it; "improvised and structureless society," as Georges Balandier describes it. Urbanization brings nearly everywhere an almost complete relaxation of traditional customs and restraints, and an emancipation which is especially visible in women and the young. It is not infrequent for the young to come to the cities with the explicit intention of escaping; even where this intention is not present, the city does not provide conditions favorable to the retention of former customs.

The only social framework which the new city dwellers, for example in Africa, had known, was a system of extended kinship from which everything else was derived: rights, duties, obligations. In the city, there is nothing of this. The kinship system has not migrated with these people, and the network of relationships it entailed can no longer function, at least fully and perfectly. Even if, as on rare occasion, a group of kinsmen has migrated in its totality, it finds itself immersed in a larger and ethnically heterogeneous mass of men. Such people then know how to behave to their kin, what is owing to them, and what can be expected from them. But they do not straightway know how to behave to men of other groups and other customs. Think, for example, of the difference involved in adherence to matrilinear custom and adherence to patrilinear custom. The result is that numerous people are thrown together who, in traditional terms, could pass for what, in the context of nation states, would be called "foreigners."

The old norms of conduct have thus been weakened and are rapidly disappearing. Generally they are not replaced by a new coherent social system; there is no structure to welcome these people. In other cases, in regions where the city has long existed and has developed its own customs and citydweller ways, it impresses all this on the newcomer. This is what happens in the cities of Europe today; it is even what happened pretty much in the nineteenth century, because many cities were already in existence with their traditions and customs before their period of growth at the industrial revolution. There is nothing like this in many cities of Asia and Africa, except for a few large old cities of Nigeria. Even in Latin America growth has been so rapid as to leave the impression of wholly new urban masses juxtaposed with the old, with no social communication.

In a word, everything must be discovered anew. The process requires all sorts of groups to be created and to develop. Time is needed, however, for this to happen. Meanwhile there are indispensable social functions which no institution seems to provide, especially the education of the young. Here is a social sector easily left in a vacuum, as long as no new educational system has truly taken root.

One manifestation of the vacuum is delinquency, especially among adolescents. Many young people come to the city without their parents or even in rebellion against them. Even those who have immigrated with their parents or who are born in the city of immigrant parents do not always receive counsel and guidance from them. In addition, the younger generation which has been raised in the cities receives a modern type of instruction, or scraps of one, and regards the older generation as outdated; the young then refuse to be guided by their elders. A further factor in the plight of the young is that marriages contracted by immigrants are often unstable, and the children are abandoned to their own devices.

Many of these children do not go to school, but neither do they find jobs, and thus they remain idle or live more or less by odd jobs. Many take up thieving, begging, pimping, drug peddling, black-market activities, etc. At Poona, India, an inquiry showed that over 50 percent of those arrested for theft did not go to school and had no job. Legislation can, at times, foolishly aggravate the situation, for example, by requiring children to go to school until they are fourteen but forbidding then to work until they are sixteen. Prostitution, too, is widespread in the new cities, because of the unbalanced ratio of men to women, the spirit of emancipation that often infects immigrating young girls, and economic difficulties generally.

We must add the wasting of their earnings by adult workers on games and drink; this is especially true among those who have no relatives in the city where they work and no social milieu to sustain them.

Despite all these serious problems, it would be a mistake to paint the picture too black, as if everything in the Third World cities were social pathology, delinquency, and prostitution. There is another side to the situation. We must not forget, for example, that migration to the city is for many the opportunity, never offered before, of escaping from oppressive custom. It is also the exciting opportunity to enter into communication with the rest of the world, to satisfy a curiosity (even if only embryonic), and to fulfill a desire for new powers and new know-how.

Furthermore, if urbanization weakens traditional social bonds, if it affects beliefs and customary values, at the same time it leads little by little to the creation of a network of new relationships in which men will discover for the first time that their problems are shared by other men, though the latter be not their kinsmen and perhaps very different from themselves. They will discover, too, that these problems can be solved by man's action, by the common effort of men together.

In the cities, then, there is simultaneously a breakdown of traditional civilization and its ethical code, and the appearance in germ of a new and more varied civilization with the freedom it brings. It is difficult to pass judgment on the whole picture. Hodgkin's remark seems accurate: "Europeans and those Africans who think like Europeans will be struck more by the aspect of breakdown; the mass of Africans is more impressed by the promise."

CHANGES IN
KINSHIP SYSTEM
AND FAMILY

In speaking of the most important characteristics of urbanization, we observed many profound social disorders affecting traditional societies today. But we must insist further on one particular characteristic which is global in its import. The family is deeply affected by the migrations, by urbanization, etc. The extended families are breaking up, being fragmented; thereby the whole kinship system is affected. But the kinship system provided almost the whole structure of traditional society. Thus traditional society is being attacked at its very roots.

In traditional society (as we have already observed but perhaps without explaining it sufficiently), relations between men are almost always based on bonds of kinship or, more precisely, on blood bonds. We must add, however: real or fictive blood bonds. for often the bond is only an imaginary one, especially in large scale units such as political entities. The Japanese were not the emperor's sons by generation, and all those who call each other brother in Africa do not therefore share blood lines. But there is significance in the very fact that people felt compelled to conceive of all relationships, even those not of blood, on the model of blood relationships. It was the only model people could use, because social relations could only be thought of as natural and because natural bonds are based on consanguinity and generation.

We do not find strictly the same thing in the feudal systems of personal relationships. But even there we are not far from the same model. We pass imperceptibly from the father-son relation to that of patron and client and the various kinds of personal relation which inspired the feudal conception. Nonetheless our primary concern here is with more strictly traditional societies. What are the effects on such societies of the economic changes we have been discussing?

Progressive Decline of the Kinship System

The privileged place for observing the decline of kinship influence is obviously Africa. Kinship relations played so important a role there as to make up the very tissue of all social life. The kinship system dominated and determined the social structure of the tribe. Nowadays, as Balandier, for example, notes: "Relations based on blood bonds (real or fictive) are yielding ground to relations imposed by new conditions of production and new types of ownership and distribution of wealth."

In the conclusion of an inquiry sponsored by the African International Institute at Stanleyville (now Kisangani), P. Clément observed: "In an urban setting the life style as a whole is largely conditioned by a fully different set of factors (for example, a monetary economy, salaried work in the service of a higher socioeconomic class, abandonment of agricultural work by women, the breaking or relaxation of connections with rural society, emancipation from the authority of custom, ethno-cultural diversity among the population, establishment of distinct residential areas for blacks and whites, limitations on freedom of movement, opportunities for instruction, etc)."[76]

The system of rights and obligations based on kinship obviously does not die overnight, but the regressive tendency is noticeable. First, the circle of kinship which a man takes into account gradually narrows as his relations with his native village become more infrequent. In Latin America where a developed kinship system never existed as in Africa but where a patriarchal family system was still alive, emigration was usually to such a distant place that there was no hope of return and the break was a brutal one; this was true, for example, of the Guarani who came from distant Paraguay to Buenos Aires. In the African villages, emigration means the absence of essential kinsmen, and this prevents the carrying out of many family ceremonies or else their accomplishment in truncated form.

At the same time, new social relations grow up which are foreign to the kinship system. We refer especially to those dictated by urban concentration as such, which makes neighbors of ethnically different groups. At times, tribal groups stay together, as did the Yoruba of Nigeria at Ibadan or Ifé, where the kinship system continued for a time to be the principle on which neighborhoods were organized. But such cases are now exceptional.

Relations of work much more obviously arise outside the kinship framework. Kinsmen, it is true, help each other find jobs and tend to hire themselves out in groups, but it is rare to find brothers or other close relatives as workers in the same factory or miners in the same pit. And even if they are together in this way, they work in a system organized by overseers who take no account of such kinship; the regulations do not acknowledge it.

More generally, the cultural evolution accompanying economic change undermines the authority of the kinship system; its hierarchy is overthrown. Men are caught between two systems: the traditional one and the one imposed by a more modern life style. In his Stanleyville inquiry, P. Clément made these observations: "Authority in the urban setting is influenced both by the traditional system of seniority and by the material and intellectual opportunities of the one who receives the newcomer and of the newcomer himself (salary, profession, level of education and culture, adaptability to new situations, etc.). Thus you can sometimes see an older son, because of his poorer education, problems in adapting, or inability to amass enough resources, occupying a lesser rank than his younger brother. But such a reversal of status is possible when brothers are in question. It is much less possible when a father arrives in the city at his son's home. In any event, we often find that the holder of a deed on a parcel of land is not the real head of the family group."[77]

The economic evolution is accompanied by a political evolution: the birth of the state and the creation of parties. The relation of all this to kinship becomes very tenuous. A corrective must, however, be immediately introduced, and it will lead in turn to an important general observation. Ethnic or tribal classification played an important part in the creation and development of African political parties. But the concept of tribe at work here has only a rather distant connection with the strict kinship system. In a looser sense, "tribe" refers more and more to people with origins in the same region or village or group of villages; it is something like "the Savoyards" or "the Bretons," from the "countrysides," as people still say in French cities. "Where African townsfolk have organized spontaneously for political ends it is the concept of tribe rather than kinship that provides the only traditional integrating factor."[78]

The new concept of tribe derives from traditional kinship but involves a nontraditional extension of it, really a transposition. "There is," says Southall, "a tendency to extend the idea of brotherhood metaphorically to all members of the tribe."[79] And even beyond the tribe, we might add, as the appearance of all sorts of new brotherhoods in the cities shows. These are modeled more or less on the kinship system, and are a venturesome transformation of it. The Stanleyville inquiry is interesting here again. "Analogous bonds and obligations grow up between people who are not linked by kinship or affinity but whose common origin—village, tribe, or region—has drawn them together in the city and who in the course of their contacts with each other have developed a solidarity and friendship hard to distinguish from those which unite people of the same blood or pledge allies."[80]

A neo-brotherhood is more easily built on a common geographical origin, especially a village, than on a tribal base in the strict sense. But it may also be formed among people working for the same boss, or among namesakes (same Christian name), or among members of a tontine. "All these fictive kinships involve duties and obligations ranging from simple mutual help to the prohibition of marriage and sexual relations."[81]

In the extreme case, similar groupings can be effected by neighborhood: neo-brotherhoods grow up between permanent neighbors and are marked by collective sharing in tasks and recreations. Here we are getting ever farther away from a kinship system, however reinterpreted. An organization on a Stanleyville street may appoint a "governor" for itself and "district commissioners," but the titles are humorously conferred. The organization may intend only to meet now and then for gossip and drink, as do the patrons at a regular table in a German tavern. Generally such brotherhoods do not have the stability given by traditional bonds of kinship. The new relations can be maintained only by frequent contact and are much less enduring than bonds of genuine kinship. But the phenomenon is interesting nonetheless and shows how the decay of the kinship system often is marked, in its beginnings, by analogous or metaphorical substitutes.

The same process can be seen in Latin America, not substituting for a kinship system, but for feudal or quasi-feudal relations which are transposed into a system of patron-client relations in the cities, with men grouped around a political or trade-union "protector." The same thing happened in the instance of nineteenth century bosses of the North American cities.

Evolution of the Family

The family obviously does not vanish with the kinship system, but it does gradually become distinguished from it and take on a new meaning. Marriage "tends to lose its significance as alliance between two families and to become essentially a union between two persons." But here again the evolution is not accomplished in one step; rather there are complex transitional situations in which some obligations of the old kinship situation are still alive, while others are already rejected.

Marriages with the newer meaning will often be contracted even back in the villages. An institution like trial marriage, often a traditional practice, frequently continues, but its meaning is different. The purpose is not now always to test the woman's fertility. The Stanleyville inquiry shows new purposes: "Our informants have often said that a man who wants a wife to give him children ought to marry a virgin. The man who sets up house with a widow or a woman who 'has already run around' rarely expects to have children by her. He takes her on a trial basis to observe her conduct and her domestic skills."[82]

This development is confirmed by the answers to questions about a wife's ideal qualities. Traditionally, she ought to be fruitful, be submissive to her husband, and contribute to the economic prosperity of the household. It seems "that in the city today the highly valued wife is one who, beyond all else, is a good housekeeper, knowing how to manage the home so that the husband feels no shame before his relatives. This implies that she must maintain order and neatness inside the home and around it, sweep the yard, clean the kitchen and dishes, wash the clothes and iron them if she is able (still a rare qualification), scrub the sheets and spread them outdoors to dry, properly receive her husband's relatives and friends, see to it that there is always food in the house, prepare meals attractively and on time, manage her money sensibly, etc."[83]

The relationship between spouses is changing: submission of woman to man is giving way to a certain intimacy between the two. But the intimacy is still limited; there is little dialogue, little communication between husband and wife. P. Clément describes the change this way: "The urbanized black man no longer requires of his wife the submission and respect that were expected of her back in the village, where she was forbidden to sit down in his presence and to come into the room when he was with his friends. These obligations took on more attenuated or at least more nuanced forms with the progress of education, with the increased responsibilities given to the woman, and with the complexity of daily life. Men esteem highly a woman who 'respects her husband's mouth,' but she is no longer expected to show the same constant reserve, the same self-effacement, the same submission."[84] That is said of Africa, but it also holds with little difference for changing India.

Let us note finally that in drawing up a marriage agreement the payments characteristic of an alliance between clans tend to be ignored or at least are not regularly required. The reason is that such payments lose their meaning in a conjugal agreement between husband and wife. If a payment does take place, it is often the man alone who pays and not his family. If the woman's family accepts it, she often makes up for it by a counter-payment, which may frequently exceed the original. "We even heard at Stanleyville," says P. Clément, "of a few cases of fathers giving their daughters a dowry after the European manner."[85] After the European manner of another day. The tendency in the developing classes of the city, then, is towards a matrimonial and familial institution quite different from the traditional system and analogous to middle-class marriage in nineteenth-century Europe. The situation is more confused in the lower classes.

Beyond these particular characteristics, we can see the general direction of the change that is taking place. The modification of family life has to do, first of all, with a transition from the extended to the more limited family, which the sociologists call "conjugal" (husband, wife, children) or "nuclear" (a nucleus as over against the larger kinship units characteristic of traditional society). The tendency is reinforced by Western example and by colonial and postcolonial legislation, as well as by the influence of the Christian missions. But one of the major causes is undoubtedly economic. People no longer feel the need for the security once offered by the extended family. The mobility which economic development has brought with it likewise helps to break down the large family group. Urbanization has now speeded up the process.

The development corresponds, secondly, to a change in the family's role. As the extended family, "the family was formerly a sociological, a juridical, and an economic unit, all in one" (G. Balandier). It thus met, by itself, almost all educational needs. This is no longer true, because no longer necessary or even possible. And as soon as the family ceases to be of itself an economic, juridical, and sociological unit, due in good measure to current economic change, then it tends to become more restricted in extent. Its makeup is adapted to the only functions it can still fulfill: intimacy; education, though only within limits; an economic function, in an even more limited way. "Some functions," says G. Balandier, "are vanishing because they now belong to specialized organizations (education, health, public protection and security, etc.); others are clearly permanent (socialization, restraint on sexuality, moral security, etc.)."

A more special aspect of evolving family makeup is the decline of polygamy or, more precisely, of the polygamous family. "Polygamy falls into disuse for various reasons: population factors in the urban centers (too few women), economic conditions (increased sources of revenue have broadened the competition for women), and cultural conditions (especially the religious efforts of missionaries)" (Balandier).

As the makeup of the family is modified, so too is the manner in which it is formed. In the past, marriage concerned primarily the extended families, the clans, and consisted in an exchange of payments between them, thus strengthening peace and understanding; marriage was much less an affair of the spouses themselves. Once the matrimonial exchanges between the clans or great families no longer seemed so necessary for economic (and political) security, the restrictions on choice of partners were relaxed. The choice became freer and depended on the individual's personal inclinations. The choice also became wider and more open; it can fall on people in groups other than those with which, in other times, matrimonial alliances had to be made.

Status of Women

The evolution of the family thus consists, in large measure, in liberation from numerous customary restrictions. In this context, observers stress the change in the status of women. We ought not, however, fail to notice a similar change for men. In a society ruled by custom, a man reached full adulthood with independence and autonomy only at a rather advanced age. The dependence of an obedient son could last into a man's forties. All that has changed. But the economic shifts that have occurred doubtless do more directly affect the position of women.

The woman is less bound to servile work, once new methods

of production and new sources of revenue are available; she is often freer than the man to engage in new activities, especially commercial ones. Or rather, where she has traditionally filled a commercial position, the sudden development of new possibilities for commerce, speculation, and business supply her with an unusual opportunity for promotion.

The change has occurred chiefly in the cities. Here a further factor works in favor of women's emancipation: the numerical imbalance of women and men. There are cases where the preponderance of men over women is really extreme and the rarity of women of course increases their value. A few years ago there were up to seven men for every woman in Salisbury, five in Nairobi, two in the cities of the Rhodesian copperbelt and at Mombasa, Kampala (Kibuya), and Brazzaville (Poto-Poto). The discrepancy was less at Dar es Salaam and at Elizabethville (Lubumbashi), because the Belgian colonial government had made a special effort to stabilize and house families. The imbalance between the sexes was at its greatest in the large plantations: those of former British South Cameroon, the sisal plantations of Tanganyika, and the sugar-cane plantations of Uganda.

To understand how important the resulting emancipation of women is, we must realize that if women leave the bush in lesser numbers than men, they do so in a more definitive way. This is doubtless because coming to the city changes their social position more radically. We must also stress the fact that a woman's position is more clearly bettered the more she has access to properly economic activities. We might compare West and East Africa in this respect. In the West, where cities are centers for commerce as well as mining, women have the opportunity to go into business. The resultant economic independence allows them all other kinds of independence as well. There are even instances of them reimbursing their husbands for the payment made at their marriage in order to assure themselves of their freedom.

The Transition

From this account of current tendencies, we ought not conclude that the process is at an end or that it is resulting or will result in the same kind of family with which we are familiar in the countries of industrial civilization. These latter themselves show great diversity, and European middle-class marriage, as we noted earlier, is gradually disappearing.

In any event, during the present period of transition the conjugal or nuclear family seems very unstable in the developing countries. "The mutual adjustment of spouses within a limited family is not very good." At the same time, "the relationships of extended kinship often remain alive, even at a distance; the large family unit helps maintain the material and moral security of distant members if they appeal to it. It can also serve as a support for economic activity of a modern kind" (Balandier). In other words, there are advantages to the narrower conjugal family, but security still often lies with the larger traditional family.

Similarly, the decline of polygamy does not immediately mean strong and perduring monogamy. Even more than in the industrial countries, we can speak rather of successive polygamy. Not long ago an observer could write: "The return of city dwellers to their villages often means for them a return to the traditional polygamy" (Balandier). The new family that is making its appearance is thus very unstable up to now; the divorce rate and the frequency of irregular unions is very high.

Neither the status nor the psychology of women has thus far wholly changed. Many former traits continue to manifest themselves even in the city; for example, among wives even if not among husbands, the desire for many children persists. Here, too, we observe a ready return to former ways when women return from city to village.

On the other hand, the liberation of women by way of economic independence (trade, for example) easily leads to prostitution. More often, the woman who has won her independence keeps it and remains single. "Women living singly, or without legal husbands, and in economic independence are one of the most striking characteristics of African towns in contrast to rural areas. In Koforidua 70 percent of the women were traders and 25 percent of them were living singly. In Stanleyville 30.3 percent of women over sixteen years old were living singly or in concubinage. In Kahama 22 percent of household heads were female compared with 2 percent in the surrounding countryside. In the Kampala suburbs of Kisenyi and Mulago 23 percent and 34 percent respectively of household heads were female."[86] The numerical imbalance between the sexes allows women easily to escape husbands who mistreat them or repudiate them for barrenness. It also allows them to claim the right to the same sexual liberty as men.

The situation of the family varies from one region to another in Africa. In some cities, in the lumber camps, and on the plantations, the observer is forced to ask at times whether there is any institutional form of family at all. In other cases, especially in West Africa, even in the cities, the older ones in particular, the family is more stable: the Yoruba family at Lagos and Oshogbo, the Akan family at Accra and Koforidua. But, even in West Africa, there are large immigrant populations, coming chiefly from the North. Although these form but a small percentage of the total population, their condition is very close to that of the immigrants in Eastern and Central Africa: the same numerical disproportion between the sexes, the same high mobility, the same lack of structured family.

In brief, wherever we find a high degree of economic change, the traditional family society is shaken and altered. In the first phase of transition no new structures emerge as yet; there are tendencies toward such new structures but also a good deal of disorder. The same is true of authority within the family: the parents generally no longer have the almost absolute authority which the elders had in the tribal environment, and the sense of educational responsibility is often weak in the new and still unstable nuclear families. The latter have not fully replaced the extended family or the village when it comes to socializing the young members, the children and especially the adolescents.

THE EFFECTS

OF COLONIALISM

We have been seeing the many profound effects on under-developed societies of such changes as have already touched them. In the present chapter we shall try to isolate the causality of colonialism in regard to these effects.

At first sight this would not seem too difficult a task, since not all developing countries were subjected to formal colonialism, that is, to formal political domination from abroad. On the other hand, we can see what has happened in countries long free of colonial domination, for example, the republics of Latin America which have been independent for 150 years.

Yet clear conclusions do not emerge. For, if not all developing countries were political colonies, almost all experienced some form of economic domination, the effects of which were not too different from those of political domination. The latter, in turn, has almost always been accompanied by economic colonialism.

Scholars have indeed succeeded in partially refuting the purely economic interpretation of colonialism: that of Hobson and especially that of Lenin (reviving Hobson's theses) in his *Imperialism, the Highest Stage of Capitalism*. It has been established that in some cases at least the motive for colonialism was not economic. This is what Henri Brunschwig, for example, intended to show in 1960.[87] His argument is that the French colonial enterprise at the end of the nineteenth century was due primarily to a nationalism embittered by the defeat of 1871 and eager to make up overseas for its loss of power in Europe; for a long time, business circles, on the contrary, were not in favor of colonialism.

Elsewhere, however, men were following a different drum. "Empire is a matter of the belly. If you want to avoid civil war, you must become imperialist" (Cecil Rhodes). In France similar sentiments soon began to come from the pens of Leroy-Beaulieu and Jules Ferry. The latter, in particular, wrote in his *Le Tonkin et la mère patrie* (1890): "Colonial policy is the daughter of industrial policy. For any state in which capital is abundant and quickly accumulated, in which the manufacturing system is continuously growing and attracting, if not the majority, at least the most alert and dynamic sector of the laboring population, and in which agriculture must industrialize in order to survive, for any such state exportation is an essential element in prosperity and the use of capital, since the demand for labor depends on the extent of the foreign markets. The European consumer can buy no more. New consumer markets must be sought in other parts of the world, or modern society will become bankrupt. Colonial policy is the international manifestation of the eternal laws of competition."

The least that can be said, then, is that if economic desire and imperialism have not always been the original source of the colonial thrust, yet from a certain point on, economic colonization, that is, economic exploitation of colonies, has everywhere accompanied political colonization. Economic colonization in turn joins forces with properly political colonization . Economic colonization was what victimized China (a few political undertakings were added, involving one-sided treaties and the formation of a few enclaves, the "concessions"). And many Latin American, and especially Central American, countries remained subject to economic domination long after they had won their political independence at the beginning of the nineteenth century.

If we thus take economic domination into account, it becomes difficult, despite appearances, to isolate the specific effects of colonialism within the developing countries. In the last analysis, there is practically no country which has not borne its mark, at least in the form of economic dependence.

The Effects of Political Domination

It is worth our while, however, first to describe the very clear effects of political colonization. We must, of course, avoid excessive generalization in speaking of political colonialism, or at least avoid generalizing on a universal scale. We can observe in past history examples of colonization which may be said to have succeeded. Ancient Greece colonized many islands and coastal regions of Asia Minor, where the populations were ethnically different from the European Greeks; yet some of the colonies in Asia Minor experienced a period of high prosperity, economic and probably political too. Other peoples on the contrary have been bled white or have declined under foreign domination.

We shall be speaking here only of colonization in modern times, for it is rather different from that of the past. It is distinguished chiefly by the fact that the modern colonizer came from a society which was scientifically, technologically, and economically developed. This fact probably also explains the most serious effects of colonization.

Even in modern times, indeed, colonization is obviously not synonymous with bad government or with inadequate or ineffective administration, and we know the importance of effective administration for any developmental undertaking. The Antillean economist W. A. Lewis, whom we have quoted several times already, worked with President Nkrumah for a long time as economic adviser; he has a close knowledge of several other underdeveloped countries and is interested in all the factors of economic development in the past. He came to the conclusion that countries are not necessarily better governed, in the technical sense of the term, when they govern themselves than when they are governed by others. To the extent that an effective government is a condition of economic progress, it is not at all clear, he thinks, that political dependence is in every respect a source of stagnation.

But in many other respects political domination had an unfavorable influence on genuine economic development. We are dealing here with a whole psychological complex which Balandier, for example, has summed up as the "colonial situation."[88]

The evil effects of colonialism were the fruit of several beliefs or convictions which, consciously or unconsciously, the colonists cherished. These beliefs or convictions were in practice inseparable from modern colonialism, whatever may have been the nobler intentions that went with them.

Among these convictions the primary one was the natural superiority of colonizer over colonized, a superiority of race, civilization, or nation as the case might be. Correlative to this was the conviction of the natural inferiority of the colonized who, successively or alternatively, were put down as savage, barbarian, primitive, backward, big children, etc. This basic conviction showed itself in the many insulting nicknames the colonists liked to use of their charges. The superiority of the colonizer was expressed ostentatiously and supported by a show of power; the effects of this outward display were also psychologically important. On the colonized the effect could only be oppressive. Instead of encouraging them to progress and to energetic effort, especially effort toward development, the colonizer's attitude cast the colonized into an outer darkness of radical and congenital helplessness.

A further conviction was closely bound up with the first: the permanence of the colonial situation. To speak of natural superiority is, of course, already to imply permanence. But the colonizer often said openly and directly that the inequality of position had to be permanent, precisely because it was natural. That, of course, only deepened the sense of oppression created by the original attitude of superiority.

To the first two convictions, yet a third was added, as a sort of inevitable consequence: the refusal of any mingling between the two societies, colonizing and colonized. In particular, there was strong objection to any marriages between the two groups, especially of a woman from the colonizers to a man who was from the colonized.

The refusal to admit any prospect of change in the colonial

situations bought with it a marked contempt for the "educated" native. In such circumstances, the latter was also regarded as particularly dangerous.

All these characteristic attitudes accompanied political domination in the strict sense. Here we must note a further decisive fact: along with the use of force (to which the observer's attention is often drawn), colonization involved the suspension of all political initiative among the colonized. The colonized people had indeed a biological and economic existence of their own. They even had a social life in subordinate communities such as the village, tribe, or district, especially in systems of indirect government such as the British established. But these subordinate communities were themselves protectorates, and the colonized had no full political life, however much independence they may have had in other areas. Strict limits were thus placed on their life as a society. Such a political situation in turn hindered economic development by fostering the lack of creative initiative.

The Effects of Economic Dependence

Political domination was accompanied by economic domination and thus had even more direct effects on the economy of the colonized countries. Doubtless it did not cause underdevelopment, but it certainly perpetuated it. It blunted every stimulus to the effort and initiative which development requires. Further, it unbalanced and upset the existing economic organization, which had no power to withstand such an attack. We find this to be the case in every instance of domination, even when the domination is purely economic.

The exchange economy put the colonized or quasi-colonized people in a dependent position, for they could not discuss as equals the terms of the exchange. They were as defenseless as the workers of other years had been in the face of industrial capitalism. They had to accept the products they needed from the colonizer to whom they had to sell their own products.

At the same time, economic colonization undermined the old economic institutions and structures without truly replacing them. It brought the beginnings of unregulated urbanization, which meant proletarization for large sectors of the population, and it had a ruinous effect on many social processes which were connected with the people's economic life.

Among the structures directly attacked, in addition to the traditional markets, we must mention the village. This was the most characteristic economic unity of the countries we are discussing. As an economic unity the village had always been marked by internal cooperation, some independence of outsiders, and stability despite national ups and downs in the course of time. Empires came and went in China; foreign or native dynasties conquered that immense country one after another. But the majority of villages, it is thought, kept their course despite political changes which, for them, were only ripples on the surface of life. The same is true of India.

Modern urbanization brought a new situation. To begin with, land was often confiscated by the colonists by direct or indirect means. This was the first cause of imbalance in village life. Then the call went out, through persuasion or force, for workers for the plantations, mines, lumber camps, and such important infrastructures as railroad construction. The effect was to rob the village of the men who formed it. In Africa—especially for example, in Gabon or the present Central African Republic (formerly Ubangi-Shari)—the human composition of the village and consequently its economic balance were permanently altered.

Confiscation of land caused areas of overpopulation, even in countries where the overall population was fairly small. Such areas of concentration were rare in the West of Africa but rather numerous in the South and East, for example, in Kenya. Kenya, as a result, was to experience the Mau-Mau (Kikuyu) rebellion, for this was caused by confiscation of land. In countries whose population on the whole was of low density, the colonists managed to create overpopulated areas.

A further effect of modern colonization was the mortal blow to skilled trades and to the embryonic industry which had flourished at times, for example, the textile trades of Asia. The colonial powers preempted the markets for their own products which were lower in price simply because of European-style industrial production.

At times the colonial powers were not content with this natural difference in price. In India, for example, the British government imposed prohibitive duties and taxes on fabrics woven in the country, in order to assure the flow of Lancashire products. A governor of Bengal could therefore write in an 1840 report: "The bones of the weavers are bleaching in the sun around the countryside." The same destruction occurred in China from the pressure of British industry, and in Indonesia from the competition of Dutch industrial products.

Everywhere the monetary and market economy forced the village, formerly a closed economy, to open itself to influences and products from outside. Traditional organizations, which were more concerned to insure subsistence for all members than personal wealth for some, and which were based on mutual cooperation, were thus attacked at their foundations by the simple confrontation of an open and a closed economy.

The most influential economic events were the development of agriculture for a world market, the development of plantations, the assignment of monetary value to land which thus became more easily transferable, and the development of individual ownership. All this brought confusion to an economy organized for subsistence and based on cooperation.

Formerly, too, the village had been homogeneous, within the terms of the caste system where it existed. Now it tended to become heterogeneous and to be composed of differentiated elements. Some villagers, for example those whose land had been confiscated, became proletarians. Meanwhile, a land owning bourgeoisie was being formed, its position based on preferred plantation crops. A cultural differentiation, too, was in the making, as a class of educated natives began to appear. "This transformation of the village," says Balandier, "led to a widespread feeling of insecurity. The villager had formerly felt quite at home in the framework of the old community, but he now felt out of place and, in some degree, threatened. It was precisely in the most deteriorated village communities that compensatory practices such as magic developed most strongly."[89]

A similar observation comes from a Ceylonese sociologist: "The village, which had been the foundation of the country's economic and cultural organization, was exposed to the destructive power of industrial technology. It ceased to be self-sufficient and found itself inextricably bound up with the city, the nation, and the outside world. Local industries now slowed down . . . . The peasant's attachment to his land and the artisan's to his trade had formerly engendered a feeling of social solidarity, an esprit de corps; the disturbance of the social balance meant the disappearance of that orderliness. The people experienced instability and frequent displacements." Again, the crucial term, "instability."

While the village was deteriorating, those even more important ancient centers of power and activity were being destroyed, which used to exist at least in some civilizations. The modern cities, sometimes created out of whole cloth, quickly left the traditional cities behind in many places. This happened, for example, in China where modern cities on the coast have imposed their presence, as it were, on the country as a whole. But the same thing happened elsewhere too. It was almost always the coastal areas that took priority, whereas the traditional centers were in the interior: for example, in Latin America (especially in Brazil) and in Africa.

G. Le Coeur provides a typical example from Morocco.[90] Azemnour, on the banks of the Oumer Rebia, inland from the Atlantic coast, was a small but powerful community since before the fourteenth century (according to Ibn-Khaldun). It decayed rapidly after 1926. The reasons were the restructuring of the Moroccan economy as a whole; the disappearance of the artisan class, due to the rapid increase in imported manufactures; and the impoverishment of the traditional agricultural economy due to competition from vast modern farms controlled chiefly by Europeans. From 1919 to 1936 the population of Azemnour fell from 12,700 to 7,700. A parallel result was a disquieting growth in traditional bourgeois conservatism, simply because the young and active people had left the city.

Economic dependence caused the downfall of the village but did not replace it straightway with inviting and humane cities which would allow men to work, to earn a living, to have a social life, and to share in a culture. On the contrary, while devitalizing the old centers of power and authority, an exchange economy led to the growth of new cities, chiefly ports, which were foreign creations. "White creations soon peopled by blacks," said J. Dresch. These are the great Third World cities of which we spoke earlier.

Thus we are confronted with many oppressive forces that destroy initiative and close the avenues of hope, and with direct attacks on the traditional system of production, which is vanishing without any attractive and satisfying alternative to replace it.

The Burden of Colonization: Second-stage Effects

Most developing countries show the mark of all the forces and influences we have described. They bear a heavy, and especially a heavy psychological, burden. We cannot, indeed, find in these influences the whole explanation of underdevelopment, although the contemporary life of former colonies still shows many psychological traits developed in colonial times. But underdevelopment was at least confirmed and reinforced by such influences.

Granting their importance, however, we must not therefore fail to see the other aspects of colonialism, what we might call its second-stage effects. For colonization, by the very violence it involved, was often the occasion for a first awakening of what today is the desire for development. In other words, colonization caused social breakdown, but the latter in turn led to the desire for growth. Without such a desire, we would not yet have the problems either of underdevelopment or of development. A comparison between colonized and noncolonized countries (though the latter are few in the present-day Third World) shows a sharp contrast in desire for development. In the first phase of colonization, the oppressive effects were the ones most strongly and almost exclusively felt. But in a second phase, reactions to the colonial situation became more frequent and carried a promise of dynamic social initiatives.

Political colonization thus evoked strong resistance to the colonizer's attitude of superiority—psychological reactions, but also dynamic social reactions. Both converged in the spirit of nationalism and the desire for independence. The colonial experience, in brief, set the history of the colonized countries in motion again. The same experience led to the desire for development, which often came as a second stage in the desire for independence.

Colonization was thus a factor, if not in social reconstruction (the term is too strong, for it supposes that some balance has been reached, and this is far from true), then at least in social questioning, such as would one day pave the way for one or other form of development.

The same ambivalence is evident in the effects of purely economic colonization. That kind of colonization undermined, damaged, and destroyed whole sections of the traditional economy and civilization and made no attempt to rebuild them. It worsened the underdevelopment of an unemployed subproletariat by destroying the only economic framework that had hitherto been effective, the village. But at the same time the shock to the old society could also stir the desire for development.

The colonizer, let us repeat, did little to restructure or rebuild. This is his great historical failure. We can without injustice hold him responsible for consolidating and maintaining a state of stagnation, even where the old economy, grown ever more lifeless, was covered over with a new modern economy and especially with its infrastructure of social services, etc. For these services remained alien to the real situation of the people. In a second phase, however, the colonial experience by the very act of undermining old structures and mentalities prepared the way for initiatives which we now see. Thus neither the serious deficiencies of underdeveloped countries with their imbalance and confusion nor the current effort at development, of which we still have to speak, can be explained except in the perspective of political and economic colonial history.

NEW

SOCIAL

STRATIFICATION

Let us pause for a moment to summarize our description of the underdeveloped societies and their present state.

Too often, as we noted earlier, people speak of the underdeveloped world as if it were nothing but an economically impoverished world. Our aim has been to bring to light, first of all, societies that are different from ours, and, secondly, societies that have been disturbed and shaken to their roots.

The disturbance or imbalance which we have described is unusually deep-going, because the old system had an all-embracing and homogeneous character, while a new and foreign system presents itself to a people at first only in bits and pieces. We recall how under the old regime people were almost completely fixed, socially, by their position in the kinship system. For this decided their economic situation, their place relative to other groups of men, and their relation as foreigner or friend to this or that individual. It also decided their marriage and conjugal status. Under the new regime, however, some types of social bonds would be determined by belonging to a business or being on the same wage scale, others by one's neighborhood in the city, still others by common interest in one kind of recreation, etc. It is not just that new social bonds tend to spring up, but that the very foundation of social relationships in general is changing. The decisive factor is no longer "nature" or blood. It is the limitless free play of human decisions. No more brutal uprooting than this can be inflicted on a man. Yet for millions, even hundreds of millions, of men this uprooting is a present reality, and the experience is traumatic for them.

But to describe how society in the developing countries has been assaulted is not to tell the whole truth. For, "summons to development" is not just a catchword. New aspirations have indeed made their appearance, and we have already alluded to them when speaking of the unstabilizing effect of colonization. Once aspirations were aroused, policies were then planned and set in motion. The state, in particular, is now a reality. We spoke of this earlier in describing the political characteristics of the developing countries, and we shall shortly be returning to the point.

On the other hand, in the past there were many social inequalities, sometimes very notable ones. In South America, for example, there were, on the one hand, the owners of large estates, and, on the other, the farmers, the renters, the peons, and the small holders with wretched incomes made even more inadequate by usurious moneylenders. We could say that there were even social classes, but not conscious social classes as long as social divisions were grounded in the traditional norms of a feudal or semi-feudal system. But we do have to speak of conscious social classes, once modern economy makes its appearance. Let us look now at this change.

Development of Social Stratification in South America

For a development most like the one that took place formerly in Europe we must look to Latin America, or at least to those countries there which are economically the most advanced. Society was once divided into two extremes: landed proprietors and serfs or quasi serfs, after the fashion of aristocratic colonial society (which was an overseas version of European feudal society). Commercial industrialism, however, quickly changed the social picture, for it brought the new industrial managerial classes and, correlatively, the proletariat.

Brazil is a good example of such a change. The country was long dominated by the landed aristocracy of ranch owners. Then, especially arter 1930, their primacy was challenged by a middle class of industrialists and businessmen. The interests of these two groups were often far from identical. In fact, the archaic condition of rural Brazil was an obstacle to the formation of that domestic market so necessary for industrial development. The landowners' interests coincided well enough with those of the commercial exporters but much less well with those of the industrialists. Landed proprietors and exporters both wanted extensive agriculture and the opening up of foreign markets, but these were not what attracted industry in its early days. On the other hand, the managerial classes, including the industrialists, were reconciled with the landowners, when they were faced with an industrial proletariat and the urban lower middle classes, for against these both felt the need of protecting themselves.

The birth of the Brazilian proletariat begins with the emancipation of slaves in 1888 and with the resultant swelling of the labor force. Later on, there were migrations from the countryside. Even today, the Brazilian proletariat is marked by heterogeneity due to the diverse origins of those who make it up. The result is great difficulty in creating a unified outlook and a common action. The members of the proletariat follow very varied leaders, often pseudo-leaders whose concerns are chiefly political. Such a situation has favored the growth of populist movements, typical of which was Vargas' Getulism.

Such a division of society into new oligarchies (landowners, businessmen, and industrialists) and a growing proletariat does not wholly correspond to the European experience in the nineteenth century. Nor, in fact, does it describe the whole social reality of contemporary Brazil. Observers lament the absence of a middle class. In fact, middle classes are developing, but of a special kind, with no analogy in the Europe of the industrial revolution but similar to those growing up today in most developing countries. The middle classes of France, England, Holland, or Belgium were basically small proprietors, artisans, tradesmen, and farmers. There is nothing like this in Brazil thus far. If there are any incipient middle classes, these are due to the bureaucracy and consist of civil servants and those civil service intermediaries so typical of Brazil. Such middle classes are comparable to those of ancient China or ancient Russia or nineteenth-century Germany. They are, in addition, unstable middle classes, because their income is constantly reduced by inflation.

Even in Latin America, then, we must be careful not to speak of classes according to over-rigid definitions and, above all, to avoid overdrawn comparisons with nineteenth-century Europe. The upsetting of the earlier social stratification has nonetheless been very radical. Especially have relations between members of different categories changed their character. Formerly, all relations were personal and still of a feudal kind; this was the all-inclusive framework. "In the traditional scheme of productive enterprise the plantation carried out its functions by means of personal relations. The employer was not only an employer but also a protector. Workers expected of him not only a salary but relief in need, medicine in illness, protection and help in all circumstances. In return, the employer could rightly expect the employee not only to do the work he was contracted to but to give the employer a personal allegiance as well, to vote as he wanted in elections, to fight for him in danger and conflict, and to show loyal submission in all circumstances. In the internal logic of such a system, employer-employee relations went far beyond the limits of the usual work relationship."[91] All this is being rapidly changed. Nothing has directly replaced the patriarchal or paternalist system in doing what it did. State intervention is far from filling the void. Workers therefore seek out other paternalist protectors and give allegiance to such men through unions and political groupings of a "personalist" kind. Such a situation is typical of the early days of industrialism, but it is complicated by the emergence of middle classes with bureaucratic origins. The Latin American countries can be classified today according to how much the old structure still stands or has deteriorated, that is, how much development there has been toward a more modern structure such as we have seen making its hesitating appearance in Brazil. The pattern is disturbed in several countries, however, by persisting racial distinctions, as, for example, wherever large Indian populations are found.

Development of social stratification is strongest in two countries with heavy European immigration and insignificant numbers of Indians: Argentina and Uruguay, which have also long had the strongest elements of economic development. There two countries have a very high level of urbanization: Buenos Aires and Montevideo each hold 30 percent of the total population of their countries. Above all, there has been a significant development in the distribution of the active population: 21 percent are farmers in Uruguay, 24 percent in Argentina. Transition from the primary to the secondary and especially to the tertiary sectors of the economy has been very rapid. The tertiary sector, which includes a large number of people belonging to the middle classes or strata, is even swollen to a degree hard to believe: up to 45.5 percent in Argentina. "This is not due, as in backward countries, to a proliferation of domestic servants, but to the increase, by deliberate social policy, of jobs in civil service, nationalized businesses, and all services."[92]

Chile is a similar but specialized case. Here 29.8 percent of the active population are farmers; there is an exaggerated concentration of city people in the tertiary sector, a large middle class, and an organized proletariat. But the rural aristocracy remains important and dominant in some rural areas where the archaic social structures of the feudal estate still exist.

At the other end of the spectrum we find that in some countries the archaic, feudal, patriarchal structure has been but little weakened. This is true of Peru, Ecuador, Bolivia, Guatemala, Salvador, Honduras, Nicaragua, Haiti, and Dominican Republic. These are all little countries and all of them, except Peru, Bolivia, and Ecuador, are in Central America. In all these countries, too, the Indians are a majority (or the Africans in Haiti). The more developed sectors of society are everywhere very localized, and the middle classes are only beginning to form in the cities. Only an embryonic urban proletariat exists. For the rest, the social regime of the large estate continues to be in the ascendant. Between urban society and rural masses relationships exist very like those of colonial times.

Between these two groups of countries there is a third. It consists of the important countries where economic progress is more rapid today and all the characteristics of transitional social structure and stratification are in evidence: Brazil, Mexico, Colombia, and Venezuela. The chief trait they have in common is the same relative numerical balance between two parts of the population, the one structured according to the norms of developed societies, the other according to the norms of archaic society. There are two Brazils, as was recently said, for in the bloc of Southern states social stratification is becoming more and more like that of an industrial society.

Birth of Social Classes in Africa

Leopold Senghor said in 1954 that in Africa there are no "classes in the strict sense. There are no social distinctions based on wealth. But there were and are castes, which have a religious basis. What needs to be done away with, then, are not as yet nonexistent classes, but the inferiority of the overseas territories (that is, of the natives), an inequality, due not to class distinctions but to the coexistence of parent-states and dependent countries."[93]

In some areas of Africa, where a more or less feudal system exists (as in some kingdoms like Burundi or, at one time, Rwanda), a situation was to be found like that of the old regions of Latin America: stratification and opposition between landed or feudal proprietors and peasants. But for Africa as a whole Senghor's judgment could, at the time, be shared by most sociologists who had studied the problem in its native setting.

Now and then, indeed, a sociologist like Jean Dresch could try to find evidence of a class system in "the antagonism of an uprooted peasant class and a developing proletariat, both of which might well have a class consciousness like that of proletariats abroad." But the prior question, as Jean-Claude Pauvert noted, "is how differentiated is the domestic proletariat, within society as a whole, as a suprafunctional group such as 'the peasant class' or 'the elite.' "[94]

Pauvert went on to criticize Dresch's Marxist position from

a Marxist viewpoint: "In fact, in the Marxist perspective, class differences within dependent countries are not a primary fact; the only decisive thing in transitional periods is the opposition between dependent countries and capitalist countries."[95]

Numerous reasons were offered, in the period when Senghor wrote, for not speaking of genuine social classes. First of all, "residence in an urban center is not enough to make a man a proletarian. Large numbers of young men come to work in the city for a while and then return to their villages and take their place within the custom-grounded structures. Such mobility and the absence of professional qualifications in the majority of workers prevent the growth of corporate bonds of solidarity, except for workers in specialized administrations (post and telegraph, for example) or in public services (transportation, for example)."[96]

In addition, the marks we regard as typical of a modern social category are often deceptive in Africa. Increased income? But this is often only a means to prestige within a traditional culture. Often a man may work for years to support his family group and then, when he has earned enough, may return to economic ways characteristic of pre-industrial society in which life style and prestige do not depend on money.[97] Such a man remains oriented to the traditional social system, which may sanction ethnical differences and even caste differences (for some kinds of work). "Within society as a whole," Pauvert concluded, "because of the coexistence of two economic systems, it is difficult to determine what goupings are based on socio-economic status."[98]

Even when the break with the traditional world has taken place, we can still be deceived in interpreting the categories we think we see operating. The people we put in such categories do not necessarily have an awareness of distinct goals and ideals. On the contrary, people in different categories often have the same ideal, for example, to raise their standard of living, an ideal "of which society as a whole is the source."[99] We tend to imagine distinct groups where there are only distinct ways of adapting to society as a whole through individual and collective roles. This is true, for example, of the "elites" and of mutual loan societies; these are "ways of sharing in colonized society."[100] There was thus a process going on of continuous ascent along the lines pursued by a whole society as it was being formed.

Paul Mercier reached similar conclusions from inquiries conducted around 1950. We may, in his view, observe various categories which are distinguishable according to criteria other than the traditional ones of membership in ethnical or religious groups. The appearance is given of socio-economic groupings. But, he adds, "Rarely are sharp discontinuities noticeable among them . . . . At first sight they are distributed, though in different ways depending on the criteria used (family structure, role of groups based on new structures, ways of life, recreations, etc.), along a line between the two poles of traditionalism and Westernization. But we cannot deduce the real existence of two groups defined by such factors. Socio-professional categories interpenetrate much more fully than the criteria allow, and social mobility remains high among people who for the most part have been only recently urbanized."[101]

"Yet we do already notice some crystallization," Mercier adds. "At the laborer level, for example, 60 percent of those whose fathers were laborers are themselves laborers. And at the level of white-collar workers, civil servants, teachers, doctors, etc., 75 percent of those whose fathers were in these categories have stayed there themselves. But we need see in these statistics no more than an expression of the urbanization process in a society which is only approaching the limits of development."[102]

To test his conclusions, Mercier polled Africans on the significance they see in such divisions into distinct categories. He tried to measure degrees of antagonism between people in the various categories. His conclusion was a guarded one. There is certainly a hierarchy of social positions, an order of ascending prestige up to the white-collar worker or civil servant. However, "among the African population the feeling of division or opposition between two or more groups is experienced clearly only in some extreme cases, as for example when the division coincides with ethnic divisions. It is less marked in other cases and varies in strength according to the phases of colonial history, diminishing to the vanishing point in time of serious crisis." On the other hand, "the traditional world, though being destroyed, still leaves many vestiges in West Africa. Its values may regain enough vitality at certain moments for fixed social positions and even broad social groupings, which have grown up outside its sphere of influence, to be temporarily suspended."[103]

Of the two phenomena, perdurance of traditional society and colonialism, the second was undoubtedly the more important in hindering the development of social classes in the strict sense. The decisive social fact was "the division of colonial society along racial lines, whether or not this was acknowledged and confirmed by a system of segregation."[104] In times of great crises, "this division came to the fore and tended to override internal dissensions within the two segments of the population." Outside such moments of crisis, "the assertion of rights by African and European workers in the professional area are separate, if not actually opposed (because of continuing differences in position and salary, the Europeans find themselves on the conservative and defensive sides . . . .Labor claims and strikes are never carried out in common)."[105] The conclusion: "The division between Africans and Europeans dominates the social scene too strongly for a diversified system of classes to form. Cultural heterogeneity continues to be the basic datum."[106]

An evolution began only with the end of colonial dependence, as men's minds were no longer focused on the colonizer-colonized distinction and became more aware of other influences on social distribution. These other factors have, in addition, been accentuated here and there by rapid economic changes.

If, then, in 1954 Paul Mercier would speak only of "social classes in germ," in 1961 Jacques Binet could, on the contrary, speak of "the birth of social classes in black Africa."[107] He had to admit that the symbiosis between city and country had not entirely disappeared. But the outlines of a new social stratification were appearing alongside the old system, within which there was little professional specialization apart from some tasks reserved to castes (blacksmiths, for example). In the past, he noted, "traditional societies were rather unfavorable to the formation of stable social classes. Power in such societies is in the hands of the elders, but they do not form a distinct class amid the mass of peasants. The existence of castes and of captives, however, had the potentiality to engender a rigid social structure . . . . Until now, there have been no social classes, but we can foresee their birth. Some groups show themselves powerful and prestigious; they are becoming conscious of their power and aware of themselves as a group."[108]

Binet then describes the same professional categories and the same hierarchy of positions as Mercier was describing some years before: laborers, businessmen, and civil servants (including almost all the liberal professions, since "most doctors are appointed by the government, while notary and bailiff functions are handled by civil servants of the judiciary").[109] These various groups, he notes, are marked off by their style and standard of living, as well as by their degree of Western-syle intellectual culture (in the cities of South Cameroon less than 1 percent of the laborers had a school certificate as against 22 percent of the civil servants). The most noteworthy fact is that these social groups have a growing tendency to become fixed. "The laborers have come to the city only recently and seek to change their status as soon as possible. But the rather advanced age of a good number of these people shows that it will not be easy to change."[110] "In 1958," says Binet, "25 percent of the civil servants in various centers of Guinea were sons of civil servants, and 20 percent of their brothers worked in the public services. The business class showed a similar exclusiveness: 30 percent of their brothers and 45 percent of their friends are also in business. The element of heredity is less strong here, however, since only 10 percent are the sons of businessmen. Marriages confirm the impression that classes are being formed. A study of the secondary school population shows it too: the sons of civil servants alone form one-fourth of the students at Konakry."[111]

What hastens the development of social stratification more than anything else is the post independence development of the politician and civil servant class. Its numbers have greatly increased and its power has grown enormously. The business of administration, in particular, has given birth to a whole middle-class style, alongside that of the new managerial class. There is a parallel here to what happened earlier in Latin America. The political role of this middle class may become quite important. "The civil servants," says Yves Lacoste, "are joined by the middle-management people in the business houses and the industries and by a part of the liberal professions. Although not very numerous as yet, these middle classes turn some quarters of the large cities into a milieu somewhat like what is found in the cities of some developed countries. It is in these intermediate social groups, in large measure, that the demand for a more just and less corrupt politics and for effort toward economic and social development is most audibly heard."[112]

Such sentiments admittedly go hand in hand with a great deal of indifference toward the most wretched citizens, those unable to organize behind their demands. The dislocation of traditional structures has created, beneath the middle classes, a proletarian or rather subproletarian stratum. "In Western Europe, the landless peasant and the ruined artisan, through a painful conversion, became 'proletarians,' who can live only by selling their ability to work. Proletarianization, which all agree in deploring, appears in the underdeveloped countries as, in fact, a happy and rare solution. For most of the people whose traditional structures have disappeared, are not able to find steady jobs. They cannot enter the proletariat, because the latter is such a small group in an underdeveloped economy where industry is quite limited. The proletariat in developed countries is victim of the exploitation described by Marx, but at least it can sell its ability to work, except in times of temporary crisis. In the underdeveloped countries, men who have lost almost all means of subsistence cannot even do that, for there is nowhere for them to be hired. A process of proletarianization has begun but is not yet complete. These people then constitute what might be called a subproletariat."[113] We are faced here with populations which are losing their own culture, and therefore have little ability to adopt conscious class goals. This is generally characteristic of the Third World.

We can thus still speak of the absence, in Africa at least, of social classes in the full and exact sense of the word. But classes in the sense which Senghor gave that term when he affirmed the absence of classes in the old villages of Africa are another matter. Senghor's statements are still valid for the countrysides which have not been touched by plantation economy, but they are no longer true of the cities and the sectors of modern economy.

We do not yet have the bourgeoisie-proletariat dichotomy of an older Europe, nor a threeway division into bourgeoisie, middle class, and proletariat. There is no genuine bourgeoisie; whatever "bourgeoisie" may exist is more political than industrial. There is no genuine proletariat, but rather a subproletariat. There is no genuine middle class, but rather strata of administrative personnel who are clients and protégés. The situation is therefore one of heterogeneous social stratification, in which tensions appear without being integrated as yet into a modern class system. But we must remember that it is an evolving situation.

The mass of Africans, we must remember, have remained peasants. Peasants do not constitute another class, but live in another world with its own, largely traditional, reference systems. They do not form one layer in a stratification, but a whole world which still exists largely for itself or coexists with that other world in which the social processes we have been describing are unfolding.

TRADE UNIONS
AND OTHER
NEW ASSOCIATIONS

The introduction of a broad market economy, industrialization, the modification of economic and social activities, and their progressive diversification and ordering give the impetus to change in social stratification. But they also stimulate the growth of new associations, quite different from the traditional groupings based on those kinship bonds which satisfied almost all social needs. Consequently we can observe a shift from natural, involuntary communities to voluntary associations. These arise more and more frequently among persons who do not belong to the same natural groups (familial or ethnic). Instead, profession or economic activity is the decisive factor, or else the cultural level a person belongs on within a modern-style culture.

New Associations

The first characteristic of the new associative life, in comparison with the older system, is its diversity. We find a large number of groups, different from each other in composition and in purpose.

First of all, there are obviously the ethnic or tribal associations to which we have already referred in dealing with the evolution of the kinship system into neo-brotherhoods. These new associations are not necessarily based on a common ethnic origin in the strict sense, but there is at least a common geographic or regional origin (associations of natives of the same place). Their formation is simple enough. Men migrating to the cities belonged at home to a compact system of kinship and neighborhood and were used to relationships of a personal kind. Since they have as yet experienced no other kind of communal life, they try to recapture it in their new, usually urban milieu.[114] It is the best means they have of adapting to the new environment.

Thus we find at times not a lessening but an intensification of tribal awareness. The Zabramas (speaking the Zerba dialect) showed a "supertribalism" after they moved from Niger to Ghana; they isolated themselves from the surrounding people in the city. The Ibos from the Nigerian North and West did the same thing for a long time to protect themselves against the hostility of their new neighbors; they set up "families," to use their own expression.

The number of tribal associations is now very large. Accra alone had niney-four in 1956. And the number of members in an association is often high too; one of the associations at Accra had two thousand members at that period.

Such associations of tribesmen or fellow-countrymen gather men together on the basis of their ethnic relationship, but they no longer belong completely to the traditional world, for their purpose is adaptation to the new demands of city life and of a modern economy. Or the purpose may be to promote the progress of the whole tribe, its city members and those back in the villages. Many associations in the English-speaking countries are thus improvement societies or progressive societies for this or that ethnic group. The same purpose marks the all-tribal federations, the first of which, a very influential group, was that of the Ibibio in Nigeria (1928); Nigeria also saw the multiplication of "state unions," federations of people belonging to the same state or province.

Tribal associations give economic and professional help to their urban members. They contribute to their education (by establishing schools, even back in the home areas, or by sending students

abroad) and to the betterment of the economic and social infrastructure in the native regions (by building bridges, etc.). Some
tribal associations have gotten into banking, in order to finance
development.

Another basis for association is religion. Such groups represent
something genuinely new because they transcend tribal or ethnic
frontiers. Some such associations are based in syncretist cults
(Atike and Tigari in Southern and Eastern Ghana, Harrism or
the cult of Deima in Southern Ivory Coast); the latter are much
like Haitian voodooism or Afro-Brazilian cults such as macumba.
The syncretist cult groups often center around healers; a ritual
communion provides assurance of protection against one or other
disease or against certain worries and cares. In some instances
the syncretist cults have developed into national political messian-
ist movements, as for example Kimbanguism (named after Simon
Kimbangu, whom the Belgian government deported in 1921 and
who was supposed to have returned to his people as an African
savior).

On the fringe of Christianity numerous African churches have
emerged, with their prophets and leaders. These are revivalist
sects of the kind familiar to English and American Protestantism.

A very large number of other associations are purely and simply
mutual aid societies, paying no attention to ethnic, tribal, or
religious distinctions. At Accra in 1954, to cite but one example,
such mutual aid societies had 26,193 members. The societies
result from the disappearance of the traditional forms of familial
and social security and are substitutes for them. Usually they
begin by providing money needed for weddings and funerals.
Little by little, they become agents for credit and loan, chiefly
in the form of tontines. At each meeting every member makes
a payment; each member in turn receives all the payments made
at one meeting, which gives him capital for some business activity;
meanwhile, he continues to contribute for the benefit of members
who have not yet been helped by the tontine.

A famous association of this type is the Nanamei Akpee (society
of friends), which, a few years back, had numerous chapters
in the cities of Ghana and enjoyed powerful protectors. "The
key is love" was its motto and a password to open the doors

of the brotherhood. This particular society, according to Kenneth Little, provided a number of social security benefits; for example, it gave each child a guinea at birth, for it saw the child as a potential member of the society. It gave gifts and toys for the ceremony of "outdooring," a week after birth. There were also benefits for illness and for the family of a dead member (ten pounds sterling, with each member contributing one shilling). It loaned the furniture and other trappings of a wake, a guinea for the expense of the service, and twelve members to attend it, console the relatives, and serve the bread and tea. The society likewise came to the aid of a member who had been robbed or suffered other financial setbacks. It even loaned 500 pounds without interest to a member who was threatened with jail for embezzlement from a business firm!

The society's funds were derived from a membership fee of five shillings and monthly dues of three pence; in need, special dues were requested, the amount per person being set after discussion at a general meeting. Charity balls and sales were another source of income.

But all this was not the most important role of the Nanamei Akpee, most of whose members were market women. Its primary purpose was to allow its members credit and savings through a tontine. In this all the women present gave what they could, and contributions were entered in individual passbooks. There was a list of members by seniority; the money collected at a meeting went to the person whose name headed the list, and the following week it was the next person's turn. The beneficiary also received a record of each member's contribution to her purse, and had to contribute to all the other members in turn the same sum she had received from each of them. Thus, each member would have a good idea of what she would receive when her turn came. In one chapter at Kumasi, the weekly total was about seventy pounds from the 300 members present.

Under various titles, such a system for providing capital is known in every area of Africa. It is *esesu* among the Yoruba (Guinea), *asasu* at Freetown (Sierra Leone), *susu* at Kumasi (Ghana), *adaski* among the Hausa of Northern Nigeria, *djana* among the Fang of Southern Cameroon, *ndjonu* in Dahomey, *bandoi* at Kinshasa, *tontine* at Porto Novo (Dahomey) and more generally in French-speaking Africa.

Other associations are recreational, especially the drumming companies and dance groups. On the other hand, there are some specifically modern associations. Such, for example, are the various Christian associations which have issued more or less directly from the missions and which look to the social and moral improvement of the members. Another example would be the many cultural associations of former students, such as the Association of Educated People at Kisangani (AES, studied by P. Clément), or the Old Bo Boys Association (OBBA) in Sierra Leone, connected with the Bo School, or the Association of Former Students of the Terrason de Fougères School at Bamako (Mali), or the Old Achimota Association in Ghana. In addition there are the private clubs.

Some associations are quite well known; many more are quite modest and not even registered. Concerning associations of regional natives, Jean-Claude Pauvert could write: "All these associations try to reinforce an organic solidarity based on custom or to make up for it when the pressures of society at large have undermined it. They usually cut across the socio-economic or socio-professional levels, and are instruments of division to the extent that to restore the balance of their members, they appeal to bonds of custom-based affinity."[116] On the whole, however, the associations are means of integrating peoples by stages into a new, still unknown, and developing society.

They welcome the newcomer, tell him what is going on in the city, give him practical help, and accustom him to urban life by obliging him to the regulations of the association (for example, making him pay fines if late for a meeting, in order to teach him punctuality). They encourage saving and thrift. They put a man in contact with people of different ethnic origin and, by assigning him a job to be done in common, teach him cooperation with "strangers."

The syncretist cults, for their part, try to handle the anxieties of the new city dweller. They also provide magistrates and arbiters for conflicts and help introduce order into a society threatened by anomie. Some impose high social and moral standards and thus contribute to the improvement of the whole community. Kenneth Little writes of them: "In taking the place of the clan and other traditional kinship associations, the voluntary associations have a wider function than the services rendered to their members. They help create new social norms for society as a whole."[117] This is true of family life, child education, and economic affairs. "The voluntary association is a means of adapting to new relationships, for it makes role specialization easier."[118] The associations take men accustomed to a unified all-embracing social structure and help them adapt to a world in which family, profession, politics, culture, recreation, and religion are all distinct and separate realities.

The Trade Unions

The unions are a particular instance of the new associations to be found in societies as they first enter into a modern economy. Like many other associations, the unions help integrate men into a new society. Along with unions in the strict sense there are many associations of the guild or corporation type, which bring together professionals, often artisans, for the purpose of organizing the profession, limiting competition, setting current prices, apprenticing young people, and defending the profession against attack.

In several countries, it is true, the unions initially have the appearance of an organization imported from outside. In South America the unions were established by immigrant workers from Europe. In Africa (British, French, and Belgian), India, Malaysia, and Vietnam, the unions were started by the unions of the parent country in colonial times. The unions in the colonies long kept their links with such parent organizations (the General Federation of Workers and the Federation of French Christian Workers for France; the General Federation of Belgian Workers and the Federation of Christian Workers for Belgium; the Trade Union Congress for Great Britain). But difficulties soon plagued these relationships, for differences arose concerning not only the connections between local unions and national political movements but also the unions' methods and goals. As a result, Indian, African, and Latin American trade unionism very early showed a great deal of originality, as the unions gradually took root in a new and developing society and played an essential part in it.

We shall try to summarize here the origin and history of Third World trade unions and then to describe their general characteristics.

In Latin America trade unionism began in the last years of the nineteenth century under the influence of European immigrants. In Argentina the first solidly organized union was that of the printers at Buenos Aires in 1878; unions began at the same period in Chile and Uruguay. These early trade unions met hostility from the government, for there was a double strain of unionism: anarchist and socialist. These unions were not meant for the masses but found their recruits in the specialized trades (printers and public service employees). Though the textile industry was already in existence, it developed no unions at this stage.

In the rest of the continent unions arose only later on, in the decade from 1920 to 1930; for example, the Brazilian General Federation of Workers (CGT) and a Colombian union on the United Fruit plantations (1928). The first Venezuelan union appeared only after the overthrow of Gómez, the dictator, in 1936.

These newer unions have a wider and less educated clientele. But they too are weak, connected with political movements, and divided. The Brazilian CGT for example drew its inspiration from the revolt of the "Lieutenants" in 1926 and remained attached to one of its leaders, Prestes, following him when he turned to Communism. Between the two world wars the division was usually between orthodox Communists and dissident national Marxists, as in Brazil, Venezuela, Ecuador, Bolivia, and Colombia. These unions are more concerned with revolution than with professional activity, and, all things considered, they reach only a small part of the working force.

Later progress, however, has been considerable. The organizations have extended their scope. Too often, however, they have grown only because they were made obligatory by governments which control their existence. The most striking example of this was Peronist unionism. Thus, "the unions became a very important political force, perhaps the most important, but they have not become an independent influence. Even more than a means of pressure by the working proletariat on employees and government, they tend to be a means of manipulation of the proletariat by the government or by a party which has been in power but is now the opposition."[119] The situation was fairly similar in Brazil under Vargas.

In Mexico things are rather different. Unionism there owes its existence to a government decision to use the unions for its own service. The Regional Federation of Mexican Workers (CRTM) of Luis Morones has in effect been an official branch of the government since 1920. "Morones could call on the police and the army to force businesses to accept his orders." The CRTM had 1,200,000 members at the end of President Obregon's period in office (1924). Under Calles in 1927 the membership rose to 2,500,000 (the government was still one deriving from the popular socialist revolution that had begun in 1910). The union's power was to diminish later on when Calles withdrew his support from Morones. A new Federation (CTM) was formed in 1936 under Lombardo Toledano, and it too found presidential support (from Cardenas) but of a more limited kind.

Latin American unionism has grown with industrialization and with the rapid growth of the labor force. In Brazil, for example, between 1940 and 1950, while the total population increased by 26 percent, the number of workers increased by 60 percent. But workers still make up a fairly small part of the population in most countries of the continent. The greatest part of those who work in the secondary and tertiary sectors of the economy are in "tiny businesses which do not allow concentrations of workmen such as are needed for the growth of class solidarity."[120]

There is, however, a real concentration today in some industrial areas: in Brazil around São Paulo and Rio, in Argentina around Buenos Aires, and in Mexico around Mexico City and Monterrey. In Chile and Bolivia there is a notable concentration in the great mining industries (copper and tin). In all these cases the trade unions now have a disproportionate importance, all the greater since the scattered rural masses remain unorganized.

In Africa, trade unions arose through the efforts of union headquarters in the parent countries to plant their organization overseas, and through progressive grants of freedom to the unions by the parent country's administration.

In French dependencies the first union seems to have been Mohammed Ali's General Federation of Tunisian Workers (CGTT) in 1924, founded against the opposition of Jouhaux, secretary-general of the French CGT. The reaction of the protectorate's authorities brought about its dissolution, but in 1932 the right to organize was given to Tunisian and Algerian workers. In Morocco, however, a law of June 1938 established a "crime of unionism," namely, the act for Moroccans of joining a union and for Europeans of admitting them; only in 1955 were Moroccan unions allowed to develop freely.

Earlier, in 1937, the Popular Front government had allowed the formation of unions in West Africa; the extension of the permission to Equatorial Africa dates from 1944. But legal status as such comes only from the Overseas Labor Code (December 15, 1952).

In the Belgian Congo authorization came first in 1946, but it carried many restrictions. The first union, the Union of Native Congolese Specialized Workers (STICS), admitted only workers who understood French. The broadening of freedom dates from January 25, 1957, and with it the development of Congolese unionism begins. In all these French and Belgian countries the Second World War did much to stimulate the rise and development of unions.

In countries of the British sphere, a circular of Colonial Secretary Sidney Webb to the colonial governors authorized trade unions at the beginning of 1930, but real progress has been observable only since the Second World War, thanks to organizational efforts by the TUC.

In this preindependence context, unions developed in most African countries until they numbered 3.5 million members by 1960. This total was distributed as follows: Morroco, 30 percent; Union of South Africa, 12 percent; Algeria, 10 percent; Egypt, 5 percent; Tunisia, 7 percent; Nigeria, 6 percent; Ghana, 4.5 percent; former French West Africa, 3 percent, with the largest numbers in Senegal, Guinea, and Sudan.

The numbers had continued to be low in the countries of black Africa. Here and there a rise began with independence. But often the increase was effected by a government which tended to impose a single union or to federate all existing unions with the single party. Unionism in these circumstances loses much of its character of voluntary association, and while it does not cease to help integrate men into a new society, it is more closely connected with politics, which have been so decisive since independence.

For the moment, the important thing here is to note the general characteristics of trade unionism as it has developed, more or less spontaneously and freely, in the Third World; we wish to prescind, in this estimate, from governmental ascendancy over the form of the unions, whether in black Africa or in Latin America. The unions of the Third World are, in general, like the European institutions of the same name, but they differ in some important ways which must be stressed.

A first characteristic is that the degree of foreign influence in the constitution of the unions has led observers at times to suspect their authenticity. In this view the unions would not be the result of economic changes as such, but purely artificial creations. Against such a view of African unionism, Jean Meynaud and Anisse Salah Bey react as follows, and with good reason: "In Africa as elsewhere the condition of the working class (in the broad sense of this last term) is the basic stimulus for forming unions. The equating of unionism with industry (mining and manufacturing) is not entirely accurate, but it does sharply define the areas into which unionism has the greatest chance of penetrating. Here, at least in appearance, we have the classic situation of workers organizing against exploitation, whether the unions arise out of individual initiatives or governmental action. Where a modern economy has not yet come on the scene, the union is almost wholly absent; where a union is established for non-economic reasons, it runs the risk of artificiality or subordination to other forces."[121]

All this is no less true because we are dealing with countries which still have relatively few salaried industrial workers in the full sense. In such countries a large part of the work force is unstable, being made up of many who have not really settled down in the cities but return rather frequently, at times for good, to the villages, to be replaced by others no more stable than their predecessors. "The industrial work force is often made up of migrant workers, intermittently absentee, temporary, of peasant origin."[122] The union members are not only few; they are much fewer than the total number of wage earners, and their numbers often fluctuate.

There are other reasons for the weakness of the unions in the developing countries. For example, there is no tradition of workers' associations and trade organizations. There is nothing comparable to the role played in the formation of European unions by the system of masters and apprentices which allows the formation of an industrial work force; the proportion of skilled manual workers is very small in the Third World countries.

Consequently, intellectuals play a disproportionately large part in the union movement. We must not deny that such men have their following, speak for others, and supply a dynamism often lacking in traditional societies. "The intellecutal," says G. Fischer, "is able more easily to throw off those ties of family, tribe, or ethnic group which remain strong among wage earners and hinder their awareness of solidarity with each other."[123] But the importance of intellectuals nonetheless gives unionism in the developing countries a special character by comparison with unionism in the developed countries.

Unions in the developing countries rather easily turn into unions of trained personnel (as contrasted with unions of the working masses). Basic organization is often neglected, and dues are collected irregularly. There are exceptions, as when an obligatory check-off is applied as in Ghana, or a special effort at basic organization is undertaken at great expense, as recently in Congo-Kinshasa by the Union of Congolese Workers.

Such a situation is often reinforced in the unions of French-speaking Africa by the important influence of central headquarters in the parent-country. The local unionist movement was immediately connected with the headquarters and great care was taken to train national leaders and to establish central institutions at the national level. All this meant greater solidarity, but it was also the cause of neglect in building up basic organization in the colony. Decentralization was much greater in the British colonies, which often had unions even within business.

The influence of the parent country could not, in any case, make up for internal weaknessess. "The parent organizations could indeed start the movement off, but the stimulus could be transformed into vigorous expression only to the extent that there existed a sufficiently large number of workers to build up the organization. There is no other explanation for the weakness of trade unionism in former French Equatorial Africa."[124]

The last-named characteristic is peculiar to Africa. But in Latin America, no less than in Africa, the influence of intellecutals and of the union cadres is disproportionate to basic organization. A further characteristic, too, is truly common to all unionism in the Third World: the preponderance and even disproportionate place occupied by some professions, civil servants, railway agents, miners, textile workers, and longshoremen. It is indeed natural that all these should come to the fore, since they represent occupations in which qualifications are higher, the concentration of workers is greatest, and contacts with the world abroad and with the various regions of the country itself are most frequent. Other categories of workers are more difficult to organize. One consequence, however, is the danger of developing, within the established unions, a caste spirit which can hinder the general progress of unionism. We see here privileged workers or at least well organized trades or services, able to protect and defend themselves. Sometimes we are close to the professional guild, mentioned earlier, but rather far from a movement toward the solidarity of the working class as a whole.

It remains true that, for all their limitations, the unions are for their members a remarkable means of betterment and of integration into a new society. This explains why, in comparison with contemporary European unions, the unions of the Third World are much less narrowly specialized for the defence of workers in collective bargaining and industrial disputes. They have many internal educational and cultural activities. This was frequently so in Latin America, just as it had been in England at the beginning of the industrial revolution.

Moreover the social problems which face the unions in the developing countries because of industrialization and urbanization are quite specific. The union must often welcome the immigrant villagers, help them adapt to their new environment, and help educate them to a professional morale and solidarity within the union.

All these roles are merits, not demerits, in a nascent unionism and an uncertain economy. We must nonetheless look forward to a day when, as industrialization progresses, there will be a greater specialization of roles for trade unions and mutual-aid societies. Most of all, there will have to be a closer solidarity of all wage earners if the betterment of all is to be promoted. But such a solidarity is unlikely to be achieved as long as a good part of the wage-earning population is as unstable as it presently is.

ROLE

OF THE STATE

IN DEVELOPMENT

Our consideration of changing social stratification and of the new social space being provided by hitherto unknown kinds of association shows that a radical renewal of the traditional, underdeveloped societies is now going on. After the long description we have given of these societies, we must still show them to be "developing," as current phraseology puts it.

Some observers will smile at the term and say that at times these societies seem rather to be underdeveloping. And indeed many social problems have been intensified by initial economic changes, while economic indicators do not everywhere show great improvement. Yet something new has in fact begun.

Reaction to Colonialism

The newness arose out of the very intensification of the colonial process, as we noted earlier but think worth recalling here. One of the second-stage effects of colonization was that it became the occasion for a first awareness of what has almost everywhere turned into the desire for development.

Colonization involved contact with the outside world, initially in the form of foreign consumer goods. Thereby men were everywhere stirred into movement—toward the cities, for example. Minds, too, were stirred—to curiosity and new mentalities.

Colonization thus caused the beginning of social imbalance. Such an imbalance is a necessary, though not sufficient condition for people opening themselves to new possibilities of organizing human life and escaping a very stable but also very rigid social and mental milieu. The colonizers disturbed and modified the inherited hierarchies of human groups and whole peoples. On the other hand, some groups made better use than others of opportunities offered by the colonizers, and this in turn introduced still further modifications of the old hierarchies.

Moreover, a political void was created by the destruction of the old chiefdoms and the imposition of a new administration. And, finally, colonization speeded up all other changes, including changes in the family and the condition of women.

When colonization became oppressive, it provoked a reaction, especially the assertion of human dignity against colonial social discrimination, even before the desire for political independence awoke. In fact, the latter was desired as a means to the former.

In the Latin American countries we can speak of a contagion which spread from places where decolonization was in process around the world. Latin America, it can also be said, showed a certain delay in reaching awareness of its situation, but education, progressively more widespread after the beginning of the century, soon speeded up the new awareness. Urbanization, for its part, affected a social imbalance like that of the last stage of colonialism.

In Asia there were analogous phenomena. Thus, the desire for development has grown everywhere in recent years—as a reaction, yes, but also as a value in itself.

There is, furthermore, a desire for cultural originality (the recovery of a people's own heritage), a desire to be different. It is probable that development will take place in all these countries in the same way as it did formerly in Europe. But the desire to recover cultural originality and the desire for development are not opposed but complementary.

The Special Place of the State

Desires, however, are not automatically fulfilled. Where, then, are the social forces able to foster development? Here we come once again upon the state, but the state in a rather special, sociological sense of the term.

It is not, for example, the peasants, majority though they be, who are the movers in development. The peasant usually remains passive, as he was in the time before independence. The active groups in political movements for independence could not rely on the peasant for help. After independence the peasant has often been aware mainly of the administrative disorganization which is, in fact, almost inevitable in the early days. We have all heard the statement put, rightly or wrongly, into the peasant's mouth: "When is this independence business going to be done with?" At the present time, the peasant world of Africa is beginning to show a veiled rebelliousness, admittedly rather negative, against the administration and the city people. But a number of young people have shown that they are able to seize the opportunities for development, despite countless obstacles put in their way by the elders (in matters of land ownership, for example). They are a promising group. But, on the whole, the peasants are not the destabilizing factor which would hasten development. Nor are they any more so in Latin America, even after rural revolts such as Northeast Brazil experienced not long ago.

In the cities, the entrepreneurs are few in number, at least true entrepreneurs and industralists. We have already noted that a characteristic of the developing countries is the fewness of the entrepreneurs and that, where they seem to occur, they are more businessmen than entrepreneurs, and often inclined to speculation in the bargain. They prefer to invest in construction, more or less for prestige, or they look for a quick profit and shy away from industrial investment which will yield only a long-term profit. There are exceptions, of course, in many countries—in the state of São Paulo in Brazil and among the Parsis in India, for example. But an enterprising spirit such as the captains of nineteenth-century industy had is very rare. In most of the recently decolonized countries the situation is even worse. Access to enterprise in any full sense was almost nonexistent in colonial days, since all entrepreneurial activity was in the hands of foreigners. The result of this, of course, wherever colonization was ruthless, was that managerial personnel, capable of taking over the various enterprises after independence, simply had not been developed, and the industrial economy often deteriorated. We ought not fail to acknowledge the very small enterprises of which we see examples all over present-day Africa. But we must also admit that it is not the entrepreneurs who today are either the leaders or the principal agents in development.

Intellectuals, wherever they exist in sufficiently large numbers, as in Latin America, have traditionally been little involved. The mediocrity of the universities there has elicited lively student protest ever since the early twentieth century, and led to the university reform which originated at Cordoba, Argentina, after the First World War. Despite all this, university teaching continued for a long period to be a part-time occupation, and many universities until quite recently had no full-time professors. Mediocrity in the universities engendered mediocrity and a marked passivity in the intellectual world. The situation has greatly changed in recent years, but as yet it is only at the student level that a dynamic new spirit is felt. In India, most intellectuals have been absorbed into the higher ranks of the civil service.

Labor unions played a political role in the decolonization of Africa; they supplied troops, and often leaders as well, for the independence movements. They exhausted their energies in the effort, however, and do not seem presently to be the force that acts to destabilize the old society. In South America they have been too dependent on the great political leaders who annex them as clients.

Tomorrow we will doubtless find all these forces at work. But the triggering of the movement toward development has not been their doing. What agency is left, then? The state. It is no exaggeration to say that everything has begun with the state. We mean by "state" the governments, but, more accurately still (in the case of the African nations), the political cadres built up after independence. We mean also the new political cadres which, for twenty years now, have at times given Latin America governments of a new kind, economically active and no longer neutral: "developer governments" according to an expression which quite fits Brazil, where the term *desinvolvimentismo* (developmentism) has been in use to designate Kubitschek's ideology. The term could even have been applied earlier to Vargas' regime.

In Africa, it has been said, the state preceded the nation. More than that: the men who run the state were practically the only social group who were modernizers, clearly out of phase with traditional society. This group accepted the mission of setting the whole of society in motion.

In still other words, the political element has generally been the most dynamic in the recent history of these countries, including their economic development. This state of affairs contrasts sharply with European development in the nineteenth century when the states, with few exceptions, were onlookers, refusing to intervene. People at that time had not even conceived the idea of active intervention by the state in the economy. The state's role in development is one of the most characteristic aspects of the scoio-economic situation in today's developing countries.

"The state's role in development": we must insist that "state" here means a stratum of men, a kind of social class or rather a kind of caste which today almost exclusively plays the role of mover of society. It is not always a brilliant group, but it is generally the only dynamic one, the only reliable trump card these countries have. And the state—this dynamic social group—has made development its objective.

For Latin America only a few nuances would have to be introduced into this picture, wherever some few industrialists of large vision have plunged into the struggle.

Development, an Objective of the State

We must recall the movement of international self-projection which early marked the new states' existence. The objective of these states would indeed be development, and that conceived seriously as benefiting the whole population. But the men of government could not fail to also see in development a means of putting their nation on the level of the other states of the world and of ceasing to be any longer a poor relation in the great international community which they had entered through independence. Or, again, development meant achieving an economic independence without which political independence is pretty much a formality. These purposes would entail certain consequences which would characterize the relationship of the Third World states to development.

To begin with, all seek development, but almost all conceive it as an action of the state, originating with the state, rather than as a general movement of society, channeled by the state but not originating in it. The whole economic doctrine of the Third World states would have to be described here in order to see how fully such a view of development reigns among them. The conception has been expressed at times with the aid of alien theories on the role of the state, for example, various socialist doctrines, but these ideologies have only been a means of expression; they hide, in fact, a profoundly original attitude and view of development.

A few examples will show this. In Guinea and Mali, people are "socialists." But the socialism is related to the problem of economic independence. "Starting with the principle that capitalism has taken shape in West Africa under the form of colonialism, the leaders of these countries share the deep conviction that capitalism is for them congenitally vitiated. This disqualifies it, in their eyes, as a method of rapid economic development."[125] They think development must originate in the action of the independent state and of the party, which is conceived in Guinea and Mali as an expression of the "people." Thus the starting point of their thinking is the idea of the state as the motive force in development rather than the Marxist idea of a collective appropriation of the means of production (the latter would be the strictly socialist approach, and it is much less to the fore than the other in the minds of these nations' leaders).

The state and its purpose, then, are primary. The initial steps taken in Guinea (including the establishment of a national bank for domestic and foreign trade) were thus necessary, according to Sekou Touré, because of "obvious bad will on the part of free commerce which was implementing an anti-Guinean policy of fomenting economic unrest."

Another very characteristic step in the economic policy of these two countries was the creation of an independent money: the Guinean franc and the Malian franc. "Monetary power," said the Malian government on July 1, 1962, "is an indispensable complement and essential attribute of sovereignty." It was necessary if the state was to be in a position to act independently. Later on, Mali had to modify its monetary practice.

In Ivory Coast, where socialism is officially rejected and private initiative is given a large part to play, the role of the state as mover in economic development is nonetheless considered fundamental. Houphouet-Boigny once defined his economic doctrine as "state capitalism," an expressive phrase. He has also sought to establish a "national civil service," for the state requires its youth to give "their sweat in defence of its true, that is, economic, independence."[126] One of the ministers, Mathieu Ekra, was more explicit: "A nation which remains poor cannot really be free and independent. And only work allows a nation to free itself of poverty; it alone allows it to escape the slavery of material cares and of waiting upon a neighbor's generous gesture."[127] Therefore the idea of a national civic service. A more generally worded resolution of President Houphouet-Boigny can close these remarks: "In Ivory Coast at the present stage of its existence, everything must be done to build up the economic and financial power of the state, for a survey of the contemporary world shows ever more clearly that the doctrines which sacrifice the state to the individual are as ineffective as those which sacrifice the individual to the state."

Within socialism as well as outside it, then, the fundamental point is the role of the state as mover in development. And for one who is a socialist in these Third World countries, the crucial point is generally not the abolition of all private ownership of the means of production, but development through state activity.

Planning and Intervention

In practice a state which takes development as an objective becomes a planner. Everywhere, then, there is planning and everywhere the active intervention of the state for development by means of a public sector. This last is considered a key factor where the state itself undertakes development.

The first thing that strikes us in the Third World countries is the rapidity with which most of the newly independent states drew up a plan. The decision to do so was taken at the time of independence or shortly after (in India, for example, as early as August 1948), and two or three years later the first developmental plan appeared. It was preceded, in some instances, by an interim plan for transition or adjustment (for example, Morocco, 1958-1959: two-year plan for economic outfitting following on plans proper to the days of the protectorate). Ghana had a plan for development right from the time of independence and covering the years 1957-1960. At the time this book was being written, most of the recently independent states had already experienced two or three or even four separate five-year plans.

Plans began to proliferate in South America at the same period. Brazil was to the fore here (Kubitschek, Santiago Dantas, Roberto Campos). From 1964 on, the Alliance for Progress obliged all countries to prepare plans, but the plans would not everywhere be carried out with equal enthusiasm and the effects of the Alliance are unfortunately diminishing.

We shall not be relating the contents of the various plans. But we should note that from the beginning they were very ambitious and some of them were directed to industrialization (a good sign of the government's developmental orientation). Later plans, India's for example, have given greater importance to agricultural development.

Another characteristic must be stressed: the generally small part played by the people and even by the private sector of the economy in the preparation of plans. The latter have generally been the work of experts alone. In a few cases, "commissions for development" have been set up with representatives from both the public and the private sectors, who can exercise some initiative with the administration. In a few instances, the plan has been widely publicized; in others, it has remained almost a state secret. In Senegal a great effort was made at the beginning to bring the plan to the knowledge of the masses; but this was the exception rather than the rule.

Theoretically the state should, of course, attach great importance to broadcasting the plan and to conscious sharing in its implementation, out of a desire that it be widely understood and put into practice by everyone. If the diffusion has in fact been generally neglected, it is because this was not the first need felt by the state. It was important indeed that there be a broad grasp of the road to be travelled and a vision of the future to be built as well as of the process of building it. But such a grasp and vision were necessary almost exclusively for the apparatus of the state itself as prime mover in development.

In this same perspective, we might expect the state itself to undertake much of the work of development. The state, remember, means a modernizing avant-garde of society. Its objective is development, but seeing itself to be far ahead of society as a whole, it also conceives such development as its own action or at least, in every instance, as originating from itself. The state is, therefore, not content with a blueprint but intends to exercise a high degree of economic intervention: it creates and manages numerous enterprises, or at least many of the most important ones.

Many problems undoubtedly arise in creating this public sector. The first is to get sufficient resources from taxation. The state might, of course, have considerable resources at its disposal through foriegn aid, but it can rely on these only to start things off, for once the initial stage is past, it must rely on domestic resources and mobolize them through taxes. "Good public services," says W. A. Lewis, "cannot be provided for 5 percent of the national income. Defense and transfers apart, the countries of Western Europe and North America use up about 12 percent of their national incomes in their public services, and the less developed countries would need even more to pay for the same standards, since incomes per head are lower."[128] The under-developed country's greatest need is to amass capital: an investment of 12 percent of the national income is desirable, whereas very often spontaneous saving will go only as high as 5 percent. (12 percent must be invested if the total revenue—not the per capita revenue—is to increase at 3 percent a year, with a resultant four-to-one ratio of capital to income.)

But such revenues are difficult to raise. The state must avoid taxes that are costly to collect, and must rely for the most part on indirect taxes. But some indirect taxes are themselves difficult to collect, especially from small businesses. Import duties are doubtless the easiest taxes in underdeveloped countries, but here again caution is needed lest the state hinder development by discouraging necessary imports.

All this means that the government must have a good measure of authority. It must be able to impose real discipline on its own services and on the citizenry. It often happens that the state income does not increase along with the national revenue, simply because the state does not want to raise the prices it controls (railway travel, postage, telephone calls, etc.) or because the tax base is set and does not follow real value, or because the state tolerates large-scale tax evasion.

Sufficient tax levies being supposed, the state tries to act through public enterprise. Such a course of action is regarded as obvious by all concerned. "The idea that public enterprise has a fundamental role in bringing a country out of underdevelopment has become almost commonplace and is admitted by antisocialist as well as socialist."[129] The only difference between the two philosophies is in the way public enterprise is used.

There are several models for "public sectors." In the first, according to Hanson, "the state acts as pioneer in a number of different areas and progressively limits its direct intervention as private enterprise becomes increasingly able to do the job. At the end, the state limits itself to maintaining an adequate infrastructure and to assuring conditions which most encourage the private entrepreneur."[130] Examples of this model are Japan and Mexico. In Communist ideology, on the contrary, private enterprise is condemned root and branch forever, and the effort is made to absorb all private enterprise into the public sector. An intermediate form would be the Indian situation in which economic policy depends on the coexistence, intended as more or less permanent, of public and private enterprises, all operating within the framework of a unified plan. This intermediate form is in fact the most widespread. Or, rather, it seems that at the beginning no one is really concerned with all these theoretical problems—for example, what will become of public enterprises later on, or whether they should extend to the whole economy. The important thing is that there should be a public sector now for development that is to be undertaken by state action.

There are other problems in organizing public enterprise. The most effective forms would seem to be developmental corporations, fairly independent of direct administration by the state, for example, the Corporacion de Fomento in Chile (since 1938) or the Bureau of Iraquian Development (after 1950). But these run the risk of setting up a state within the state. Beyond this, the government is very sensitive to any limitation of its own authority and therefore tends to bring all economic enterprises under its own direction. The hold of the state on the public sector tends to become stronger rather than weaker, as has happened in the marketing boards of Ghana and even of Nigeria.

A further difficulty in fostering a public sector is the lack of personnel, for there is no way of guaranteeing a dynamic public personnel when there are no dynamic private entrepreneurs to draw from. But despite all these obstacles, the public sector of eonomic enterprise has a primary importance for the Third World states in their effort to be prime mover and agent of development.

The dangers of the situation should also be pointed out. There is danger of the state being too isolated, operating too much in a void: drawing up fine plans for ministerial portfolios and blueprints for office walls, but experiencing great difficulty in coming to grips with living social reality. There is danger of the state going even a step further and building huge factories but not operating them profitably and not inserting them into the nation's economic life as a whole (or even forcing the latter to conform to the former). There is danger of having a state of civil servants, almost a technocratic state before technology spreads among the population as a whole. There is danger, finally, of a gulf between this "social elite" and the rest of the people.

Our remarks on the state's role in development explain some of the characteristics we met in Third World political regimes. First of all, there is the oligarchic character of the leadership—of governments, political bureaus, party cadres. At the same time, oligarchy is affected with impotence and corruption if it is not headed by a personalist, charismatic leader. We find the characteristic single party whose role is primarily to be an agent of communication to the membership, for the leaders feel how difficult communication is. At the same time, we find too much disinterest in the very serious problems of national unification and integration, because the society is being built from the top and by means of a future-oriented project, namely the developmental plan. In this perspective, the plan even seems at times to be an escape into the future. We have seen this evasion before, in the way in which the new states have tried to project themselves onto the international scene. But we must add that states which are concentrating on development also tend to have a strong and effective government, not only because development is regarded as important, but also because development is regarded as primarily the business of the state (there is no one else whose business it could be).

DEVELOPMENTAL
POLITICS

The state as developer cannot be satisified to plan and to establish a public sector. It must make the developmental spirit permeate society as a whole, and, to this end, it must remodel society as much as possible, while also facing up to the social consequences of economic change.

Economic plans are therefore accompanied by many and varied measures for modifying society. Largely paper measures, no doubt, and only a beginning. Once again, it is an operation from on top, with the risk this involves of ineffectiveness, since decrees do not change the customs, mentalities, and institutions of traditional societies. On the other hand, there is no easy way of confronting the social ills that flow from the imbalances and disturbances which economic change already undergone inflicts on these traditional societies.

We shall discuss here some of the more typical developmental policies of the new nations: demographic policy, land and agrarian policy, and efforts to mold the family. In a further chapter we shall look at policy for education and for community development.

Demographic Policy

We have already referred to the important quantitative changes brought about in the Third World countries by the rapid lowering of the birth rate, well before any real growth in productivity (and, more significantly, well before any serious growth in agricultural yield). In the light of this complex event we can understand why developmental plans are so often accompanied by efforts to slow down the population growth, that is, the birth rate. There is today hardly a single country in the Third World which does not have some kind of policy on population growth.

The problem, indeed, does not arise everywhere in the same terms. We saw earlier that there are still areas where the rate of growth is not very high. There are regions and countries which cannot, absolutely speaking, be called overpopulated. In several the relation of population to land area or, more generally, to natural resources is favorable. In a few places, people are even beginning to think that a larger population would bring greater economic effectiveness, reduce the general expense of infrastructures, and thus be beneficial, and that it is practically indispensable to economic development.

In such cases, however, there remains the problem of how fast the population growth should be if it is to be beneficial. For, even where happy results may be expected from growth in population, not every rate of growth is equally desirable, since every increase demands new investments.

This consideration is admittedly of limited importance whenever ample investments can be gotten simply from an increased amount of human labor, without the need of a great deal of financial capital or improved equipment such as a country cannot yet produce. Such is theoretically the situation of many countries in black Africa. They would gain by a larger population, on the condition that a minimum of investment can be made without any great contribution from financial capital or improved equipment. These countries would thus be better prepared for a second stage of development. In a number of Latin American countries, too, natural resources and the prospects for their use are good enough that the disadvantages for develoment from a fairly large current population growth would be more than compensated by advantages at the term of the growth. The difficulty is, however, that we cannot expect many countries today to follow such a Spartan method of accumulation. But if these countries have recourse to more costly kinds of investment, they will have to modify their population growth or else sacrifice the fruits of the investment, namely a better use of natural resources and a better distribution of general expenses.

On the other hand, there are here and now very serious situations in many countries of the Caribbean area, North Africa, Egypt, and Southern and Southwestern Asia, where the density of population is already very high in relation to land area and to resources available in the near future. In these places, very rapid development is needed, not in some second stage, but right now if the countries are to meet the demands of increased population. It is possible that in a later stage of development the huge populations of these countries might be an advantage, even an economic advantage, but at present the difficult first step of starting development has yet to be taken. It is at this point that India seems to be stumbling despite its large resources and Egypt despite its efforts at irrigation and industrialization.

Thus, there is a great diversity of situations, ranging from extreme overpopulation to relative underpopulation. Nonetheless many countries are faced with the problem, set perhaps in different terms, of at least a reduction in population growth. A policy of population limitation depends on a number of factors: the existence of effective means, the possibility of making these available, and their acceptability.

Effective means range from sterilization and abortion to various chemical and mechanical contraceptives and various forms of abstention. Research into means of contraception is active at present, and the situation is changing quickly. Thus only a few years ago many concentrated all their hopes on an oral contraceptive, the pill. Today we hear much of the intrauterine device (with people asking, however, whether it is not an abortifacient as well as a contraceptive). The device is now favored by several policies on contraception.

But effectiveness turned out to be a rather complicated idea in this area. Even where effectiveness in biological terms is fully guaranteed, the means must be used regularly and according to prescription for it to produce its demographic results. Such use cannot be taken for granted among simple peoples. It generally presupposes instruction, whether in observing the thermal curve (basic to the method of periodic abstinence) or in taking a regular dose of contraceptive pills. The intrauterine device requires less instruction but does suppose a good network of doctors.

Above all, there is the problem of psychological and moral "tolerance" or acceptance: acceptance of the various means of contraception, but also acceptance of a deliberate limitation of the birth rate to begin with. A state can only act with caution, if it is not to do direct violence to its people and to risk turning them against its policy.

A final problem lies in wait for us. Though we have not reached such a point as yet, we must face the possibility of demographic policies being perhaps too effective. The effects of such policies will not be simply quantitative, they will be qualitative as well. Demographers know that there is danger in suddenly overturning the age pyramid of a population. Systematically to reduce the number of active men and women of tomorrow is to prepare for each of them an ever heavier burden of unproductive old people (within thirty years Japan will surely be facing this formidable situation). Consequently, even where a policy of population limitation seems an immediate necessity, the amount of limitation desired must be calculated with an eye to the future.

In brief, the problem is not simply to reduce population—a goal which may be achieved someday, even if not immediately. The problem is also to master the population growth. In this perspective, those methods which require, and can presuppose, an education in responsiblity have a great advantage. No method, however, should be broadcast without accompanying education, and such education is today too neglected in the policies being tried.

Demographic policies are in their infancy. They do not take sufficient account of psychological, cultural, and moral factors, nor of what will happen to the age pyramid. In addition, there is a serious political problem: it is too often the rich and secure countries which most insistently promote policies of birth limitation in the Third World!

Land and Agrarian Policy

The second stumbling stone in the path of economic development is usually the land and agrarian system. What can the states do here?

In black Africa, as we have already seen, the chief problems are not the redistribution of property concentrated in too few hands nor the protection of small owners against exploitation by middlemen. The most urgent need is to adapt a law system with uneconomic characteristics and purposes to the demands of a productive and progressive economy.

In fact the peasants have for a long time tended by (new) custom if not by law, to assert individual ownership, especially where crops for export and not just for subsistence have become common. Among such crops are fruits (coffee, cocoa, bananas); the owners of the fruit trees have tended to become owners of the ground. Often, even, planting trees has been a good way of becoming de facto owner. This, of course, has made people distrust a stranger who wanted to plant trees.

Various steps were taken in colonial times to establish and register property rights and to fit them into a modern system of law. The steps were usually not very effective. People rarely took advantage of the possibilities opened to them, for they probably understood them but poorly and, besides, the new opportunities were contrary to the old customs.

Other measures in recent years, beginning at independence, have had the effect of confirming customary rights which had been poorly defined by tradition. The new states wanted to do away with the concept of "empty and ownerless land" which the colonizers had introduced in order to gain governmental control over lands little used by the tribes. It was a colonial concept which had never really been accepted by the native population. In Cameroon, to take one instance from among many (the problem had also been a burning one in the Belgian Congo, for example), a law voted by the first National Assembly in 1959, even before independence, abolished this concept. There would henceforth only be lands subject to tribal law (whether the lands were registered or not, and whether the rights in question were individual or collective) or lands expressly coming under the jurisdiction of the state (public domain or the "private" domain of public groups or private parcels registered as properties). And it was understood that the first category included all lands not explicitly belonging to the second; the presumption, therefore, would favor tribal law.

At the same time, in a decree more favorable to economic development, every Cameroonian who under tribal law had held a parcel of land at his residence for five years could have his right confirmed.

The insistence on tribal law was too strong, and the limitation on the state's rights over lands subject to tribal law was too great; but this was an understandable reaction to colonial practice. However, after independence (1960), the situation would change. There was not a return to the concept of empty and ownerless land, but a concept of "national patrimony" was developed. An ordinance of 1963 provided that all land not effectively in the hands of individuals or groups according to tribal law or not, in the public or private domain, or not privately owned according to the civil code, was to be "national patrimony." Only lands actually cultivated or lying fallow escaped, along with those needed to make development possible and to allow for population growth. The state can transfer other lands to public entities (for use), keep them in its private domain for later distribution, or make grants to individuals. A decree of 1964 brought further determinations. There was no indemnification for lands not cultivated or improved. Confirmation of collective rights (a collective request for confirmation of ownership) could no longer be sought except for communal use (by individuals designated by name).

The same tendency to restrict customary rights to the benefit of the states shows up in more than one country. Several have adopted a similar concept of national patrimony for all land not actually cultivated or necessary for the immediate needs of traditional groups.

These restrictions were followed by a strong trend toward the creation of individually owned properties. Resistance to the trend arose at times in the name of socialism, but we must recall that socialism itself supposes a dissociation between a man's right to possessions and the religious and familial bonds that attach to these possessions.

If individual ownership is made easier, it is also necessary to avoid making transfer of ownership or mortgaging too easy, for these allow the formation of the more or less large estates which are rightly regarded as undesirable.

In practice these various problems are far from being generally resolved. The chief difficulty is to give the law a hold on matters so subject to custom. Perhaps there is also a tendency to underestimate the developmental powers of custom in matters of the land.

In Asia the major problems were the large properties with absentee owners, the methods of fragmentary cultivation, feudal-style rents, and various forms of usury practiced by agents. Some solutions to these have been adopted in a number of countries.

In Burma, for example, laws of 1948 and 1953 provided for the expropriation of properties larger than fifty acres in the South or twenty-five acres in the North. These appropriated lands have been put into the hands of farmers who previously were tenants of owners who did not cultivate the land for themselves. Such farmers now are 50 percent of all the peasants in Burma.

In the People's Republic of China, the first step in agrarian reform was of a similar kind: suppression of the great landed estates and introduction of peasant ownership. Of course, later on there was a regrouping of the parcels into "production cooperatives" (1,400,000 at the end of 1955), then a gathering of these into people's communes (26,500 in November 1958, with 99 percent of the peasants belonging to them), then a softening of this radical formula in turn.

On Formosa, the effort was made to better the condition of tenants by putting a ceiling on farm rents (which were not to exceed 37.5 percent of the crop, whereas formerly rents had been as high as two-thirds of the crop), and by increasing the number of cultivator-owners (by selling estates so as to allow cultivators to become owners). The government also launched a program called "the land to the cultivator," and in its name expropriated land to sell to the farmers. These measures were implemented by low-interest loans and by sending out consultants for improving farm techniques.

In India, where 40 percent of the land had been let to agents who sublet it in turn, the rights of the agents were abrogated in principle, and twenty million farmers are now directly related to the state. Moreover, all the states of the Union have legislated a ceiling on rents and payments in kind (previously amounting to at least half of the crop). The maximum was fixed at one-fifth of the crop in Maharashtra, Gujarat, and Rajasthan, at one-fourth in Kerala and Orissa, and at one-third in most other states. These are stages; the goal is to achieve the right of permanent occupation for a large number of farmers. The application of the plan has admittedly run into much resistance regarding the conditions of leases.

In Pakistan, the law of 1950 for East Bengal (on acquisition of estates and on tenant-farming) meant the suppression of most agents; the problem with them had been the same as in India. Cultivators now own 70 percent of the land. In West Pakistan where a very large part of the land was owned by a very small number of proprietors, a law of 1959 set a maximum size of five hundred acres for irrigated lands and a thousand acres for others. Two and a half million acres were redistributed under this law.

In the Philippines, the most important law is the Agrarian Reform Code of 1963 (there had been earlier efforts at rural colonization). The code contained a program for land redistribution and a new program for rural colonization. Further dispositions suppressed various forms of rent in kind, and defined the clauses for land leases and the rights of farm workers, as well as the freedom to join a union and minimum salaries.

In Asia generally, before or after such reforms, the average size of a holding is very small. In India, 55 percent of the rural families have parcels of less than two and a half acres; 75 percent of the cultivated parcels are less than five acres. In Java the average size is four and a half acres; in Japan two acres. Size continues to be a serious difficulty even when reforms are effective in redistributing the land or protecting the various kinds of renters.

In Latin America, where the amount of disposable land is generally greater, the problems of agrarian reform are currently more urgent than elsewhere. They have, in fact, long been the order of the day, ever since Mexico, for example, undertook a first agrarian reform around 1915. More recently, Guatemala undertook an agrarian reform in 1952, Bolivia in 1953. Many other countries have passed laws in this area since 1960. The Alliance for Progress made agrarian reform a condition for receiving North American aid.

Progress has been slow, however, and resistance strong. One reason for the fall of Joao Goulart's government in Brazil in 1964 was his project for agrarian reform. The situation is troubled in many countries. An estimate in 1964 considered 35 percent of the cultivators in Venezuela, 47 percent in Paraguay, and 67 percent in Panama as squatters on lands belonging to the great public or private estates.[131]

Let us look in greater detail at some agrarian reforms of the fifites. In Bolivia, reform began before 1953. Maximum sizes were determined for holdings: one thousand to two thousand acres on the Andean altiplano, two hundred in the fertile valleys, five thousand in Oriente province. At the end of June 1963, 196,184 deeds had been distributed for 9,737,500 acres to 123,403 heads of family. Moreover, indirect cultivation via renters had been abolished. The attempt was also made, in order to relieve population pressure on the altiplano, to start rural colonization in the lowlands and in the valleys where many sections of land have not been adequately cultivated. The major problem with such colonization is the lack of infrastructure: roads, education, technology.

In Chile a law of 1962 aimed only at easing the acquisition of property by farm workers and at raising the standard of living in rural areas. President Frei's government attempted a much more radical reform and achieved some success.

In Colombia, a law of 1961 dealt both with social security and with agrarian reform. It gave an important place to rural colonization (especially in the Ariari district). The Colombian Institute for Agrarian Reform is empowered to expropriate and indemnify, to redistribute waste lands, and to encourage colonization (by creating family holdings).

In Costa Rica the government took steps in 1961 to help farmers acquire property as in Chile a year later and provided for expropriation under certain conditions.

In Cuba reform was much more radical, even more so than in Bolivia. The maximum size of a parcel of land was set at a thousand acres; foreigners were forbidden to acquire and inherit land. All estates larger than the legal size were divided among peasants and farm workers. Payment of rent in kind was prohibited. Later the effort was made to establish peasant cooperatives, with the "people's farms" being managed directly by the Institute for Agrarian Reform.

Other laws may be mentioned. A law of April 1962, aimed at improving living and working conditions for the peasants of the Dominican Republic. An Institute for Agrarian Reform was set up, and redistribution of large estates was envisaged but no maximum size for future holdings was set. The law of July 11, 1964 in Ecuador established an Institute for Agrarian Reform and Colonization, whose function was to determine the principle for a more equitable distribution of land. The law eliminated outmoded forms of land tenure and of hiring labor, especially the institution of *Huasipongo* (work for a hacienda in return for a minimal salary and the right to work a parcel of land). The lands formerly worked by laborers under this system were to be given to them, or else a cash indemnity according to the length of their service.

The Peruvian law of 1962 envisaged a progressive redistribution of land with limited possibilities of expropriation (if the owners were using farmers to cultivate the land or if the estates were poorly cultivated or lying waste) and with a progressive land tax on excessively large rural properties. In 1963 an Institute for Agrarian Reform and Colonization was established in order to apply the reforms. It began with pilot projects in the valleys of Convencion and Sares in the Cuzco district. The new military government is now speeding up these reforms which had been moving too slowly.

In Venezuela a law of 1960 provided for redistribution of land and for the expropriation of large estates and their break-up into family parcels of between four hundred and five hundred acres.

It is estimated that under this law 3,750,000 acres were distributed to 56,000 families in 1963.

Many observers continue to be skeptical about the effectiveness of reforms undertaken in many Latin American countries on the grounds that they are too progressive. The plans do indeed meet much resistance in practice. A number of plans are more concerned with colonizing new lands than with redistributing existing farmland, and colonization is somewhat risky. But the plans must be given time to produce results; more rapid but also more improvised agrarian reforms do not have exclusively good effects (as René Dumont's studies of Cuba have shown). In any event, important steps have been taken with the passage of these various laws which could not have been passed at all only a few years ago.

Family Law

Agrarian and land reforms look directly to the improvement of agricultural production. They have a wider impact, however, and this is perhaps their more important aspect. The attempt is being made to form a new type of man, one who is freed of enslavement to various estate and feudal systems and to traditional tribal restraints, and who is acquiring a new outlook on progress, the value of which he now sees since he can profit by it. It is difficult to succeed in such an undertaking. Failure often lies in wait because peasants do not have the necessary education nor the social framework to sustain a new outlook. But it is also true that the very attempt at agrarian reform upsets old habits and attitudes. Even where the means of carrying the reforms through are lacking, the desire for them is awakened, and new possibilities rise up for men to grasp at. To the same end of recreating men themselves, reformers dream of reforming other social structures in a more or less authoritarian way. The goal is to put men in new situations where they will react in ways new to them and, hopefully, more favorable to development.

This is what lies behind reforms of family structure. If development is possible only when minds are sensitive to economic values, and especially to the appeal of comfort, then it may easily be inferred that some forms of familial society and kinship system ought to be modified so as to allow for economic development. For example, in the extended family system all the "brothers" and distant cousins may expect to share the new income of one who has taken a job in a modern economic enterprise. But then the danger is that this individual may lose the stimulus for his own development. This is precisely the kind of situation we often find in underdeveloped countries, especially in Africa.

If the only aim were to foster progress within the framework of traditional technology and to improve the production of foodstuffs within a closed economy, the extended family would be an adequate instrument. But the development sought today involves exchange between agriculture and other economic sectors. It involves industrialization, the use of new technology, and some urbanization. The realization and extension of all this seem to require a social system in which men are mobile and in which, consequently, the bonds of the extended family and clan are not too strong. It should be a system in which income reverts, if not exclusively to the worker, than at least only to a limited group—the nuclear family for example—so that the possibility of enjoying the fruits of work becomes a real stimulus.

It is obvious, however, that such a transformation of the family cannot be achieved purely and simply by legislation. To belong to the clan or extended family or to belong to the nuclear family is not a matter of more or less arbitrary choice; one does not simply make a decision on such matters. If men are to abandon the extended family, if the strong bonds of such a family are at least to be relaxed, individuals must be able to do without the securities and guarantees which the extended family gives. Substitute securities and guarantees must be within reach: economic and social security within their new sphere of activity, and psychological security within other human groups (nuclear family and political community). Yet in transitional situations it is precisely these securities that are lacking. The breakup of the extended family may be succeeded by family anarchy, as we pointed out earlier, and not immediately by a stable nuclear or conjugal family. And a new political community is far from offering the satisfactions of tribal security. Economic and social security is but minimally provided by economies in full transition for the latter are most often plagued by inflation and exploitation.

Laws can, however, do something in these circumstances. This is especially true of laws effectively assuring the protection of workers and their social security to the extent that the economy will permit, and of laws which protect the functioning of cooperative forms of economy. In addition, efforts to achieve a deep national unity within a renewed political community will also serve to weaken the social bonds of the extended family or clan.

Such means of indirect action on familial structures and customs are fundamental. But they can be combined wtih more direct action. Thus, for example, Christianity has exerted a radical influence on familial structures by spreading the idea of the stable monogamous family; it has often helped strengthen conjugal bonds in the nuclear family which seems better adapted to modern economic development. Today various governments are undertaking legislative efforts in this area, and the results will probably be real, even if long-term. We present here, simply as examples, some of the new laws on the family in Mali and Ivory Coast (codes very unlike each other in other areas).

First of all, the codes decree that there is no marriage without consent. They likewise impose a period of "widowhood" on a woman whose marriage has been dissolved by divorce or death and who wishes to marry again.

They sanction the preeminence of the husband: he is head of the family and determines where the couple is to reside. The Malian code says: "The husband owes protection to his wife, the wife obedience to her husband." Both codes, however, consider the wife to be helper to her husband. The Malian code notes: they "assume together, by the very fact of marriage, the obligation of directing the family morally and materially." But the wife is obliged to have her husband's permission to engage in business (Mali) or to exercise any profession by herself (Ivory Coast). There are limitations to this obligation, however: "If the husband's opposition is not justified by family interest, the wife can be authorized by the courts to go against his wishes."

On the other hand, the Malian code recognizes "either joint or separate ownership of goods." The Ivory Coast code says: "Marriage effects a community of goods between the spouses," but it stipulates that matrimonial agreements may not derogate from the woman's right to exercise a separate profession. Thus some independence is granted the woman by reason of her profession, even if she be married under a regime of joint ownership.

The two codes are also alike on the question of divorce and separation. Mali, a Muslim country, now outlaws the Koranic repudiation still allowed in several Islamic countries (Morocco, for example), because it gives the husband undue rights. The Ivory Coast code does not recognize separation simply by mutual consent, as the Malian code does. But both tend to put the spouses on an equal footing when it comes to divorce or separation.

On two points, however, the codes diverge: polygamy and dowry. These illustrate the many issues which remain hotly debated in the current evolution of mentality on the family. The Malian code: "The woman cannot contract a second marriage before the first is dissolved. The same holds for men who have chosen monogamous marriage. But the man who has opted for polygamy has the right to revise his marriage contract with the express consent of his wife." The Ivory Coast code, on the contrary: "No one can contract a new marriage before the old is dissolved." It provides for a delay in application of the law, after which "the polygamous spouse will not be able to contract a new marriage under the new law until all the marriages in which he is involved have been dissolved."

As for the dowry, the Malian code fixes the maximum for dowry and marriage gifts: no more than twenty thousand francs for a young girl, no more than ten thousand for a mature woman. The Ivory Coast law, however, abolishes all dowries.

The difference on these two points shows how difficult a task it is for a government to adapt familial practice with a view to development. Juridical reforms, in addition, do not produce immediate massive results. But in fact they ought not to be judged by such a standard of results. They are to be judged rather by the possibilities they open up, however few in number, to people who are able to behave in new ways, to enter into a nontraditional family system, and to free themselves of the burdensome obligations of the extended family, especially from the parasitism it often begets. People who have changed their behavior in so crucial an area as the family or procreation will be more disposed to behave in new ways in other areas of life. At least they will be less inhibited.

EDUCATION

AND

ANIMATION

The various measures we have spoken of, concerning population, land law, and family law, are direct interventions in society and its institutions. The effort is to adapt these institutions to the requirements of development.

Other measures are indirect interventions: policies of education and community development, and the spread of ideology. The intervention is indirect at least as regards institutions. Yet it is probable that education is infinitely more decisive in producing a change of mentality than any modification of laws on land or family. Once mentalities have changed, institutions will follow suit. However, the desire for instruction and modern education must first be roused.

Educational Policy

Every developing nation today regards education as one of its most important political concerns. But we can ask whether the basis for educational policy is broad enough; this is a matter of great consequence.

The general tendency is to suppose that education, and indeed any education whatsoever, will have immediate and direct utility. Thus there is a tendency to indulge in education in a vacuum, without adverting to the unpreparedness of the economy, or indeed of society generally, to absorb the new educated individuals. The danger then, as has often been noted, is of producing unemployed "intellectuals." This group includes not only lawyers and men of letters and science (all intellectuals in a stricter sense of the word), but also at times young people who have gotten a diploma and cannot now think of themselves as anything but civil servants or white-collar workers, whereas they could really be helpful to the economy in other kinds of work.

All this is, of course, well known. Our point in speaking of simplistic views on the productivity of education is to stress that no immediate usefulness ought to be expected of all education. For education transforms milieu and mentalities in other ways than by giving immediately useful instruction.

It is possible, indeed, to distinguish education as an investment from education as a consumer product. In our present perspective the nations must resolutely choose education as an investment. René Gendarme wrote: "Education as a consumer product and education as an infrastructure have grown in the Western countries as their economies found the necessary resources and were able to delay the age at which people had to go to work. Now, with the shortening of the time it takes for innovations to become wisespread and with the growth in specialization, teaching must anticipate the economy's need for researchers and skilled personnel. Educational outlays must henceforth be regarded as productive investments. This is why recent years have seen a good deal of economic research into the area of education." These remarks must be properly understood. There can be education which is apparently only a consumer product, yet which nonetheless transforms the mental infrastructure and thus represents a considerable investment of indirect value.

It is important to keep this aspect in mind, even while respecting the viewpoint according to which education is an investment with direct and proximate results. Viewed as an investment with long-term results, a widespread primary education (even one that is rather mediocre in quality) or simple literacy can radically affect society; yet these may be questionable in terms of immediate value.

The difficulty is keeping the two aspects balanced, for the cost of education in underdeveloped countries turns out to be very great; it is often even greater, proportionately, than in the developed countries. This may seem paradoxical. For certainly the money not earned by a person during his time of education is a small sum. "The real cost of education in the underdeveloped countries," says René Gendarme, "that is, the value of the goods and services that would be turned out if productive people were not removed from the economy, is difficult to evaluate, and it varies from one economy to another. But in all countries where population and unemployment are high and the extra productivity of work is near zero, it seems that this real cost of education is very low, to the extent at least that teaching employs manpower in the form of professors and students and demands but few material aids."[133] However, we must unfortunately insist on the words "to the extent." For education is difficult today without many material aids. We can imagine students whose status involves few new consumer goods and whose time at school does not represent a serious loss of productivity, but we can hardly imagine professors being had at so small a cost. Generally, too, the situation of a student does imply considerable new consumption. Education often removes him from his natural setting, and then there are the problems of housing and feeding him in the city or rural center, whereas food and housing were much more readily had in the traditional situation.

Even the absolute cost of education is higher at times in the developing countries. Here are some figures given by W. A. Lewis in 1962: in Ghana boarding schools for five hundred students and twenty professors cost 250,000 pounds sterling to build, while a good secondary school cost only 50,000 pounds in England at the time; at universities the cost per student was three to five times higher than at European universities.[134]

Many factors determining this high cost are clearly provisional.

The cost results partly from too small a student body in the first days of a new facility (so that, according to Gendarme, there may be one professor for three students in Africa, compared to one for eight in Great Britain and one for twenty in the United States). The number of students is so small at the universities because many students prefer universities abroad. In this phase, there is also a heavy dropout rate.

In any case, the cost of education is always relatively higher than in the developed countries. That is, the amounts required for a complete primary system, for example, form a greater part of the national budget in underdeveloped countries than in developed ones. Here again are some figures given by Lewis: "To allow all children eight years of primary education costs .8 percent of the national revenue in the United States, 1.7 percent in Jamaica, 2.8 percent in Ghana, 4 percent in Nigeria."[135] Again the salary of a primary school teacher represents one and a half times the average per capita income in the United States, three times the average income in Jamaica, five times in Ghana, seven times in Nigeria. These figures also show that the major factor in the higher costs is the salary of teachers. If it were possible to lower these salaries a good deal proportionately, the situation would be considerably improved. But this is out of the question in the immediate future for many localities because the personnel is from abroad. In the states of French-speaking black Africa and Madagascar it is true that primary education is almost completely in the hands of Africans and Malagasy; foreign help chiefly takes the form of improvement and formation (travelling teams of educational advisers), furnishings for educational establishments, and the setting up of pedagogical centers for educational adaptation and teacher improvement. But at the secondary level the French still make up three-fourths of the teaching staff, and even if the number of native teachers is growing rapidly, their proportion will grow less rapidly if secondary education has to be considerably expanded, as seems likely.

High costs are thus a notable hindrance to educational development. It can be calculated that "at the primary level, for states with only 25 percent of their children in school, a rapid increase in this percentage (its doubling within five years, for example) would demand an effort disproportionate to the financial and human resources of the states. A large attendance at school (more than 50 percent) is a heavy burden on public finance, and the effort must be made to hold down expansion rather than to encourage it."[136] In some countries public investment in education already represents one-fifth or one-fourth of the national budget, and education for all would absorb the whole present budget.

A pragmatic viewpoint has generally dictated the development of primary schools, but at times we also find a rather rapid development of higher education on a narrow secondary school base. Today the secondary level is still weak. It seems that an optimum proportion between different levels of education must be respected or established if education is to be effective for economic progress. René Gendarme notes on this subject: "Suppose that five hundred illiterate workers are occupied in traditional activities or are unemployed. With one engineer (but not with one or with ten diploma-holders) at their head, they will be able to dig irrigation canals and build roads. With one engineer, some foremen, and some skilled workers, you will have an industrial unit. Thus there is a kind of job-ladder: one engineer allows you to use five foremen, and five foremen can manage one hundred laborers . . . . Ten medical aides per doctor would allow you, while continuing to supply the outlying rural areas with the kind of help they now receive, to use the doctor to his full capacity for serious cases sent to him by the aides and for the organization of hygiene programs and disease eradication campaigns, etc. At present, we find doctors doing vaccinations in many places and engineers doing draughtsman's work. An adequate number of auxiliaries would multiply the effectiveness of the professionals."[137]

These observations lead to the conclusion that the various levels of the educational system should form a harmoniously proportioned pyramid. René Gendarme, using statistics furnished by UNESCO, has tried to reconstruct the pyramids actually found in various countries, putting the students in primary education at the base, the secondary students in the middle, and those in higher education at the top. The pyramid is well proportioned in the United States, France, Denmark, and Japan. It is less so in India, and we find a very thin secondary level in Mexico,

Cuba, and Iran. Nigeria shows a rather limited secondary level and a very limited upper level. The situation would probably be even more serious in many other countries of black Africa. Belgian Congo, too, before independence had intensively developed the primary level, but had no concern for the secondary and upper levels. "Yet," says Gendarme, "the secondary level is the most indispensable one. Primary level education brings no utilizable knowledge or technical skill, except for the lower-echelon office worker. Apart from trained personnel a developing economy needs only a few university graduates and can import them from abroad at less expense than it would cost to educate them. Two or four years training beyond the primary level, on the other hand, will provide all the specialized personnel needed: technicians, medical aides, middle-level and high-level entrepreneurs, agricultural instructors, and teachers."[138]

Today Africa lacks personnel for both secondary and upper-level instruction. Asia and South America have more upper-level personnel, but lack people to work at the intermediate level. Consequently there is serious unemployment among the highly educated, and many professionals (doctors, lawyers, even engineers) emigrate.

Obviously, a good distribution of educational levels is not enough; education adapted to real needs is also necessary and, therefore, well-chosen disciplines and methods. Yet, at the upper level, for example, realism is often still very limited: far too few students take up technical studies. It can be estimated that about half of them should choose sciences, technology, medicine, agriculture, and pharmacy; one-fourth normal school; and another fourth, law, letters, social science, and business management.[138] Yet Gendarme notes, "At present those matriculated in the sciences and technology at the upper level total only 19 percent in Africa, 16 percent in Latin America, and 23 percent in Asia."[140] (The figure is 31 percent in India.) Similar imbalances are evident at the secondary and primary levels. In the present situation specialized, well-adapted instruction is important, for straight primary instruction is generally inadequate.

In fact educational planning is turning in these directions today. "Educational policy has been undergoing an evolution for some time. The African governments are stressing the improvement rather than the extension of general instruction, and the development of professional education, in order to avoid the anarchic growth of poor education and the proliferation of unemployed intellectuals."[141] The first rule is to continue education far enough, even if for fewer people, for it to be truly useful; it is better to let ground lie waste than to sow it and not plough it.

Such a policy of intensification is gradually replacing a policy of extending education to as many as possible, and it is becoming policy in some places where there has been none. This is an important step forward. Yet, in conclusion we must add that the aspect of education we noted above ought not to be neglected, namely the fact that education is always useful for changing mentalities and awakening curiosity. This is not to turn education into a pure consumer product, simply because it does not yield faultless results in terms of economic productivity. The viewpoint we are stressing here is valid above all in a first phase, when development has hardly begun and social resistance is still manifold and strong. At this moment, it could be said, almost any education is good, for no one yet knows to what it will lead. At least we know that it helps upset the kind of balance which means stagnation. The day will soon come, however, when it will de necessary to introduce corrections and balances so as to render education more productive. At such a moment if education were to refuse to become a real investment, it could indeed become a purely unproductive consumer product which is more and more distrusted.

Community Development and Animation

As prolongations of educational policy, the various actions grouped under the titles community development and animation[142] require our attention. There are two different techniques, even if we bring them together here. Furthermore, the two do not have quite the same relation to education. We must insist on these preliminary points before considering the roles played by these policies.

Community development and animation belong to different cultural universes and traditions. The expression "community development" and even the techniques summed up by the name belong to the English-speaking world of India and former British East and West Africa. Animation and its techniques have been developed in the French-speaking world, in former French Africa and Madagascar.

The idea and, we might also say, the ideology of community development can be translated, at least in principle, as "self-development of the community (or collectivity)." Or perhaps we might better say that community development supposes a belief in the power of communities to develop themselves. The impulse from outside may be weak. But men, gathering together, united into a community, debating and working together, must be regarded as capable of important initiatives toward development within the community framework.

The idea of animation is rather of organized effort toward leading populations, especially peasant populations, to an awareness of their problems. It is a matter of waking them up and enlightening them. The whole enterprise rests, of course, on their native abilities, and the effort is made to develop natural leaders while removing them as little as possible from their milieu. But a large role is played by outside effort in the awakening of latent abilities and in the discovering and forming of leaders.

There is a certain similarity between efforts at rural animation in, for example, Senegal and Madagascar, especially by the Institute for Research and Application of Methods of Development (IRAM), and various efforts to arouse rural populations in Latin America, for example in Northeast Brazil before 1966. These latter efforts have the well-known name *conscientizaçao*, "the action of making aware." The name was perhaps not always exact, because the effort often took the form of literacy campaigns. But awareness was the goal pursued, or at least an essential purpose of the enterprise.

A difference between *conscientizaçao* and animation ought to be noted. *Conscientizaçao* was embarked upon with no clear idea of where it would lead, and it had rather a revolutionary tone. It sought to bring men not only to awareness but also to rebellion against injustice and wretchedness, which until then had been borne with resignation, apathy, and ignorance. The efforts at rural animation, for example in Senegal in the time of Mamadou

Dia, were not wholly foreign to such perspectives. But in general, the aim of animation is to form associations of people for achieving well-defined goals in a planned way. In this undertaking, any revolutionary outcome of the new awareness is regarded as a deviation or failure to be avoided. The danger is there, and real. But what is aimed at is not a vague revolutionary state of mind, but an active and aware collaboration in a well-defined process of change. This is expected both to save men from a vague revolution and to be more profitable for them.

A further difference emerges from the preceding one. It is difficult to think of a rural animation program being led by any but the public power or at least without its approval. A good deal of the recent *conscientizaçao* in Brazil, on the contrary, was done without any links with public authority and even in opposition to it.

Let us note finally, in passing and still with reference to South America, that in the cities these undertakings have yet a different character, belonging rather to community development. This is true, for example, of many attempts to organize "communities" (and cooperatives) among the marginal shantytown populations.

If we relate all these enterprises to educational policy proper, further remarks are in order. Community development, strictly speaking, has no direct educational goal. It does indeed provide the education which common action brings with it. But the primary goal is the organization of the community. At times the most express and direct goal, even if it is hardly attained, is the economic improvement of the activated community. Animation, on the other hand, if not conceived entirely without relation to economic production and to structures for that purpose, is nonetheless an educational technique in the strict sense. It intends, often explicitly, to complement the educational system. And its promoters regard it as highly opportune: they believe that in the first phase of education instruction which does not remove people from their natural milieu is more important than general education which uproots them, causes emigration, and creates unemployed and alienated intellectuals.

What is the status today of the two techniques? We can provide only a few elements of the answer.

The most extensive community development undertakings are in India. The attempt has been made to cover the 558,000 rural villages with a network of community development units, organically linked with one another and forming an ensemble that will help in the development of the country as a whole. In India, as elsewhere, the time of enthusiasm is long past. The community development system is far from having done all that was expected of it and from producing all that was hoped for in immediate results.

There had been high hopes of economic effects, among them increased productivity. In fact, however, the initial chief effects were only indirectly economic—such as the connection of previously isolated villages with the national system of roads and railways. The villagers likewise built many schools. But, as René Dumont reported, "all these actions did not attack agricultural problems or land improvement, especially through hydraulics: irrigation in one place, drainage in another, flood protection in a third, and everywhere reforestation, the planting of orchards and the fight against erosion. It did not do so, because all this was the concern of private property owners."

The Indian land system in principle did not allow villagers, individually or collectively, to really profit by projects they might have undertaken; therefore they did not undertake them. "Every renter who contributes further work or capital bears the whole burden of such an effort but gains only half of the further crop which his extra effort produces. When the consultant agronomists advised following Japanese methods of growing rice, the question of who was to pay for the necessary ammonià sulfate arose (a cost of 75 to 100 rupees per two and a half acres): the owner who would take half the extra crop without spending a penny, or the renter? Since the cost of fertilizer is 55 percent of the value of the additional crop to be gained, the renter would lose money and therefore he does not enter into the scheme. A number of intelligent landowners grasped the situation and agreed to pay for half the fertilizer. In these instances the use of chemical fertilizer has been continued. But the intelligent landowners are in the minority."

These observations help us to better understand the role of

community development. It has probably been somewhat overesteemed as the sole technique for development or as a self-sufficient technique. Today people realize more and more that community development cannot be fully effective in the absence of various important structural reforms. It is not the panacea some believed it to be. This is not to say that it is useless. It is even, we judge, of primary importance, provided it is integrated into an ensemble of economic and social measures aimed at development.

Another defect has cropped up in India. The community development agents had so much to do that they had no time for popular instruction and farm problems proper. Besides, they were not prepared for this latter role.

We find here a deficiency that also marked early efforts at rural animation. Much was done to awaken the confidence of peasants and to stimulate their desire. At this propitious moment, however, there was often no one who could present them with techniques, however modest, that would allow them to profit by their new awareness and interest. The danger is that the peasant will then become discouraged or that his new awareness will turn into rebellion pure and simple—that is, into a vague revolutionary awakening which can hardly lead to anything but a peasant uprising. (The more probable result in the first stages of the process is discouragement.)

The remedy for this situation is, in part, improved competence of the agent who has many roles in both community development and animation. But we quickly reach limits on this front. It is necessary, therefore, to have other men available to take over the work at the right moment, to be popularizers of agronomy and agents of further rural development. But it is difficult to find such men, to form them, pay them, and fit them into the whole operation. When we look at things from this angle, we can see again that neither community development nor animation is a short-term panacea: modern development always requires a whole set of complex measures into which they can and must be integrated.

A final point should be raised in conclusion: the problem of relating the various structures which community development or animation supposes to the public administration. The situation would be simple if the public authority were to remain neutral, occupied only with general matters, with paper work, with police, etc. But we must plan on having to deal, in fact, with an active, interventionist, ambivalent administration. In a developing country, the administration must be an administration for development, with its agents active in the economic and social areas. If people do not realize this and provide for it, there is danger of confusing frames of reference and the roles of various agents.

There can also be an opposite danger: an administration which sees all activities as belonging to the civil service may crush community initiative that operates in a more flexible way. This danger is greater in a society which has not yet fashioned solid social institutions for itself. And the danger is a real one, for there is a tendency for developing countries simply to transpose for their own use an administrative organization borrowed from the developed countries, when what is really needed is a new and original approach.

IDEOLOGIES

The state, through all the agencies described, is the chief source of developmental energy in the means of exercising public action on the economy. It attacks traditional structures through modification of land law and family law and, even more radically, by making available a modern education, which is complemented—in order to reach the masses—by techniques of mass education, community development, and rural animation.

Our final subject will be ideology. Paradoxically, what we have to say about it prolongs rather directly the observations made in earlier chapters on state action for development or on socio-cultural steps taken to foster the social changes which will facilitate development. For, in the developing countries, ideologies too are instruments of social change. This does not prevent them from being, in part, something spontaneous as well. We shall see, however, that a deliberate choice lies behind some at least of these ideologies. Ideology is itself, in addition, a sign of development; strictly traditional societies are unaware of ideologies, and live instead on continuity and tradition.

The Need for an Ideology

The need for an ideology is often explicitly felt in the developing countries, and views on this point are current which would not be particularly acceptable in other societies. One example will illustrate; it is taken from a 1961 report prepared at Dakar by a study group on African socialism considering the role and necessity of an ideology.

First of all, said the group, an ideology is needed for national development. "A shared ideology is necessary for every human community that wishes to deal with the situation in which it finds itself." An ideology? That means an overall scheme or conception, embracing both the goal and the means of achieving it. An ideology is a matter of "a human group taking up the totality of its problems" (in our context, the problems of development) and building the nation.

If there is no shared ideology, what happens? "The group may let itself be crushed by its situation. Then, for lack of dynamism within itself, it will inevitably fall under the sway of external forces. Or else the group will be guided by a weak nucleus of men who impose their solution on the masses. Then it is to be foreseen that this oligarchy, promoting a totalitarian solution to problems, will block the native spirit of the group and prevent its growth in accordance with its own values. Then the group enters a prerevolutionary period, for the ideology of the masses can, in such circumstances, develop only outside the apparatus of power."

Let us note some further details of this report's definition of ideology: "A projection of a system of solutions, coordinated with a value system to which a human community adheres as it faces its destiny and masters its situation." There is question here not of an abstract philosophical system but of a system of concrete values and solutions; not a static vision, but a future-oriented conception of things: "a system of solutions." Such an orientation does not mean that the ideology cannot be rooted in a tradition, "in a past, in a history," that it cannot arise out of "a chain of traditions." It is impossible, in practice, to create values totally outside history. If an ideology is deeply to inspire a human group, it will have to show, even in its forward thrust, a certain fidelity to the group's authentic character and consequently to its history and tradition.

Let us also note the following words which sum up the position

here adopted on ideology: "An ideology is necessary for the progress of humanism, especially at the present time when the
individual can less and less find his fulfillment outside a group."

The need for an ideology is especially great, we are told, when
we are faced with the problems of development. "When dealing
with the development of a young nation, it seems absolutely
necessary that all the human cells of a population be guided by
a shared idea of their human growth and their common fulfillment
(always respecting the irreducible diversity among men), an idea
whose fundamentals are not only accepted, but willed, chosen,
created. A people can be inspired to a great common work only
by such conditions as these." The report adds, as it further com-
ments on and documents the need for an ideology, "The nations
in the best situation are those whose growth rests on a strong
ideology, to which the people adhere firmly but freely and which
itself emerges out of the people's being and life."

Finally, the recognition of a people's need for an ideology does
not exclude the notion of progress toward human unity; it does
not necessarily carry with it the strengthening of particularism.
"If we admit that the human condition is the common starting
point of all men despite all differences among them, then it follows
that the ideologies of all human groups should converge on a
common platform which the nations will have to define in con-
cert." This, it is thought, is today true above all for an African
nation (among all the Third World nations). "Aware of the drama
now unfolding or shortly to unfold, an African nation which
is not yet caught up in the net of ideological warfare can only
refuse to enter such a war, that is, refuse to be alienated for
the profit of a Western or an Eastern or a neutralist bloc. It
must first face its own condition and that of other peoples, that
is, understand the dynamism at work in the creation of an African
nation, for the latter is naturally open to trans-national communities, which in turn are a provisional form of future nations.
It must then determine its own ideology, without being influenced
by any blocs. It ought not only refuse to align itself with these.
On the contrary, despite its limited material forces and in the
name of a permanent human truth which is not determined by
material forces, it ought to engage in dialogue with all the other

nations, so that these may come to renounce the dialectic of power or pure technology and work out a common humanism as they project the world of tomorrow."

These lines are clearly inspired by Mamadou Dia's *Nations africaines et solidarité mondiale*.[143] All those concerned with ideology in the developing countries do not have the same clear vision of universal brotherhood, nor do all so clearly express the need and function of an ideology. But almost everywhere the need is felt and inspires the search for an ideology, whether in black Africa or North Africa or Asia. In Latin America it is rarely the governments which engage in the search (except in Cuba or, at times, in Argentina under Peron). But important groups do conceive in like fashion the need for an ideology of development, one that can stir men to the pressing tasks at hand.

Nationalism

The elements which in varying mixtures make up the ideologies of the developing countries are primarily nationalism and socialism. In many instances the first ideology was nationalism, and it remains perhaps the most important element still.

In this context nationalism does not have quite the same meaning as it did in the French Revolution. At that time the question was freeing the people from the tutelage of absolute monarchic sovereigns. But there are parallels, since the issue today is to establish a people's independence and its autonomy to decide its own destiny and organization. There is evidently no question, initially at least, of establishing the nation's supremacy over other nations (this is another meaning of the term nationalism).

Nationalism in the Third World has to do chiefly with gaining independence, but it is also related to development. Buchmann explains this for the black African world.

A first aspect: "Nationalism as applied to Africa is rather fundamentally different from nationalism as generally understood in Europe. In Europe it refers to the existence of 'nations' with fairly well defined frontiers and to their striving for their own political existence, for existence as a national state. The term can therefore be used in the black African context only if we make it clear that here there is nationalism without a nation, a nationalism that is thus unsure of its concrete basis."[144] This statement is true at least of nationalism before independence, but for some years now we have perhaps been watching the birth in various states of nationalism along more classical lines. However, we are discussing for the moment the first form which nationalist ideology took in Africa.

It is before all else a matter of protest, refusal, and self-vindication in the face of the colonial situation, and is accompanied by the affirmation of a people's own personality as translated, for example, in the word "blackness" *(négritude)*. "Against the background of a black Africa which became the dependency of another continent only because it was 'colonizable,' the claim to autonomy is seen to be not so much a positive principle of cohesion as a simple demand for human dignity."[145]

Nationalist ideology is, further, the expression of a "right to development," and this gives such nationalism a more explicit social context. "The foundation of these claims is evidently the underdeveloped state of black Africa, viewed much less in its objective components than in its psycho-sociological components. Underdevelopment today contains a new constitutive element, which is doubtless the most important element of all: the peoples of the underdeveloped countries are aware of their situation."[146] The problem of development thereby becomes part of a nationalist ideology: "Awareness of their wretched state and especially of the contrast with the wealthy developed countries; awareness that the immense economic inequality is increasing and at an ever accelerating rate; awareness of the developmental possibilities offered by technology and therefore awareness that the wretchedness they experience is not necessary; awareness of the responsibility of Western liberalism for this radical inequality. The initial feeling of frustation, springing from initial awareness, is changed, with deepening awareness, into a sense of injustice and finally into a desire for, then a claim to, change and development." The claim may be accompanied by a demand for "equalization" (Nehru's word) of conditions throughout the world.[147]

Thus, as Buchmann noted, the "mystique of development

becomes an essential component of black African nationalism."[148] Tibor Mende has shown in his books that this component is present on other continents as well. Gunnar Myrdal, too, has stressed the same phenomenon: "The strong emotional relationship of the drive for economic development to the fight for national political independence is a very important fact, distinguishing it from the historical industrialization process in the now advanced countries. Indeed, the very fact that there is a political drive for economic development is a new and different thing."[149] The desire for economic development in the underdeveloped countries is not the empty dream of an economist enamored of his plan, but a political force of great and irresistible power in the present-day world.

Nationalism that is focused on the right to development can be an ideology and accomplish the purposes of an ideology. "It is a powerful idea," says Buchmann, "and capable of uniting the varying groups and interests within a heterogeneous society."[150] It is also one of those ideologies which is not immediately shared by a whole people, but is an instrument of development in the sense that the leadership elite must bring all to share it. A further component marks this kind of nationalist ideology: the idea of and claim to nonalignment.

We must add that African nationalist ideology not only makes claims but is also a "mystique" (Buchmann's term) and thus reinforces its power over men. Mystique here means that this ideology is rooted "in the instinctual collective life of Africa."[151] Black African nationalism is thus grounded in an exaltation of the black African past, as evident, for example, in the enthusiastic writings of Sheikh Anta Diop. With Nkrumah we reach messianism. "When Africa is free and independent," he said at the second pan-African congress (Accra, December 1958), "we shall see an unparalleled flowering of the human spirit." An extreme statement, indeed, but such extreme statements are part of a dynamic ideology which can consolidate the energies needed to build the future and develop a nation, unless of course they are mere slogans and one never moves beyond them.

In brief, this nationalism is quite new, even if the term is old. "The criteria for the nation state, as nineteenth-century Europe seemed permanently to have determined them, are likely to be questioned today by some, perhaps by many, of the new non-European nationalisms. Given the fluidity and ambiguity of some of the ideological concepts being used, it seems possible to move from the nation state, defined territorially by its present boundaries, to a whole civilization, defined by language, culture, or religion. It is posssible, for example, to move from Algerian nationalism to Arabic nationalism."[152]

Yet the term nationalism is not being used here by accident. First of all, the new stirring began in many instances with the claim to a land, to a fatherland, against its invader. This is true especially of colonized territories which had earlier had their own fairly well defined political existence—Vietnam, for example, or Dahomey. We may cite the words of Behanzin to Ballot, lieutenant-governor at Porto Novo, in 1892: "Did I ever go to France to make war upon you? No, I stay in my own country, and if another African nation harms me, I have the right to punish it. That is none of your business."

In a similar but looser way, nationalism is grafted onto the *memory* of ancient local political units: e.g., Congo, Mali, Ghana. "In the very early years of the Christian era, long before England had become important, long before its people had even formed a nation, our ancestors had built a great empire which lasted until the eleventh century, when it succumbed to Moorish attacks from the North. At its height this empire stretched from Timbuktu to Bamako and even to the Atlantic. It is said that lawyers and scholars enjoyed great prestige in this empire and that the inhabitants of Ghana wore clothing of wool, cotton, gold, and textiles, and wore jewels and carried arms of gold and silver. Did not our ancestors hold the reins of government before the white man ever came to our shores?" (Nkrumah). The members of the Lukiko (parliament) of the Kingdom of Buganda addressed a memorandum to Queen Elizabeth II in 1960, which was filled with the same spirit: "Buganda is an ancient kingdom with a long history; its dynasty counts thirty-seven kings in uninterrupted succession. Buganda's history began with a king, and it has crossed the centuries under royal leadership down to the present day."

Such nationalism recalls the wellsprings which fed traditional European nationalism—for example, that of the Slavs in the nineteenth century. But we find other nationalist movements whose background contains no distinct political entities. In these cases, nationalism is inspired by the outcry of a society against a discrimination and inequality which wound the human spirit. We can speak of nationalism because the discrimination is the work of foreigners, men from other traditions and cultures. "Our spirit has been choked by foreign overlords," said Tran Trong Kim, Vietnamese prime minister, a nationalist and historian, on August 17, 1945. The feeling is found not only in well-defined historical units like Vietnam, but also in countries like Algeria whose historical antecedents are much more obscure; there has been an Algerian nationalism no less than a Vietnamese.

In the nationalisms of the developing countries, then, political themes are frequent, especially the criticism of colonial powers for their policy of domination and suppression of freedom. Social protests are also essential: "Exploitation, wretchedness, starvation," said a Vietnamese pamphlet in 1945. But the chief protest is against inequality. The same document said: "The French doorkeeper of Hanoi University earns fourteen hundred piasters a month, whereas the salary of an Indochinese engineer from the Polytechnical School is no more than four hundred, and a Vietnamese workman earns hardly more than fifty."[153]

At one period, the social aspect was even primary in dealing with the colonial problem. Writing of the French-speaking community, Senghor said in 1945: "France does not have to justify her colonial conquests any more than she does Brittany and the Basque country. She needs only to reconcile her own interests with those of the natives. The colonial problem is only the human problem of dealing with a province." Patrice Lumumba likewise wrote before 1956: "The essential desire of the Congolese elite is not to refuse recognition of. all the good that was done, but to be themselves 'Belgians' and to possess the same freedom and rights, with the merits of each man taken into account." We can also cite the African Democratic Rally's 1946 manifesto: "We solemnly proclaim our loyalty to the French Union. The loyalty is justified by a realistic approach to the world's political problems, by confidence in Africa's future, and by the assurance that despite reactionary opposition we shall obtain liberal, democratic, and humane conditions in which to freely develop the native abilities of the African genius."

These are words foreshadowing the nationalism of the intellectuals, which is a reaction to cultural oppression. These men have the sense that native culture has been scorned, trodden down, uprooted. Some sentences of Césaire express the thought clearly: "Everywhere that colonialism comes, native culture begins to wane, and from its ruins is born not a culture but a kind of subculture. It is condemned to a marginal existence at the fringes of European culture. It is the possession of a small group of men, an elite, who live an artificial existence, cut off from life-giving contact with the masses and with popular culture. This subculture thus has no opportunity of flowering into a genuine culture. The result is vast territories or zones of cultural emptiness or, what comes to the same thing, cultural perversion or subculture. Such is the situation which we men of black culture must courageously face."

All these nationalisms springing from social or cultural protest finally took the step of claiming independence, without thereby ceasing to feed on their earlier protests and claims. Indeed, the moment came when they had no choice but to seek independence. "The Annamite people," said Tran Duc Thao, "came to the clear awareness that it could not fully develop except as an independent part of the international community." Senghor, Houphouet-Boigny, Bourguiba, and Patrice Lumumba all followed the same path.

However, soon after independence, nationalism took on the complex character it had had in the earlier period. Now, the political theme does not stand by itself; it is accompanied by an economic theme. But even in this new stage the word nationalism remains valid.

It quickly became evident that political independence was limited and inadequate without the necessary foundations. Economic dependence continued, and the strongest nationalist protests and claims flowed from that fact. Their expression was no longer moderated, for now they were the protests of an independent state. Economic dependence indeed has a more abstract character than the former problems of the masses, but it is strongly felt by the political leaders who brought about independence. These leaders now rouse their people's feelings around the theme of economic independence.

In this way, nationalism has spread throughout the developing areas of the world. For even countries long independent politically have felt economic dependence. Here is a Brazilian speaking: "In Third World countries at least, contemporary nationalism is aware that political submission is not the only, nor perhaps even the most dangerous, form of dependence. Economic hegemony, though more subtle, is no less a form of colonization, and political independence remains an abstraction until it is matched by economic liberation. Such total sovereignty is not for the taking. A country inadequately equipped is necessarily dependent on the industrialized countries; the vulnerability of its economy means it is subject to the vicissitudes of the rich nations. The help it needs for its development almost always implies a more or less close satellization." In this respect, the author notes, "the situation is the same for the Afro-Asian countries as for the Latin American nations."

Latin America does not lag behind when it comes to nationalist ideologies. "Those nations which thought themselves free and sovereign and were proud of their past and confident of their future, discovered in the nineteenth century that they were behind economically, and that catching up would require costly reforms. They found they were so dependent on American capital that their political liberty was illusory. This new awareness is the origin of nationalist awakening in Latin America." Juan Perón put it well: "Our revolution is our nation's second epic story. The first was the winning of political independence. Now we are engaged in the second, as we strive for economic independence" (Declaration of Economic Independence, July 9, 1947).

At this point, nationalism generally enters into a compact with socialism, especially in Latin America. A complex alliance it is, and we will have to look closely at its socialist component in a moment. But we must stress the fact that we are still dealing primarily with nationalism. For domestic social foes are reduced to enemies of the nation and its independence; or else economic independence is made the condition for socialism. "I maintain that without economic independence there is no possibility of social justice" (Perón). Perón fell from power the day that he abated his nationalist intransigence a bit, for that was more important than his position on social justice. The day came in 1955; his enemies could accuse him of making scandalously favorable grants to Standard Oil. Frondizi, the "oil industry nationalist," met the same fate when he too relaxed his initially intransigent attitude.

In the case of national Marxism, so frequent in Argentina and the rest of Latin America, Marxism is in fact abandoned, but it is typical that the national or nationalist element in the compound is kept. At a now rather distant time, the Peruvian Mariategui was the first genuine Marxist on the continent, but he was also openly nationalist. "He claimed to be a Marxist," says one commentator, "but wanted freedom from the dialectical schemas and dogmatic affirmations of a party whose structures had hardened. At the Communist congress of Montevideo, his proposals for agrarian reform were not in conformity with Moscow's directives and they won him the label Trotskyite. From that moment he broke with the party. He remained faithful to the Marxist theses but rejected the rigid internationalism of Russian Communism with its desire to centralize all decisions."

All this happened back in the thirties. But it has happened periodically ever since, in various Latin American countries. It happened with Rodolfo Puiggros, for example, in Argentina, and is perhaps happening now with Fidel Castro. The tendency of international Marxism, it seems, is always to grant less importance to the national factor and to accept alliances with the middle and lower middle classes, rather readily, whereas the intransigent nationalist regards these classes as the most dangerous possible allies. On the other hand, international Marxism is more attentive to domestic class struggles and interested in imperialism abroad only as the prolongation of these; for a national Marxist this is a reversal of priorities.

Economic nationalism has a close relation to the problems of development, and undoubtedly is more in evidence the more development gets underway. It appears in economies already strong and well consolidated. For the new needs of a growing

economy can lead to a real dependence greater than in the intermediate stage. Thus a dividing line passes today between the
African and Central American countries, on the one side, and,
on the other, some really growing countries of Asia and South
America, for example, India, Argentina, and Brazil. "In contemporary Brazil," one observer notes, "the main nationalist positions
are a function of a certain stage in economic development."

The new nationalism is not only sensitive to long-standing
kinds of dependence—for example, the existence of foreign companies with concessions for supplying water, gas, and electricity
to the cities. It is much more sensitive to the new burdens which
must be taken on when the country goes in for large productive
investments. The need for capital—foreign capital—increases;
occasions on which one's dependence is brought home become
more frequent. Consider, for example, Brazil when it wanted
to build an ironworks. "The building of a large iron industry
required a great deal of capital. Borrowing from American banks
was difficult because up to the Second World War the United
States wanted the Latin American countries to remain producers
of raw materials, who would then buy back the finished products
of American industry. American production had to become
absorbed by the war effort for Brazil to obtain from its 'good
neighbor' the cooperation it needed for developing a national iron
industry, and even then it had to allow American bases in Brazil.
In this way there arose the first plan for a Brazilian heavy industry,
the Nation Iron Company."

In its economic form, then, nationalism arises from contact
with development; it is produced by development. It is also an
ideology for development, to the extent that a nation sees foreign
countries setting obstacles to its development.

In summary, despite some paradoxical traits (such as being
a nationalism without a nation, or even embracing more than
the nations, as in the early days of independent Africa), Third
World nationalism certainly has a future. It is a genuine nationalism, especially in the sense that it is very attentive to foreign
nations and asserts itself over against them, even when it is not
very sure of its own frontiers.

Socialisms

The other great theme for ideologies in the developing countries is socialism. We have already pointed out the relations which often exist between nationalism and socialism. We also said that socialism is not as universally found in Third World ideologies as nationalism is. This is not only because there are regimes which do not allow socialism (in Africa, for example, the government of Houphouet-Boigny, whose watchword instead is "state capitalism"). It is even more because there is a large difference in the reaction of the masses to nationalism and to socialism. Perhaps we must add that socialism is a more complex matter, more difficult to grasp. Above all, it makes greater demands on many people, those for whom it could mean a modification of social position and those who would have to undertake a hard struggle to bring it into existence.

There is also historical reason. At the moment of independence socialism seemed to be just the ideology for nations that were asserting themselves against the colonizers. Colonization was identified with the capitalist countries. Why not adopt socialism, then, since it was the doctrine opposed to capitalism within the colonizing countries themselves? Not much thought had been given to the fact that the current themes of socialism looked to a social situation typical of industrialized countries and quite different from the situation in the developing countries. All that the latter countries could retain of socialism was the element of nationalist anti-imperialism, but that was not a major element in socialism. Thus one could keep the word socialism and mean by it the search for economic independence. Or one could keep the word and mean nothing by it. In fact, the term is now less widely used than it was eight or ten years ago.

In brief, socialism in the developing countries still has trouble forcefully developing ideas really pertinent to the domestic social situation. This is true especially in Africa and Asia. In Latin America we are much closer to situations in which classical socialism prospered.

On the whole, however, socialist ideologies are fairly well represented in the Third World countries. But the socialism is not everywhere the same. We must distinguish some broad types (and these cut across one another at many points). In several of them we find a typically nationalist desire for originality.

The Marxist variant likes to label itself "scientific socialism," or at least socialism with no geographic limitation. At the beginning it is the most vigorous form of socialism. But it has trouble at times in relating itself to a social situation quite different from the one in which Marxist socialism developed. It is difficult to nationalize or collectivize the means of production when there are practically no means of production. It makes little sense to talk of collectivizing the land when private ownership has hardly developed. There are cases in which capitalists to be flushed from hiding—native ones at least—do not exist. People would certainly be willing to create needed capital on a public basis. But, in such situations, the typically Marxist notion of revolution cannot play a predominant role.

Over against classical socialism that is poorly adapted to many countries, other variants of socialism present themselves as specific to the developing countries and their situation. These refuse to imitate the socialism found in industrial countries. Since they in principle respect the most deeply rooted traditions of the developing nations, such socialisms do not tend to be very revolutionary; thus they do not have the inner drive which Marxist socialism has, at least in principle. It is among these variants that we find the socialisms with limiting modifiers—African, Arab, etc.—which so displease the authorities of international Communism or at least the Soviets.

African socialism is a typical example. We cannot speak of it without at the same time speaking of all socialisms in Africa. It is true there is opposition between the types, but often the distance separating them is not great, since it is extremely difficult to apply Marxist socialism to strictly local circumstances.

The complexity of the situation can be seen in the evolution of Senegalese socialism and Malian socialism. We recall that the two countries were for a time linked in the Malian Federation. The federation broke up rather quickly, for many reasons no doubt, but in particular because of incompatible ideologies, especially when it came to planning. When the break came in 1961-1962, the opposition between the two countries was strong: "African socialism," on the one side, "socialism" unqualified, on the other. In Senegal, due especially to Mamdou Dia's influence, "African socialism" was the watchword. The Malians poked fun at it and called it "Senegalese socialism." The September 5, 1961, issue of *Essor*, organ of the Malian African Democratic Rally, said: "The whole Senegalese economy is conceived, directed, and managed by international monopolies, and thus is objectively opposed to the interests, present and future, of the Senegalese masses. Mamadou Dia's pompous boasting about the famous five-year plan, the cooperatives, the infantile, obscure, and confused literature of 'Senegalese socialism' cannot prevent the Senegalese masses from daily experiencing the truth of the matter, as they sit by, powerless, and watch the managers shamefully enriching themselves."

Before listing the elements of Senegalese "African socialism," it is interesting to underline some characteristics of the Malian theses, that is, of a socialism more orthodox in principle, at the very time of its violent opposition to Senegal. "As far as revolution is concerned, the African revolution need not look just like other revolutions." Africa has not known and need not know an internal "class warfare." This is rather different from the doctrines of scientific socialism which banner the Malians considered themselves to be carrying.

Further: "We are dispensed from a struggle against capitalism at home . . . . The African revolution takes the form of liquidating colonialism which brings capitalism and capitalist exploitation in its train." Does this not mean that to liquidate foreign colonialism is by that very fact to establish socialism? We will not be surprised, then, to find the Bamako socialists themselves using the phrase "African socialism"—though they distinguish it from the "African socialism" of Dakar, or "Senegalese socialism." The explanation offered is that the new revolution taking place in Africa, which is nothing more than completion of the struggle against colonial dependence, leads of itself to an "African socialism which has been exempted from passing through one of the usual stages and which will not be created in vain." Thus socialism turns out to consist of preventing capitalism from making its entry: a socialism of prevention. "In the absence of private capitalism, the formation of which was happily prevented by the colonial regime, only the state, as an emanation from the masses, can quickly and rationally organize a supply of national capital. To leave this task to private initiative would be a defect in the building of the nation. For the characteristic of private capitalism is to concentrate the national revenue in the hands of a few privileged individuals. History shows that the initiatives of private capital are never good; moreover, delays, base calculations, deceptive maneuvers are all legion in such a system. In such conditions how can those responsible for building the state expect a class of men, with such a deadly reputation, to arise and take up the struggle against obvious underdevelopment, a struggle which cannot be put off for even a day?"

There speaks the radical Marxist distrust of private initative, although the revolutionary element is missing. But is it missing because there was no occasion for it? Yes, and therefore we can recognize here, despite its limitations, a variant of socialism which does retain some bit of Marxist character.

How are we to define, in comparison with this socialism, the type called "African socialism," represented by Senegal among others, and never repudiated to the present day? It is, to begin with, more a cooperative than a statist socialism. "People often err," said the proponents of African socialism at Dakar, "by confusing statism and socialism. For the state to take charge of a sector of activity is not in itself a mark of civilization, but can be understood only in the light of the common good and justified only in the measure, and for the time, that contemporary human communities are not able to assume direct responsibility. In light of this, the cooperative movement represents genuine socialism in action." This view does not exclude nationalization, but only systematic nationalization.

It is true that in Mali, too, positions on nationalization were rather nuanced. For example: "Domestic (not foreign) private business will build its own future, to the extent that it collaborates faithfully with the government." Only in case of failure "will the party and the government turn to other solutions." And Modibo Keita wanted to foster "autonomous management," "self-management." The party journal said: "We will watch with special care the movement of our nationalized organizations towards autonomous management, with a broad and increasing autonomy of their personnel as a way of preparing them for self-management. The success of such a regime cannot be assured without an effort to educate the workers." But African socialism at Dakar was even less favorable to nationalization and more explicitly leaned to cooperation. It wanted cooperatives based on "contemporary human communities" and not just self-management within nationalized organizations.

At the institutional level, African socialism was primarily aiming at bringing the traditional village community to its flowering or reflowering, even if in ways that were adapted to modern times. Socialism did not need to be invented or built so much as rediscovered, revived, and continued. "There is no contradiction," Mamadou Dia wrote, "in saying that the traditional economy of Africa was indeed a socialist economy . . . . How can an impartial observer . . . continue to deny that African collectivism is a continuation of the old socialist economy? . . . The simple ways that excluded luxury, the principle of common life which automatically assured an equal distribution of goods and proscribed superfluities and the taste for luxury—all that meant a natural regulation of demand, so that supply found its best stimulus in the enthusiasm which inspired the various members of the community. Need we recall the part played by those typically socialist societies, the peer-group fraternities, whose success came from the fact that they were spontaneous, friendly, and local?"[154]

This outlook has not been abandoned. In 1968 Senghor bore witness to it: "In the social sphere, the special qualities of the black community lead us to use original methods, different from those used in Europe . . . . This year all our peasants have been put into cooperatives, and we foresee that each group of ten villages will form a rural community. This will strengthen collective activities and the community sense of the villagers. Clearly, we must give up some aspects of traditional society and gradually arrive at the monogamous family, which will replace the present tribal practice. But it is essential to preserve the values of collective communion in all that concerns leisure, sports, and art in particular."

Once again, we must not overdo the contrasts. Modibo Keita, for his part, also said: "Well before the colonial period, the community spirit was strong in our villages and formed the foundation and roots of our society. The village was our basic cell, and its vitality engendered the vitality of the whole nation. No regime can be viable which is not based on the village." The differences begin when Modibo Keita adds: "The party itself has its roots in the village, as does our administration. This is why you have a political committee and an administrative council in the village."

African socialism proper insists, even more than on institutions, on the basic values and the whole philosophy which are necessary to this ideology. We have just heard Senghor speak of "the values of collective communion." The *Eléments pour un manifeste du socialisme africaine* insist on two complementary aspects, which are judged to be deeply African: liberty and solidarity, linked together in a humanism.

Solidarity: "The socialist believes that human fulfillment is impossible, as a general rule, apart from a living, coherent society, and therefore from a community. This means a harmonious balance in implementing the destiny of each man in the community—what 'human economics' [the allusion is to Francois Perroux and Father Lebret] expresses in the formula 'the development of the whole man and of all men.' This means, in turn, the rejection of egoism, whether of the individual or the group, and of certain kinds of solitude."

Liberty: "There is no solidarity under coercion, except perhaps the solidarity of resistance to such coercion, which is itself the affirmation of a freedom. A socialism in which one regards the common good as a shared value requires, then, a free adherence. An unfree socialism is no longer socialism, even if it wears the name, but totalitarianism."

Thus, solidarity and liberty, but, we must add, "in the African manner." "Liberty is established in Africa essentially through the word, through dialogue." Solidarity is connected with the communal village structures which we have already mentioned. These are the essential themes, along with "blackness" *(négritude)* and with black African vitalist philosophy. The whole socialist project is thus presented as anchored in a past which was already socialist. There is no brutal revolutionary break, and there is a bit less attention to foreign colonialism than in the more Marxist variants of socialism in Africa.

What is true of Mamadou Dia and Senghor holds likewise for Nyerere in Tanzania, for African socialism has representatives in the East no less than in the West.

Nyerere, too, is convinced that socialism lies in the past as well as in the future. "When a society is organized to watch over the well-being of its members, no one who is willing to work need worry about what will happen to him tomorrow, should he fail to amass wealth. Society watches over him, his widow, and his orphans. Traditional African society achieved this ideal. Rich and poor were both secure in it. Natural catastrophes indeed brought famine, but rich and poor alike suffered from it. No one was deprived of his human dignity simply because he lacked personal wealth. Each one could count on the wealth of his community. This was socialism . . . . Socialism is essentially distributive." Nyerere makes explicit here a characteristic implied by Senghor and Dia.

For Nyerere, as for Senghor and Dia, socialism as a state of mind is more important than socialism as an institutional affair. "Socialism, like democracy, is an attitude of mind. In a socialist society the important thing is the socialist attitude which sees to it that each individual is concerned for the well-being of the others." Thus socialism is ethical, as well as distributive.

The years have passed without this vein of thought being exhausted, despite the attacks of orthodox Marxism which will allow only a socialism that is universal, not an African or a European or a Russian socialism. In 1965, for example, there appeared in Kenya from the pen of Tom Mboya, with a preface by Jomo Kenyatta, a white book "African Socialism and Its Application to Planning in Kenya."

Here, in comparison with documents previously cited, the

source is more public and official, and the solutions proposed
are more political and more specifically economic. The white
book insists on the necessity of a radical evolution in traditional
community structures. It also asks for a more exact determination
of the vague traditional property rights. Modern cooperatives,
it says, will require greater discipline and better formation.
However, Kenyan African socialism agrees that it must build
on the community spirit and acknowledge the principle of "social
responsibility inherited from our tradition."

The ideology presented is one which distrusts ideologies. On
this account, it rejects dogmatic, fixed, "theoretical systems,"
be they capitalistic or communistic. The white book seeks rather
to open the way to a practical and practically useful economic
system. The "Africanness" of this system is played down, for
the economic and political project is one of less cultural originality.
But it is not any the less distinct from Marxist scientific socialism.
The two variants thus continue to be at loggerheads in contemporary Africa.

"Arab" socialism, too, includes, in fact, a great variety of forms.
On the one hand, there is the socialism of Nasser's Socialist
Union; its charter contains the words "scientific socialism." On
the other hand, there is a whole spectrum of native socialisms,
shading off into very distant forms. Lebanon, for example, presents us with the Druse, Kamal Jumblat, who calls himself a
"socialist" and is influential especially because of his name and
family, which is traditionally one of the most important in the
Druse community. But then there is also the Syrian People's
Party (PPS) of Antun Saadeh, who claims to be a socialist or
rather a national socialist. This party intervened in events in
Lebanon in 1958; it is now disbanded, but seems to persist as
a clandestine organization. There was also a National-Socialist
party, founded by Suleiman Nabulsi in Jordan, which was prohibited by King Hussein after 1957.

Bourguiba likewise adopted the name socialist. In Morocco,
Ahmed Reda Guidira, an adviser of Hassan II, gave the new
name of Democratic Socialist Party to an organization which
had first been called the Liberal Party and later the Front for
the Defence of Constitutional Institutions. This was opportunist

socialism indeed by comparison with Mehdi Ben Barka's National Union of Popular Forces.

According to the constitution of September 8, 1963, the Algerian Democratic People's Republic wished explicitly to be "socialist." What was meant was an economic system in which elements of state administration and self-management were to coexist with private enterprise; it represented a pragmatic effort to reconcile Algeria's colonial past with its actual present. Then, in 1964, a single-party program was adopted. Strongly inspired by the Marxist conception of history, it recommended the application of Marxist methods, urged "democratic centralism," called for class warfare against the upper and lower middle classes, against proprietors large and small, and against exploiters of private property, and promised agrarian reform and industrialization in order to solve the country's problems of unemployment and underdevelopment. All these ambitions were a good deal toned down after the fall of Ben Bella.

We must mention, finally, what is perhaps the most important of the Arab socialist parties: the Arab Socialist Party of the Resurrection (or Baath), inspired by the theorist, Michel Aflaq, who was a Christian. The Baath program inspired the socialist charter of Nasser. It was the Baathists who urged the union of Syria and Egypt in 1958, thinking thereby to provide the Egyptian revolution with a doctrinal basis. They occupied many posts in the United Arab Republic government. Later Nasser almost totally eliminated Baath from the Egyptian political scene, but, after 'this parting of the ways, Baath recouped its strength and put its program across in Syria and Iraq.

There are more than minor differences among all these versions of socialism—which range from a socialism in name only to a socialism apparently quite Marxist in its outlook. But we must see that, even in the genuine socialisms, we are faced with a complex reality. In them nationalism, or rather Arabism, holds a very considerable place, perhaps even the primary place. Unlike African socialism, Arab socialism is Arab not so much because it claims to find socialism in the Arab past, as because it is useful for the defense and promotion of the Arab world. This latter movement, itself highly complex, is not explicitly socialist. Thus, in Arab socialism, nationalism is never missing, and very often it is the predominant element in the mixture.

Here, for example, is how the Algerian constitution looks on Arabism: "Islam and the Arabic language have been effective forces in resistance to colonial attempts to depersonalize Algerians . . . . Algeria affirms that Arabic is its national and official language and that Islam is the source of its basic ideals." The party program, formulated later on, would insist just as strongly on Arab unity. "The division of the Arab world into individual geographic and economic units should not make us forget the bonds of unity forged by history, Islamic culture, and a common tongue . . . . Algeria is an Arab and Muslim nation. Algerian culture must be national, revolutionary, and scientific. As a national culture its primary role must be to give Arabic its dignity as a civilized language, for it is the expression of our nation's cultural values. In this way the Arab will overcome cosmopolitan culture and Western influence."

Baath, for its part, is the party of Arab resurrection as much as it is a socialist party. Its goal is to "secure the unity and freedom of the Arab nation." "The Arabs," says Baath, "are a single nation and have a natural right to live as one nation and freely to develop their full potentialities. . . . The Arab nation has an eternal mission. That mission is to take the form of a total regeneration through the stages of history, leading to the transformation of human life, the progress of mankind, and harmonious cooperation between the nations." The means to this end is revolution: "The Arab Socialist Party of the Resurrection is revolutionary because it believes that its chief goal, the awakening of Arab nationalism and the building of socialism, cannot be attained except through revolution."

What is the connection between the Arab awakening and socialism? The program says that socialism "will allow the Arabs to fulfill their own potentialities and will allow their genius to develop in the fullest possible way." This socialism implies, indeed, the redistribution of the national wealth, agrarian reform, and nationalization of public services, transportation, and large industries. But, in the spirit which we have met often before, the chief insistence is on the principle that "all foreign companies and all foreign concessions must be done away with. Thus, with the weight of the foreigner off their backs, Arabs will be able to fulfill their own potentialities."

Baath Arabism, be it noted, is a pan-Arabism. "Every citizen of the Arab fatherland must identify himself with it and break with his racial group. Anyone who keeps up relations with a racial group which is hostile to Arabs or who enters the Arab fatherland for colonial purposes, must be expelled."

Nasserism, finally, was no less Arabist and bent on Arab unity. The socialist theme was added only later on and is not always easily fitted in with the rest. Here, for example, is a text of Nasser's which attempts a "dialectical" harmonization that is really an acrobatic feat. "The existence of differences within the Arab nation is in fact a proof of its unity. The differences arise from the social struggle going on in the Arab world (unity has created disunity, which is a sign of unity). 'Unity of purpose' must be the watchword for Arab unity, as the Arab world passes from the stage of political revolution to the stage of social revolution." Nasser continued, "Slogans which were useful in the stage of political struggle against imperialism must now be abandoned. . . . Arab unity by no means implies a uniform constitutional regime to be everywhere rigidly applied. There is a long road still to travel, and the stages and forms will have to be many until the final goal is reached." Obviously, two forces or two aspirations mingle here, without being perfectly fused: socialism and the drive toward Arab unity. Arabism always comes first.

What is Arabism itself? It is a complicated matter, because many factors enter in. It is difficult to dissociate Arabism and Islam, for the latter has been the dominant current in the stream of Arab history. There does exist today a secular Arabism; the Baath program, for example, makes no reference to Islam or the name of Allah. But most Arabisms, including the Algerian, do relate themselves to Islam. Today, when there is so much insistence on Arab culture and the Arabic language, it is rather difficult to separate language and religion. But there is immense complexity in this area, for there are non-Muslim Arabs, the Christian Arabs for example, and it is often they who have been the protagonists in the Arab renaissance. There are also non-Arab Muslims: the Turks, many Asiatic Muslims, etc. It is this whole complex reality, so difficult to define yet so strong a force, that is associated with socialism in every form of Arab socialism.

We have seen that several elements, nationalism and socialism especially, enter in varying proportions into the ideologies of the developing countries. We may ask, in conclusion, whether ideologies so compounded match the ideal of an ideology for developing countries and for development itself, which we described early in this chapter. The answer would have to be carefully qualified. Here or there, we meet with an attitude of rigid defensiveness and even an exaggeratedly traditionalist outlook, rather than a forward-looking spirit. But the ideas of constructiveness and resurrection are almost always present. They are enough to show that we cannot prescind from ideologies when we try, as we have done in this book, to shed light on characteristic traits of underdeveloped societies which are seeking their own development.

CONCLUSION

The analysis we have presented is certainly an incomplete one. Completeness would require several further steps.

We would have to move from the general to the particular and apply to each country and society the general categories which we have worked out through comparison of many diverse and even heterogeneous situations. Not only likeness and common traits, but differences too would have to be shown, and above all the immense differences between continents. For it is definitely misleading to lump Africa, Asia, and South America together without distinction under the name "Third World." Our overall presentation, however, should at least make highlighting such differences easier.

But, above all, after our look at the present, we would like to try to anticipate the future. It is true that today the political class, for all its defects, is the dynamic social class, and that development, especially in Africa and Asia, is the work of the state. But everything points to the emergence of new forces: groups of educated men, groups of economic agents who have exercised initiative and tasted success, groups of opressed and hitherto neglected men who can organize sufficiently to reverse the present mode of development. Such an emergence is highly likely, and it is the interplay of these new social forces which will shape the future.

But once we move beyond this basic conviction, any further prognosis will have to be very reserved. Are we, for example, to expect a revolt of oppressed and dissatisfied social groups? In other words, is revolution around the corner? Not in most parts of the world, it seems. Except in some industrialized regions of Asia and South America, the really oppressed people are still peasants—scattered, and in no position to organize and find effective means of action. In Latin America men have long talked of revolution and for fifteen years we have heard the same diagnosis repeated: a revolution is in the making. But no real upheaval has occurred, except in Cuba which quickly became isolated. A peasant revolution, in any event, is not very likely, because the peasant world is not united, and the working classes, however oppressed, also remain divided.

We must indeed expect many disturbances, many social convulsions. Society and social stratification are so changing that adjustments will be difficult and painful.

Education and science will soon be making a more decisive contribution. Especially in the new countries, they will probably take up the work of the political class which started things off. But will this require a revolution? Possibly, if the presently dominant political classes refuse to recognize the regenerative power of education and science. But such a refusal is not assured, whatever we might be tempted to think when we see student unrest in the developing countries and the threat of unemployment which hangs over them for the immediate future. If there is even minimum success in the first stage of development, a great deal will probably then be expected of education and science; this is what happened in the Soviet Union after the initial and highly political stage of development.

We must anticipate a real variety in the socio-economic future of the presently underdeveloped world. Therefore we cannot exclude the possibility that in some countries groups of enterprising economic agents, issuing from more modest social strata, may take their place alongside tomorrow's political and technical elites.

Finally, there is the role of the military. The military plays a notable part today, and has long played it in South America, and there is no reason to think that it will not play it for quite some time to come.

On the other hand, the likelihood of change or revolution cannot be estimated solely as a function of forces at work within the developing countries. Their destiny will depend at least as much on the evolution of relations with the developed world. This fact renders prognosis all the more difficult. But it also makes us aware once again of the importance of international relations between the developing and the developed nations.

APPENDIX

UNCTAD III:
An Exercise in Global Consciousness

The real issue debated at the third United Nations Conference on Trade and Development in Santiago, Chile, in April, 1972, was the power of the poor countries to determine their fate relative to the controlling interests of the world's rich nations. As at any gathering of international civil servants, reams of resolutions were approved relating to various and sundry development problems and plans. Yet, at the core of most all of UNCTAD III's actions is the locus of international power politics. Is it just, indeed is it tolerable for three-fourths of the world's people to be disenfranchised in the international community?

The United Nations Conference on Trade and Development was founded in 1964 in an attempt to assert the rights of poor nations before the developed world's governments. The dignity of the world's poor could never be secured without concessions from the rich—on trade arrangements, commodity agreements, technical cooperation, etc. The very formation of such a "labor union for the poor world" represented a significant shift in the consciousness of the international community. The conditions of underdevelopment could not be ameliorated solely by the internal adjustments of the less developed countries with token assistance from the world's wealthy nations. In the final analysis, as Don Helder Camara of Brazil says, "The First World is the problem!"

Those delegates and observers that expected hard policy results from UNCTAD III could not help but be disappointed. The industrialized nations do not consider UNCTAD to be a "decision-making" body. Rather, UNCTAD is a forum for an exchange of opinions and intent on matters of rich-poor relations. The rich nations would much rather relegate matters of international economic policy to those forums which they control. The poor nations, on the other hand, pressed hard at UNCTAD III to reform such international institutions (e.g. International Monetary Fund) and to upgrade the status of UNCTAD itself to assume certain policy-making functions.

The UNCTAD III resolution adopted on monetary reform has already been partially implemented with the IMF's recent action to expand its governing committee to include representation of developing countries. Another UNCTAD III agreement of like importance concerns the equitable representation that the poor countries will get at the 1973 international trade negotiations to be held under the auspices of the General Agreement on Tariffs and Trade (GATT).

UNCTAD's 144 delegations also managed to agree on a code of 13 principles to govern international trade relations and trade policies conducive to development. Among these principles were recognition of the sovereign right of every country to freely dispose of its natural resources in the interest of economic development and the well-being of its own people, as well as agreement on the principles of adding no new tariffs and the reaffirmation of the desirability of extending trade concessions to the poor countries. Such resolutions, it is true, were the stuff of heated debates at UNCTAD I and II. So agreement on these "principles" seems hardly encouraging. Yet the fact that matters which in 1964 were construed to be of unusually radical character by the world's rich nations could be overwhelmingly approved less than ten years later suggests an uncommon change in consciousness.

UNCTAD III also marked a significant shift in the attitudes of the poor countries toward each other. The developing nations caucus, the group of 77, was unable to present a united front in Santiago since traditional Latin-African tensions continued to prove strong. Yet, despite these differences the conference unanimously adopted a resolution specifying measures to be taken internationally for the benefit of the "least developed" among the developing countries. The delegations further adopted without objection a list of 25 poor nations identified as "hard-core" least advanced among developing nations. The fact that the Latin Americans agreed to such resolutions urging preferential treatment for African nations is noteworthy indeed.

Countless other issues of concern to the world's poor nations were vigorously debated at UNCTAD III. Matters of controls on restrictive business practices in the developing world to regional integration to commodity agreements to a Generalized System of Preferences were explored in Santiago and referred to the UNCTAD Secretariate to puruse. Some progress was made on the terms of developing financing, debt service, foreign private investment and the transfer of technology.

Yet non-binding resolutions themselves can hardly be considred "authentic" progress until policy implementation results. UNCTAD, though, is not a policy-making body. The LDC's relatively universal dissatisfaction with UNCTAD III, therefore, was predictable. One cannot expect a golden egg from a common goose. Given UNCTAD's "advisory" capacity only, then, issues of the economic and hence political independence of the Third World will still be determined by the "benevolence" of the world's rich nations alone.

Yet, the significance of UNCTAD III lies in the increasing awareness of the rich world that what today might be construed as benevolence is rapidly becoming a matter of global survival. Because, as President Salvadore Allende of Chile said in his opening address to the UNCTAD delegates:

the people of the world will not allow poverty and wealth to exist side by side indefinitely! They will not accept an international world order which will perpetuate their underdevelopment. They will seek and will obtain economic independence, and will overcome underdevelopment. Nothing can prevent it: neither threats, nor corruption, nor force.

It depends upon the urgently necessary transformation of the world's economic structure, upon the conscience of countries, whether the progress and liberation of the vast under-developed world will be able to choose the path of cooperation—based on solidarity, justice, and respect for human rights—or whether, on the contrary, they will be forced to take the path of conflict, violence and pain, precisely in order to apply the principles of the United Nations Charter.

History will record whether or not such an admonition prompts the industrialized nations to act.

_____

Time did not permit the author to prepare a reflection upon UNCTAD III. With his approval, this report was prepared by Paul A. Laudicina, Associate Fellow of the Overseas Development Council, Washington, D.C.

NOTES

---

1. P. Gerbet in Jean-Baptiste Duroselle and Jean Meyriat (eds.), *Les nouveaux Etats dans les relations internationales* (Paris: Colin, 1962), pp. 465-66.

2. Michael Virally, "Driot international et décolonisation devant les Nations-Unis," *Annuaire francais de droit international* 9 (1963) 511.

3. Virally, *art. cit.*, p. 521.

4. Marcel Merle, "Les liens institutionnels du nouvel Etat avec l'ancienne métropole," in Duroselle and Meyriat (eds.), *op. cit.*, p. 177.

5. Merle, *art. cit.*, p. 185.

6. Merle, *art. cit.*, p. 188.

7. Merle, *art. cit.*, p. 191.

8. According to Myron Wiener, "The Politics of South Asia," in Gabriel A. Almond and James S. Coleman (eds.), *The Politics of the Developing Areas* (Prince: Princeton University Press, 1960), p. 158.

9. Jean Buchmann, *L'Afrique noire indépendante* (Paris: Librairie Générale de Droit et de Jurisprudence, 1962), p. 286.

10. Jacques Lambert, *Amérique Latine: Structures sociales et institutions politiques* (Paris: Presses Universitaires de France, 1963), p. 304.

11. Lambert, *op. cit.*, p. 379.

12. Lambert, *op. cit.*, p. 380.

13. O. Cintra, "Explication politique du Brésil," *Projet* 1 (1966) 255.

14. *Ibid.*

15. Lambert, *op. cit.*, p. 376.

16. Lambert, *op. cit.*, p. 389.

17. Lambert, *op. cit.*, p. 390.

18. *Ibid.*

19. Lambert, *op. cit.*, p. 292.

20. Buchmann, *op. cit.*, p. 178.

21. Buchmann, *op. cit.*, p. 210.

22. Buchmann, *op. cit.*, p. 213.

23. Lee Hamon, "Les nouvelles constitutions africaines," *Notes et études documentaires*, no. 3175 (March 26, 1965), Introduction, p. 7.

24. Pierre Chauleur, "L'Afrique noire à l'heure des militaires," *Etudes* 327 (1967) 483.

25. James S. Coleman and Carl R. Rosberg, Jr., (eds.), *Political Parties and National Integration in Tropical Africa* (Berkeley: University of California Press, 1964).

26. Coleman and Rosberg, *op. cit.*, p. 657.

27. W. Arthur Lewis, *Politics in West Africa* (London: Allen and Unwin, 1965), p. 29.

28. On the unions, see A. Lecomte, "Liberté sydicale et panafricanisme," *Revue d l'Action Populaire*, no. 174 (January, 1964), 102 ff.

29. Buchmann, *op. cit.*, p. 280.

30. Sedou Madani Sy, *Recherches sur l'exercise du pouvoir en Afrique noire: Côte d'Ivoire, Guinée, Mali* (Paris: Pedone, 1965), p. 167.

31. Madani Sy, *op. cit.*, pp. 172.173.

32. Madani Sy, *op. cit.*, p. 186.

33. Madani Sy, *op. cit.*, p. 202.

34. Madani Sy, *op. cit.*, p. 176.

35. Madani Sy., *op. cit.*, p. 179.

36. *Cf.* note 27.

37. *Cf.* note 25.

38. Coleman and Rosberg, *op. cit.*, p. 655.

39. Coleman and Rosberg, *op. cit.*, p. 657.

40. Yves Lacoste, *Les pays sous-développés* (Paris: Presses Universitaires de France, 1958), pp. 49-50.

41. J. G. Dumoulin, in *Le monde*, October 13-14, 1693.

42. Richard F. Behrendt, *Soziale Strategie für Entwicklungslânder: Entwurf einer Entwicklungssoziologie* (2nd enlarged ed.; Frankfurt: S. Fischer, 1965), p. 81.

43. *Cf.* M. Reuchlin, *L'utilisation des méthodes psychologiques pour la promotion humaine dans les pays sous-développés* (Paris: Presses Universitaires de France, 1960).

44. René Gendarme, *La pauvreté des nations* (Paris: Cujas, 1963), p. 15.

45. L. Bouthilier and L. Thoré, *Rapport sur les structures foncieres de Haute Volta* (unpublished dissertation, 1961), p. 8.

46. *Ibid.*

47. Reported by Gendarme, *op. cit.*

48. Bouthilier and Thoré, *op. cit.*, p. 8.

49. Placide Tempels, *Philosophie bantoue* (Paris: Editions Présence Africaine, n.d.).

50. O. Mannoni, *Prospero and Caliban: The Psychology of Colonization*, trans. by Pamela Powesland, 2nd ed. (New York: Praeger, 1964), p. 158.

51. Pierre Bourdieu, "La société traditionnelle," *Revue de sociologie du travail* (January-March, 1963), 24-43.

52. Bourdieu, *art. cit.*

53. Bourdieu, *art. cit.*

54. W. Arthur Lewis, *The Theory of Economic Growth* (London: Allen and Unwin; Homewood, Ill.: Irwin, 1955).

55. Bourdieu, *art. cit.*

56. Bourdieu, *art. cit.*

57. Elias A. Gannagé, *Economie du développement* (Paris: Presses Universitaires de France, 1962).

58. Edward C. Banfield, *The Moral Basis of a Backward Society* (Glencoe, Ill.: Free Press, 1958).
59. Bourdieu, *art. cit.*
60. Emile Pin, "Catholicisme et changement sociale en Amérique Latine," *Revue de 'lAction Populaire*, no. 178 (May 1964), 600.
61. Pin, *art. cit.*, p. 601.
62. *Ibid.*
63. Pin, *art. cit.*, pp. 601-2.
64. Lewis, *The Theory of Economic Growth*, p. 102.
65. *Ibid.*
66. Lewis, *op. cit.*, p. 103.
67. *Ibid.*
68. Lewis, *op. cit.*, p. 104.
69. Lewis, *op. cit.*, pp. 105-6.
70. Gendarme, *La pauvreté des nations*, p. 85.
71. Lewis, *The Theory of Economic Growth*, p. 106.
72. *Ibid.*
73. *Ibid.*
74. Lewis, *op. cit.*, pp. 106-7.
75. Peter B. Hammond, *Yatenga: Technology in the Culture of a West African Kingdom* (New York: Free Press, 1966).
76. P. Clément in *Aspects sociaux de l'industrialisation et de l'urbanisation en Afrique au sud de Sahara* (Paris: UNESCO, 1956), p. 416.
77. Clément, *op. cit.*, p. 396.
78. Aidan W. Southall, "Introductory Summary" in A. W. Southall, ed., *Social Change in Modern Africa* (New York and London: Oxford University Press, 1961), p. 33.
79. *Ibid.*
80. Clément, *op. cit.*, p. 399.
81. Clément, *op. cit.*, p. 400.
82. Clément, *op. cit.*, p. 423.
83. Clément, *op. cit.*, pp. 423-24.
84. Clément, *op. cit.*, p. 424.
85. *Ibid.*
86. Southall, *op. cit.*, p. 81.
87. Henri Brunschwig, *French Colonialism, 1871-1914: Myth and Realities*, trans. William Granville Brown (New York: Praeger, 1964).
88. *Cf.*, for example, Georges Balandier, "Contribution à une sociologie de la dépendance," *Cahiers internationaux de sociologie* 12 (1952).
89. *Ibid.*
90. G. Le Coeur, *Le rite et l'outil* (1939).
91. L. A. Costa Pinto, "Economic Development in Brazil: A General View of Its Sociological Implications," in *Implications sociales du progrès économique* (Paris: Presses Universitaires de France, 1962), pp. 140-41.
92. J. Lambert, *op. cit.*, (*cf.* note 10), p. 40.
93. Léopold Senghor, "L'avenir de la France outre-mer," *Politique étrangère*, October 4, 1954, p. 421.
94. Jean-Claude Pouvert in *Cahiers internationaux de sociologie* 19 (1955) 77
95. *Ibid.*
96. Pauvert, *art. cit.*, pp. 81-82.
97. *Cf.* Melville J. Herskovits, "The Problem of Adapting Societies to New

Tasks," in Bert F. Hoselitz, ed., *The Progress of Underdeveloped Areas* (Chicago: University of Chicago Press, 1952; Glencoe, Ill.: Free Press, 1964), p. 96.

98. Pauvert, *art. cit.*, p. 83.

99. Pauvert, *art. cit.*, p. 87.

100. Pauvert, *art. cit.*, p. 91.

101. Paul Mercier, "Aspects des problèmes de stratification sociale dans l'Ouest africaine," *Cahiers internationaux de sociologie* 14 (1954) 51.

102. Mercier, *art. cit.*, p. 52.

103. Mercier, *art. cit.*, p. 57.

104. Mercier, *art. cit.*, p. 58.

105. Mercier, *art. cit.*, p. 60.

106. Mercier, *art. cit.*, p. 64.

107. Jacques Binet, "La naissance de nouvelles classes sociales," *Revue de l'Action Populaire*, no. 151 (September-October 1961) 956-64.

108. Binet, *art. cit.*, p. 958.

109. Binet, *art. cit.*, p. 959.

110. Binet, *art. cit.*, p. 960.

111. Binet, *art. cit.*, p. 961.

112. Yves Lacoste, *Géographie des pays en voie de développement* (Paris: Presses Universitaires de France, 1965), p. 82.

113. Lacoste, *op. cit.*, p. 91.

114. Kenneth Little, *West African Urbanization: Voluntary Associations in Social Change* (Cambridge University Press, 1965), p. 24.

115. Little, *op. cit.*, p. 25.

116. Pauvert, *art. cit.*, p. 90.

117. Little, *op. cit.*, p. 99.

118. Little, *op. cit.*, p. 102.

119. Lambert, *op. cit.*, p. 240.

120. Lambert, *op. cit.*, p. 236.

121. Jean Meynaud and Anisse Salah-Bey, *Le syndicalisme africiane* (Paris: Payot, 1963), p. 8.

122. G. Fischer, "Le syndicalisme des nouveaux Etats," in Duroselle and Meyriat, *op. cit.* (*cf.* note 1), p. 239.

123. Fischer, *art. cit.*, p. 240.

124. Meynaud and Salah-Bey, *op. cit.*, p. 43.

125. Madani Sy, *op. cit.* (*cf.* note 30), pp. 4-34.

126. Houphouet-Boigny, in *Fraternité*, January 13, 1964, p. 4 (*Fraternité* is published by the Ivory Coast Democratic Party.)

127. In *Fraternité*, February 2, 1962, p. 5.

128. Lewis, *The Theory of Economic Growth*, p. 397.

129. A. H. Hanson, *Le secteur publique dans une économie en voie de développement* (Paris: Presses Universitaires de France, 1961).

130. Hanson, *op. cit.*, p. 7.

131. *Conférence internationale du travaile* (1965), *Rapport VI: La réforme agraire* (Geneva: B.I.T., 1964), p. 10.

132. Gendarme, *op. cit.* (*cf.* note 44), p. 474.

133. *Ibid.*

134. W. Arthur Lewis, "Les priorités dans le développement de l'enseignement," in *Politique de croissance économique et investissement dans l'éducation* (publications no. 3 [February, 1962] of the Organisation de Coopération et de Développement Economiques, Paris).

135. Lewis, *art. cit.*, p. 40.
136. According to a report of the Secrétariat d'Etat à la Coopération, Paris.
137. Gendarme, *op. cit.*, p. 480.
138. *Ibid.*
139. According to Harbison, "Politique de croissance économique et d'investisse-ment dans l'éducation," in *Les exigences de l'aide au tiers monde* (publication of the Organisation de Coopération et de Développement Economiques, Paris).
140. *Ibid.*
141. Lewis, *art. cit.*
142. There is no satisfactory single word to translate the French *animation* in the technical sense it has in the present context. The English word "animation" has been used elsewhere as an equivalent. Tr. note.
143. Paris: Presses Universitaires de France, 1963 (2nd ed.).
144. Buchmann, *op. cit.*, (*cf.* note 9), p. 105.
145. Buchmann, *op. cit.*, p. 113.
146. Buchmann, *op. cit.*, p. 114.
147. *Ibid.*
148. Buchmann, *op. cit.*, p. 122.
149. Gunnar Myrdal, *An International Economy: Problems and Prospects* (New York: Harper, 1956), p. 160.
150. Buchmann, *op. cit.*, p. 122.
151. Buchmann, *op. cit.*, p. 134.
152. Raoul Girardet, "Autour de l'idéologie nationaliste," *Revue Française de science politique* 15 (1965) 444.
153 *Témoignages et documents relatif à la colonisation française du Vietnam.*
154. Mamadou Dia, *Réflexions sur l'économie de l'Afrique noire* (Paris: Editions Présence Africaine, n.d.), pp. 108-10.